List of figures and tables

Contents

CHAPTER 7

APPENDIX 1

Preface

Economic theory has a long tradition of examining the role and functioning of government interference in markets. In the late 1700s and early 1800s 'laissez faire' ruled economic thinking, with government interference seen as an impediment to the 'natural' functioning of the market mechanism. In the second half of the 1800s government intervention was increasingly seen as necessary to clear up problems *caused* by the market mechanism. In the late 1930s and 1940s the influence of two people, Keynes and Beveridge, laid the basis for active government intervention in markets as an essential and pervasive feature of economic and social policy. By the postwar period government intervention at the macro and micro levels was the norm and remained so for the next 30 years or more. Interventionist policy lives on even now, although in the 1980s and '90s a new wave of 'laissez faire' thinking has influenced government policy. This has caused a partial or full return to the market for many government industries and services.

The market for sport in Britain has reflected these changes in economic thinking and government policy. This book charts the shifting ground of government-sport relations, particularly in the last twenty years. The catalyst for the book is the great potential change in the relationship between government and sport brought about by compulsory competitive tendering of local authority sports facilities. This legislation and other similar moves to change the relationship to a contracting basis are seen as an enormous threat to sport by some and a great opportunity for sport by others. As we hope to prove, economic analysis can illuminate this debate.

This book is written for three clear markets, with no priority intended between the three: first, practitioners in leisure management and administration, many of whom will *of practical necessity* have to understand the possible effects of government policy for their facilities and services; second, students of leisure studies and leisure management, who *must* understand the relationship between government and their field of study; third, economists interested in the application of their discipline to an important and interesting area of study.

As always, the most important debt of gratitude goes to our long-suffering partners, Christine and Janice, wihout whose support both publishers and readers would have had to wait much longer . . . .

1 Introduction

This book is concerned with sports policy in Britain. It attempts to chart the historical developments of the role of government in sport, to analyse the rationale for government involvement in sport, to specify the objectives implicit in that rationale, and finally to evaluate the extent to which government policy in the post-war period has succeeded in meeting those objectives. The perspective from which we approach this task is that of economics.

Sport is by far the most important area of government expenditure on leisure in Britain. It is also in the area of sport, and in particular indoor sport, that public expenditure on leisure has been increasing most rapidly since the mid-1960s. There has been substantial new investment in sports centres and swimming pools in the last twenty years, and it is this new wave of investment that is the central interest of this book. After this major new investment, these same facilities were belatedly added to the Local Government Act 1988 so that from 1993 onwards all local authorities in England, Scotland and Wales will have to subject the management of these facilities (together with other local authority sports facilities) to compulsory competitive tendering. The sports market, and government intervention in it, therefore provides an interesting case study of the appropriate role for government in the economy in the 1990s.

During the 1980s the conventional economic wisdom regarding the nature and extent of government involvement in the economy changed radically. It is not surprising, therefore, that the role of government in the leisure market in general, and the sports market in particular, became a major focus of interest given that this area of the economy attracted an increasing share of public sector investment in the 1960s and 1970s. In this book we attempt to describe the changing economic thinking in the latter half of the twentieth century regarding the role of government and markets by analysing the changing relationship between government and sport.

As a background to these relatively recent developments, which are the main focus of this book, in this introductory chapter we begin by looking at the historical role of government in sport. We first of all describe how leisure markets have developed and the importance of sports in this development. We then indicate the types of government intervention in these markets over the last 300 years.

Pre-industrial leisure (pre-1800)

If we go back to the early 1600s we find a picture of the ordinary worker faced with a relatively rich and diverse set of leisure activities. Drinking (alcohol) was virtually a universal activity; holidays were more numerous than they were in early industrial Britain, some sports – football, cricket, horse racing, boxing, cock-fighting, bull-baiting and dog-fighting – both participant and spectator, were highly popular. Many of these leisure pursuits were complementary: holidays such as Shrove Tuesday, Christmas, or May Day were the occasions for long drinking sessions where sports were organised for entertainment. The ale-house, or tavern, was the centre for many of these activities: one survey of South Lancashire villages in 1647 indicated that there was an average of one ale-house for every 12 households (or approximately one per 57 inhabitants) (Malcolmson, 1973).

However, people of the seventeenth century would not have identified leisure as we do today. Leisure in modern industrial Britain is something that derives its definition from work: a leisure activity is something we do in non-work time. In seventeenth century, rural, agricultural Britain, there was no such clear distinction between work and leisure. Agricultural production itself followed the rhythm of the seasons with times of hard, intense work (eg during harvest) followed by quiet periods. During these less active times, leisure and work would be occasionally indistinguishable. It was certainly common for agricultural workers to drink while they were working. Documents from the time record complaints of workers observing 'Saint Monday', that is taking Monday off for extra leisure time (often because they had worked the whole of Saturday). It seemed that workers often 'voted with their feet' for a five-day week (Reid, 1967). Many sporting activities would take place in these periods of 'stolen' leisure time. Equally many sports were engaged in during the working day out in the fields.

It is certainly the case that nobody prior to the nineteenth century had ever considered the notion of a government policy for leisure. As indicated above, leisure itself was hardly a meaningful concept in pre-industrial, rural, agricultural Britain. There were attempts though to ban the worst excesses of popular culture. As Judd (1983) explains:

> In pre-industrial England the culture of the inarticulate poorer classes had been expressed in the symbolic performances of the yearly festivals

(both religious and secular), bread riots, songs, tales, parochial sports, charivaris and trade rituals. This 'low' or 'vulgar' culture was predominantly oral and its observation was mainly local and depended on face to face contact between the participants.

Occasionally such 'face to face' contact got out of hand, particularly since these occasions were always accompanied by heavy drinking. As Walvin (1978) comments:

> popular leisure activities were hard won and hence all the more important, and the rowdiness which heralded the breaks from work were often feared by their social betters. Not surprisinglty it was often felt that leisure itself ought not to have a place in the lives of the poor.... Indeed the history of popular recreations before the late eighteenth century could be written in terms of the attempts made to curb and forbid them by men in authority. Yet such pastimes could not be wished away or dispelled by acts of legislation, and the fact that these recreations survived for generations in the teeth of recurring opposition suggests the degree to which they were unshakedly rooted in popular culture.

This increasing opposition did lead to a series of local acts to ban certain blood sports and the cruel treatment of animals (eg cockfighting, bull-baiting, and throwing at cocks) in the eighteenth century. Clarke and Critcher (1985) list specific instances:

> throwing at cocks was banned in Worcester in 1745, Bewdley and Kidderminster in 1750, and Liverpool in 1778. In 1780 London magistrates banned the playing of skittles outside taverns. Additionally there were sporadic attacks against football, horse racing and fairs. Towards the end of the century especially, developments in the economy, in politics, in religion, and in the leisure of the non-labouring classes began to shape more stringent attitudes towards popular culture.

All the quotes above indicate the move to greater control over leisure, particularly working-class leisure, as the eighteenth century progressed. The motive was mainly that of social control: it was the fear of violence associated with large crowds, animated by heavy drinking, gambling, and sport, that led to such measures.

These popular recreations were also under attack from the puritan movement. Much of the puritan antagonism was focused on activities that took place on the Sabbath. The fact that much of the drinking and many of the sporting activities took place on a Sunday led puritans to direct their attack against such popular recreations. However, although evidence is patchy, it seems that puritans were notably unsuccessful in changing the basic pattern of leisure activities during this period. They were aided, though, in their task in the late eighteenth and early nineteenth century by the dramatic change in people's leisure caused by the Industrial Revolution.

Early industrial Britain (1800–1850)

The movement from agriculture to manufacturing industry, involving the movement of the population from a rural to an urban environment, completely altered leisure in Britain. The most significant change was in the availability of leisure time. Factory work typically involved a six-day week, with working days of at least twelve hours for men, women and children alike. There was no seasonal rhythm to this work – every week was the same. Holidays also decreased: in 1750 the Bank of England closed on 47 holidays; by 1830 this had decreased to eighteen, and by 1834 it closed on only four – Good Friday, Christmas Day, and the first days of May and November. During the same period many of the popular recreations of pre-industrial Britain virtually disappeared.

The rise of factory working not only reduced the availability of leisure time for the average worker; income was also a major constraint. In the towns and cities leisure activities increasingly had to be paid for, and the early industrial workers hardly received a subsistence income. The recreations of the working class in this period were largely restricted to the pleasures of the tavern, that is alcohol and prostitution. These activities were predominantly male-orientated; leisure activities for women were even more restricted.

Time and money were not the only constraints facing the new industrialised working classes. Space was also a major constraint. Many sports, football in particular, could not flourish in the new industrial towns because of the lack of space. These activities still survived in rural areas, but by 1851 the majority of the English population lived in towns and cities.

Coalter, Long and Duffield (1986) argue that industrialisation created a new force towards greater control of leisure activities:

> New forms of work organisation required a new sense of time and work discipline which were in opposition to many popular pastimes (Thompson, 1967). The systematic organisation of work into specified times and places required reciprocal forms of 'rational' non-work activities.

As indicated earlier, work and leisure time were never completely separated in an agricultural economy. Manufacturing industry however required a complete separation of work and leisure. Coalter *et al.* indicate that whereas drinking while working in the fields was commonplace, drinking while working with the machinery in the new factories was both disruptive and dangerous. Industrialisation involved heavy capitalisation and working with this capital not only required a sober work-force but also it required that workforce to work long hours so that the capital equipment was kept fully employed.

The role of government in the early nineteenth century was to support the new manufacturing industries in providing an effective labour workforce. This involved "criminalising and suppressing 'popular recreations'" and 'regulating and rationally organising the temporal parameters of leisure' (Coalter *et al.*, 1986). As far as suppressing popular recreations was concerned, some blood sports (eg cock-fighting, bull-baiting, and dog-fighting) were made illegal. Leisure time was regulated and 'rationally organised' by the passing of various Factory Acts which established clear divisions between work time and leisure time. In this early period of industrialisation therefore the role of government was one of suppressing popular working class sports and recreations.

If this was the picture of leisure for the new urbanised working class, the rich had a wider choice of leisure pursuits. They were the leisure classes with time and money to do as they wished. Although concern for animals led to legislation to ban cock-fighting and bull-baiting, other activities such as fox hunting, shooting, and fishing were considered respectable for gentlemen.

It was not only the very rich, however, who enjoyed a wider choice of leisure activities. The Industrial Revolution had created a new affluent class, the industrialists, who, though having less leisure time than the aristocracy, did have the money to adopt the leisure pursuits of the very rich. It is noticeable that their choice was to copy the leisure habits of the aristocracy – a process of 'filtering-down' of leisure activities that is identifiable throughout the history of leisure. For these more affluent classes, there was a significant lack of government suppression of their sport and recreation activities.

The re-emergence of mass leisure (1850–1914)

As the nineteenth century progressed the twin constraints of time and money were gradually eased for the mass of the English population and leisure activities began to expand. By the 1850s, Saturday afternoon was no longer a regular work time and, because of the strong influence of the Sabbatarian lobby, it became the regular sport and recreation afternoon. Initially it was the better paid of the working class, the skilled, that led the move to a more varied leisure lifestyle. A new influence emerged to shape the leisure demands of the masses, facing increased time and money income – technology. The same technology that led to the Industrial Revolution and the restrictions of factory working, started now to widen the opportunities for enjoyment. The largest single change was the coming of the railways. The day out to the seaside became a mass leisure pursuit, now possible with this new, relatively fast cheap form of transport.

But it was not only technology that was changing. Real wages increased by about 40 per cent between 1860 and 1875 and by a further 33 per cent between 1875 and 1900. The idea that time should be set aside for leisure interests was encapsulated in the Bank Holiday Act of 1870 which established a day's holiday in August. Although originally only intended for bank workers it was quickly accepted as a general holiday. It was this day in particular that became the day of the mass trip to the seaside. Nobody foresaw that the Bank Holiday Act would lead to the surge of demand for holiday trips that followed. It is interesting to note that the first thing the working classes wanted to do, when faced with more time and more money, was to copy the leisure pursuits of 'their betters'. Brighton, Scarborough, Southend and other resorts were established initially to cater for the leisure demands of the landed and the wealthy. Gradually they were taken over by the new emerging, but fairly rich, middle classes. By the end of the nineteenth century, it was working people that flooded into the resorts at Bank Holidays.

There developed a new theme to government policy in leisure in the mid-nineteenth century. Again quoting Coalter *et al*:

> there was also an increasing concern with the location of leisure activities and their cultural content. Here we can see the emergence of a number of themes which have, in varying degrees, remained central to public leisure policy – the physical health and moral condition of the working class, the socially intergrative properties of leisure, the contribution of recreation provision to the solution of urban problems and the proper relationships between public provision and voluntary effort.

Many leisure activities, but particularly sports, were encouraged by local government in providing parks, open spaces and swimming pools. One of the problems with the move from country to town was that there was no longer any space in the new urban areas for the conventional pre-industrial popular recreations. As the nineteenth century progressed local governments accepted the responsibility for the provision of both space and facilities for leisure in the towns and cities. In 1847, legislation was passed enabling local authorities to provide public parks. The Bank Holiday Act showed that national government would intervene to provide people with leisure time; local government set about the task of providing areas where this free time could be used 'productively'. The need for these open spaces was brought home by the 1911 census figures which showed that 80 per cent of the nation's population lived in towns and cities.

These initiatives were the first signs of government adopting a more positive role in leisure. In the past the role of government had been to restrict leisure activities that were socially undesirable: cock-fighting, bull-baiting, dog-fighting, prostitution, gambling and drinking. In this latter half of the nineteenth century the emphasis of government policy in leisure shifted from control and prevention (through legislation and policing) of unsocial leisure pursuits, to encouragement and support (through provision of facilities and subsidisation) of desirable recreations. A whole series of Acts appeared in the mid-nineteenth century which enabled local governments to improve the leisure opportunities for their populations: the Museums Act of 1845, the Baths and Wash-Houses Act of 1846 (leading to the provision of swimming pools) and the Public Libraries Act of 1855. It is interesting that these government initiatives were not in response to public demand, rather it was the first sign of the paternalistic role of government in encouraging leisure activities that were socially desirable. The Local Government Act of 1894 and the Open Spaces Act of 1906 allowed local governments to provide both indoor and outdoor facilities for sport and recreation. It should be emphasised though that the Acts mentioned above were permissive rather than mandatory: local governments were not forced to provide such leisure facilities. Also the Baths and Washhouses Act of 1846 was more concerned with public health and sanitation than with health and fitness through sport.

There is one area of sports facility provision, swimming pools, for which we have statistical evidence dating back to this period (Sports Council, 1983). Although several pools and plunge baths were built in the seventeenth and eighteenth centuries (the oldest still in existence in 1977 was built in 1688), public swimming pool provision did not start to develop until after the Baths and Washhouses Act of 1846. By 1870 nearly 100 pools were in existence mostly in and around the industrial cities of Manchester, Newcastle and London (see Figure A.1, Appendix I).

However, the real boom period in construction was between 1870 and 1900, when over 200 swimming pools were established, again mostly in and around London and Manchester but also in and around other cities in the Midlands and Yorkshire (see Figure A.2, Appendix I). This expansion continued into the twentieth century so that by 1914 over 500 swimming baths were open to the public in England (see Figure A.3 Appendix I). Thus the first major investment boom in public sector indoor sports facilities occurred in the 1870–1914 period. Of these pre-1914 pools, 201 were still open in 1977.

Sports became more commercial during this period. Football had been tamed by the public schools to become an organised, respectable sport with a rigid set of rules. In 1863 the Football Association was established and in 1872 came the first F.A. Cup competition. The game started to attract large numbers of spectators, and football stadiums were constructed to house them. By the 1880s professionalism in soccer was well-established. In 1895, professionalism also entered rugby when some northern clubs split away from the Rugby Union because they wished to allow 'broken-time' payments to players (Mason, 1980).

The nineteenth century therefore signalled the beginning of a new, more positive attitude in government policy towards sport. As Coalter *et al.* (1986) point out, there was an emphasis in improving the public provision of sport and recreation facilities as a means of improving the quality of life in urban areas. Sport and exercise was also encouraged because of worries about the physical health of the population (and hence about its ability to fight wars).

Also during the nineteenth century there were significant developments at the élite end of the sports market. Cricket, rugby, and soccer already had developed international competitions. In 1896, the first modern Olympics were staged in Athens. However, élite sport was the sport of 'gentlemen' to a large extent. Except perhaps for soccer, it was the rich who participated and the poor who watched. There was no clearly defined role for government at this end of the market at this time. Finance came either from the aristocratic participants or from patronage.

The interwar years (1918–1939)

The interwar years were characterised by a major leisure expansion. This seems to contradict the popular view of the 1920s and 1930s as years of economic depression and mass unemployment. For those in work, however, real income was improving. Money wages and prices both fell during this period but prices fell faster than wages and real incomes increased. Real wages grew by 11.4 per cent between 1920 and 1938. Also, the average family size decreased and the price of food decreased at a faster rate than prices in general, providing more discretionary income for the working-class household. The other major constraint on leisure activity – non-work time – also increased. This was particularly the case in the years immediately following World War One. The average working week in 1920 was 48 hours compared with 54 hours before the war. This was probably the largest fall in working hours experienced during any decade of the twentieth century. For the rest of the interwar years the reduction in working hours proceeded at a sluggish rate, reaching only 47.7 hours by 1938. An additional boost to leisure was the fact that the price of leisure activities fell during this period. These changes meant that, on average, demand for the output of the new emerging leisure industries increased. But there was a large minority of the population excluded from such activities. The unemployed bore the full brunt of the recession, and for them the interwar years were not a period of expanding leisure opportunities.

World War One necessitated State control and regulation of economy and society to an extent not seen before. Part of this new government control and intervention was in the field of leisure. Control of drinking was a major priority during the war because of the dangers of drunkenness amongst the forces and munition workers. In 1915 the Central Control Board (Liquor Traffic) was set up to regulate the sale and consumption of alcohol. Although disbanded in 1921 the State control of licensed premises continued after the war (Jones, 1986).

There was also evidence, however, particularly in sport, of continuing public investment in facilities. After World War One, investment in swimming pools continued but at a reduced rate. Interestingly, of the 250 pools built between 1915 and 1945, almost half were open-air. All of these open-air pools were opened after 1930, indicating a new fashion for sun and fresh air in this period (see Figures A.4 and A.5 Appendix I). Nearly all of these pools built in this period were still open in 1977. Only seventeen indoor pools had been closed.

Probably the most significant government intervention in leisure in the interwar years was in the area of physical recreation. There was growing concern with the physical fitness of the nation's youth and this turned into worries about the fitness to fight in a war with Germany as the 1930s progressed. In 1935 the Central Council for Recreation and Physical Training was formed. In 1937 the Physical Training and Recreation Act was passed, aimed at achieving a higher level of fitness through the provision of a wider range of sports facilities. The National Fitness Campaign followed immediately afterwards and the government allocated £2 million for grant allocation towards new facilities. A National Fitness Council was set up to allocate these grants and Table 1.1 indicates how the money was allocated. The entire £2 million was not spent, however, as war intervened in 1939 and the Council was suspended. The Table shows that grants were allocated to two major sources: local authorities and voluntary bodies in sport. As we will see in the next chapter, this was to be the pattern of government financial support for sport in the latter half of the twentieth century.

Table 1.1 – Grants offered by the National Fitness Council (up to 31 March 1939)

Type of project	Grants offered to: Local authorities	Voluntary bodies	Total
Swimming baths	439,427	2,625	442,052
Clubs	–	289,297	289,297
Village halls	500	12,935	13,435
Other recreative centres	187,888	145,483	333,371
Gyms	3,200	3,070	6,270
Youth hostels	–	12,575	12,575
Camps and camping sites	5,050	17,900	22,950
Equipment	1,510	9,361	11,141
Playing fields	302,947	34,264	337,211
Total	940,522	527,780	1,468,302

Source: National Fitness Council, *Report of the Grants Committee to the President of the Board of Education*, HMSO, 1939, p. 8. (from Jones, 1986)

Towards a new leisure age

During World War Two expenditure on leisure and entertainment doubled. When the war finished there was an even greater demand for enjoyment after the seven years of hardship. The commercial sector in leisure expanded in the interwar years and this sector was only too keen to cater for the pent-up demands of a nation still subject to constraints on other outlets for its spending power due to rationing. Real incomes increased during the war years and by necessity much of this increase in earnings was saved. When savings are high (as long as inflation is low) leisure normally flourishes. The immediate postwar years saw peak attendances for many leisure outlets. British holiday resorts saw the best visitor numbers ever recorded, with Blackpool and Scarborough heading the records. The record attendance for cinemas is 1,635 million and this occurred in 1946. Professional football achieved its all-time record attendance of 41.25 million in the 1948–49 season. People spent their savings on leisure activities and the prewar leisure industries sat back and enjoyed their prosperity. But it was to be short-lived as progress and technology gave consumers other things on which to spend their money.

Two major technical innovations changed the face of British leisure. Television meant that spectating activities could continue without the need to leave home. Watching live sport was a major loser in this, as was the cinema. The car also opened up a whole new field of leisure activities, and getting out of the towns and cities was no longer confined to Bank Holidays and the annual holiday. The decline of Saturday morning working and the emergence of 'the weekend' as a designated leisure time signalled a new leisure era.

The rest of this book is concerned with analysing the role of government in sport in this rapidly expanding leisure market of postwar Britain. There are many questions to be answered. Later chapters deal with the economic rationale for government intervention in sport, arguments both for and against such intervention, and an analysis of the likely impact of compulsory competitive tendering on public sector sports services. However, before we consider these issues we look at the process by which government became more involved in the sports market in postwar Britain in Chapter 2.

2 Government and sport: policy and finance

In this chapter we look at government intervention in the sports market since 1945. It is possible to identify a radical change in the role of government particularly since the late 1960s. In this period we have a much more adequate statistical base than for the pre-war period and the statistics on public expenditure on sport that we examine later indicate a sharp rise after the 1960s. We first of all describe the development of government policy that led to the eventual rise in public expenditure.

Postwar sports policy

There was little movement on sports policy in the immediate post-war period. Despite the increasing consumer interest in sport and leisure activities, government had more pressing priorities. This is illustrated most starkly by statistics on public swimming pool construction in the immediate post-war period. Between 1946 and 1959, only two indoor swimming pools (Hornchurch in Essex and Wombourne in Staffs) were opened (see Figure A.6 Appendix I). A major reason for this is that investment expenditure by local authorities during this period required loan sanction from the appropriate central government department and, during post-war reconstruction, loan sanction was generally not given for sport and leisure facilities. Housing, education, and infrastructure were much higher in the public investment priority list.

In fact it was in 1960 that the first major development occurred in sports policy with the with the publication of the report of the Wolfenden Committee, *Sport and the Community*. The report suggested that the government set up a Sports Development Council to promote sport at all levels. It also pointed out the shortage of sports facilities.

There was little government reaction to Wolfenden until 1963 when the Conservative government announced increased financial aid for voluntary sports clubs. However the idea of a Sports Development Council was rejected.

The election of a Labour government in 1964 led to a change of policy and the Advisory Sports Council was set up in the same year. The role of the Sports Council in these early years was 'to advise the government on matters relating to the development of amateur sport and physical recreation and to foster co-operation among statutory bodies and voluntary organisations'. (*Hansard*, House of Commons, 3 February 1965: quoted in McIntosh and Charlton, 1985).

A more precise definition of a major aim for the Sport Council came from the Council of Europe which adopted a 'Sport for All' policy in 1966. The United Kingdom government, as a member of the Council of Europe, accepted 'Sport for All' 'as an appropriate description of one of the aims of its own policy for sport' (McIntosh and Charlton, 1985). It was not only 'Sport for All' though that concerned the Advisory Sports Council. The Council also worked closely with other non-governmental organisations in sport to promote international sporting success by Britain's élite sportsmen and sportswomen.

The role of government during this period was therefore one of giving a 'gentle push' to the already established system of provision which was essentially a voluntary sector administrative system using many facilities provided by local authorities. The aim was simply 'more of the same': government's role was essentially one of finding discrepancies between supply and demand and encouraging the voluntary sector and local government to increase supply in those areas of greatest excess demand (see also Figure A.7, Appendix I).

Coalter *et al.* argue that the setting up of an executive Sports Council in 1972 fundamentally changed the relationship between sport and government and the role of the voluntary sector. In particular, they argue that instead of merely encouraging provision for those people wanting to take part in sport and recreation there was a new direction in sports policy – sport as an integral part of social policy. In the Royal Charter for the executive Sports Council it was stated that the council had responsibility:

> to develop and improve the knowledge and practice of sport and physical recreation in the interests of social welfare and the enjoyment of leisure among the public at large.

The Sports Council became the main agency involved in the setting of policy objectives in sport. The Council tried to achieve these objectives through the allocation of its grant-in-aid support to all aspects of sports and recreation. It also had a wider role to play by developing 'national plans'. The first of these was *Provision for Sport* (1972), which established 1981 target levels for the provision of indoor sports centres, indoor swimming pools, and golf courses. A second volume followed in 1973 which outlined target levels for other specialist sports facilities. *Provision for Sport* called for over 800 more indoor sports centres in England and Wales, and over 500 more indoor swimming pools. The report laid out for each sub-region the difference between existing provision and the target level, and urged local authorities to plan to reduce the deficit by 1981. *Provision for Sport* illustrated the way that the Sports Council led policy developments in sport and recreation by influencing other agencies, in particular the local authorities.

What is often not realised is how amazingly successful *Provision for Sport* turned out to be in meeting its objectives for increased supply of facilities. *Provision for Sport* set out a case for:

> spending £370 million of public money in the ten years to 1981 for facilities which it believed every community should have (a sports hall, an indoor swimming pool and a golf course) as well as facilities for minor, specialist and national needs. This level of public investment was twice that then prevailing. The plans produced a target figure for each type of facility and in many cases extended to recommending locations. (*Sport in the Community . . . The Next Ten Years*, Sports Council, 1982).

Table 2.1 – Increase in the provision of sports centres and swimming pools 1970–71 to 1980–81

			Sports centres	Swimming pools
1970–71	–	Provision	12	440
1981	–	Target from *Provision for Sport*	759	857
1980–81	–	Provision	461	964
		Achieved	61%	112%

Source: Sports Council (1982)

Table 2.1 shows the incredible rise in investment in sports centres and swimming pools in the 1970s. In 1970 there were only 12 indoor sports centres in England and Wales. By 1980/81 this had risen to 461. The *Provision for Sport* target for swimming pools was exceeded. Golf course provision was the one area in which the *Provision for Sport* target was not achieved. However, over the 1960 to 1979 period, new golf course construction was at one of the highest levels this century, except for the 1900 to 1920 period.

The Sports Council report into the historical development of the swimming pool stock (Sports Council, 1983) shows that it was the post-1970 period (Figure A.8, Appendix II) that saw the biggest investment in swimming pools in the twentieth century. A total of 394 new pools were opened in the eight years, 1970 to 1977, 385 of them indoor pools. As the Sports Council report indicates:

> This astonishing total accounts for nearly 30 per cent of all pools ever built in England. Over 40 per cent of the indoor pools operating in 1977 were now 'new' pools, opened in the 1970s, and for the rural regions the proportions are nearer two-thirds. Of the new post-1974 local authorities almost 100 had no public pools in 1970, but by 1977 only twenty authorities out of 365 were not providing a public or jointly operated indoor pool, and at least six of these had outdoor pools. (Sports Council, 1983).

From 1977 to 1982 the rate of new provision slowed down. The Sports Council report suggests explanations for this:

> Perhaps the most significant of all has been the pressure put on older pools from a number of directions. Public expectations of what a swimming pool should provide have been greatly influenced by the modern pools built in the early 1970s. Older pools therefore became less attractive to the user and in many instances attendances fell. Thus local authorities were often faced with accelerating maintenance costs as the fabric became outdated and declining constraints in public expenditure added further pressures. In response to these pressures, many older pools were closed, whereas others were 'upgraded' or 'refurbished' in an attempt to increase the number of users, make them more economic to run and extend their lives.
>
> All of these factors have combined to produce a marginal net increase of only eighteen indoor pools over the five-year period, and a more dramatic net decrease of 55 outdoor pools.

Between 1983 and 1988 there was a further wave of investment with 144 new pools opened (offset by twenty closures). As a result, the current capital stock of swimming pools has been substantially updated since 1960. In addition to the new pools, many of the old pools have either closed or been refurbished. There has thus been a major public investment in this area of sport and recreation provision.

Investment in sports centres showed a similar dramatic rise. The indoor sports centre hardly existed prior to 1970. The rise in construction in the 1970s continued into the 1980s. A total of 387 halls came into public use over the period 1983 to 1988. Most of these, 282, were of the large (four badminton courts or more) purpose-built variety. This new investment represented a 75 per cent increase in the provision of indoor sports centres over this relatively short period.

It was the local authorities who provided most of the funds for this new investment although the Sports Council did provide 'pump-priming' capital grants. The early 1970s were a period of increasing local government expenditure generally but the major boost to investment in sports facilities was local government reorganisation in 1974. Many of the old County Boroughs and Urban and Rural Districts spent excess funds on sports centres and swimming pools before being amalgamated into larger authorities. This effect was seen most notably in 1974–5 when 137 sports centres and 190 swimming pools were opened.

While all this new capital investment was going on, there was a gradual change in the nature of public sector objectives for sport and recreation. This was signalled in three White Papers (Department of the Environment 1975, 1977a and 1977b). The first, *Sport and Recreation*, established that 'recreation should be regarded as one of the community's everyday needs and that provision for it is part of the general fabric of the social services'. For the first time, the idea of providing for effective demand was questioned. Public policy was concerned with more than simply providing facilities for those that wanted to take part in sport. The targets were now to be those that did not participate. The concept of 'recreational need' emerged in public policy discussions and allied to this was the concept of 'recreational deprivation'. Recreation deprivation was closely associated with other forms of environmental and social deprivation: it was concentrated in the unemployed, in low-income groups, in single-parent families, in young married women with small children, and in the elderly and the disabled. Since these groups tended by necessity to live in run-down areas of inner cities there was a spatial dimension to the problem.

Policy for Inner cities (1977a) emphasised this new direction for sports policy indicating that sport could 'improve life for many who would otherwise be attracted to delinquency and vandalism'. *Recreation and Deprivation in Urban Areas* (1977b) again stressed the concept of recreation deprivation and the potential of recreation as a socially integrative force.

This new direction for policy involved the Sports Council in a different role as regards the promotion of investment in sports facilities:

> The recognition that fewer people were attracted to the conventional (formal) facilities and programmes led to calls for more 'relevant' and

accessible forms of provision. Therefore policy gradually shifted from exhorting local authorities to build large, prestigious leisure centres to smaller, more local forms of provision. (Coalter *et al.*, 1986).

The difficulty was in persuading local authorities to undertake any capital investment at all during the mid-and late-1970s due to the general financial crisis in local government at this time.

The new emphasis was reflected in the next Sports Council policy document, *Sport in the Community . . . The Next Ten Years* (1982):

> The council recognises that the only way of reconciling growing demands with limited resources is to set priorities, and to concentrate resources either where need is judged to be greatest, or where it will produce the greatest social or economic return. This is the basis of the Council's strategy for the 1980s, proposing selective but effective investment in limited age groups, in particular kinds of facilities and in the continued fostering of sporting skills and the developing of new partnerships with other providers.

Targets were again provided as in *Provision for Sport* but the targets were now in terms of 'target groups' of paticipants, in particular the age groups 13–24 years and 45–59 years. Facility provision should be geared to attracting the 'recreationally deprived' groups into sport for the first time. Policy now was to be demand-based rather than supply-based: it was not to be judged on how many facilities were built but on who was using such facilities.

The latest policy document, *Sport in the Community: Into the 1990s* (1988) emphasises the same direction for policy:

> Sports reflects an increasingly polarised society. In the foreseeable future there will be two broad markets for sport: the first is generally affluent, in work, healthy, well educated, and will increase its expenditure on both leisure and other goods. This market offers considerable opportunities for the providers of sport and recreation, especially those in the commercial sector, to offer an increased range of activities, of a better quality, and generating an economic return.
>
> The second market is generally poor, has poor health, may be unemployed, often lives in inner cities or rural areas with a poor economic base, and contains many ethnic community groups. The benefits of increased leisure and 'Sport for All' have largely passed it by. This market offers not an opportunity, since it often eschews participation in sport, but a challenge. It is a market to which successive Governments have consistently directed the attention of sports providers, and continue to do so. It is, however, a market where the commercial sports provider has relatively little impact, and the voluntary sports club only a modest one. In the last twenty years local government has played the key role in expanding sporting opportunities for the general public, and to meet the challenge of this second market the need for a strong public sector will be vital. (Sports Council, 1988).

This quote indicates that the current role of government, in terms of the mass participation objective, is mainly to cater to the needs of the recreationally disadvantaged since other demands can be met by the commercial and voluntary sectors. The 'target groups' outlined in *The Next Ten Years* were extended to include specifically women, the unemployed, ethnic minority groups, and the disabled.

However, the document is less clear in how these overall objectives can be achieved other than reverting back to the old policy of providing more facilities (in particular, 500 new Sports halls and 150 new swimming pools by 1993). The focus of policy has clearly changed; the means used to achieve policy objectives look somewhat familiar.

Sports policy aims at both increasing participation and increasing standards of performance. The participation objective, however, has always been the major objective. It could be argued that it is only by increasing participation that standards of performance at the élite level will increase. It is also the case that policies aimed at excellence have always been much more difficult to identify than those aimed at mass participation.

During the early years of the executive Sports Council there were two main strands to the Council's excellence programme. The first of these was to provide facilities that would become centres of excellence. National facilities such as Holme Pierrepoint (water sports), Bisham Abbey (tennis and weightlifting), Lilleshall (football), Plas y Brenin (canoeing and climbing), and Crystal Palace (athletics, swimming and diving), are owned and financed by the Sports Council.

The second main strand of Sports Council policy for excellence is in its support for the governing bodies of sport for coaching, training, administration, and the staging of national events. As we will see in the later sections of this chapter, such expenditure has taken up a substantial part of the Sports Council's grant-in-aid in the 1970s and 1980s. There has been a change, however, since the mid-1980s, in the relationship between the Sports Council and the voluntary sector as represented by the governing bodies of sport. During the 1970s grants were awarded to governing bodies but the latter had a fairly high degree of independence in the way such grants were used. Since 1985 applications by governing bodies for grants must take the form of three to five year development plans with specifications for major functional areas such as membership services, coaching, excellence training, and competitions. Block grants are then awarded after due consideration of these functional needs. Further grants are available from the Sports Council for one-off contingencies such as competitions and training trips available at short notice and thus not anticipated in the development plans.

Coalter *et al*. (1986) see this as an attempt by the Sports Council for stronger direction of the voluntary sector. John Wheatley, then Director-General of the Sports Council, outlined the new policy:

> They only get money from us if they have got a development programme and they achieve their targets. So some will not achieve and will get their money withheld and some will get more money against development. (Quoted in Coalter *et al*.).

The implication is that it is the Sports Council that now makes policy and the voluntary sector must follow.

It is not always clear, however, what the Sports Council's policy is in relation to excellence. In *Sport in the Community . . . The Next Ten Years* the following quote appeared:

> The Council will continue to emphasise excellence and to encourage it in numerous ways, but sees its role mainly in the better use of proven approaches rather than seeking any major new actions. Some countries invest vast public funds in special facilities, training programmes and financial and status rewards for élite athletics, in order to win prestige and trade internationally.
>
> It is neither tradition nor policy to treat top level sport in this way in Britain. (Sports Council 1982).

The quote seems to suggest that the Sports Council does not want to adopt methods that have proved successful in producing outstanding athletes in other countries! It could also be interpreted as meaning that it is not the tradition or policy in Britain to produce such quality. Perhaps realistically the quote simply highlights the secondary nature of the excellence objective in British sports policy.

The latest Sports Council strategy document (Sports Council, 1988) is much more positive about support for excellence, but remains vague on the resource implications of this support:

> The Council itself cannot deliver winners and gold medallists . . . . However with the government's help, it is in a better position than any other organisation to make sure that the essential ingredients for achieving international success – coaching, sports science, facilities, sports medicine – are co-ordinated and harnessed to best effect.

However, there has been a recent movement of public policy at the élite end of the sports market. This could be termed the 'Sport as Tourism' movement and is concerned with using major sporting competitions as an opportunity for the upgrading of facilities and infrastructure in a city and the attraction of tourists. This movement has been typified by Birmingham's bid for the 1992 Olympics, Manchester's bid for the 1996 Olympics, and Sheffield's successful bid for the 1991 World Student Games.

Before 1984 the Olympics looked like an excuse for running up a large public debt. Munich (1972) lost £178 million, this loss being shared between the Federal Government (50 per cent), Bavaria (25 per cent) and Munich itself (25 per cent). Montreal (1976) lost £692 million this being shared between Quebec Province and Montreal. However, Los Angeles (1984) turned the tide and made a surplus of $215 million. This trend was continued in Seoul (1988) with a surplus of over $300 million. It seemed as if the Olympics could achieve economic regeneration without the cost of municipal debt.

Public expenditure on sport

Not surprisingly the increasing emphasis given to sport in public policy since the 1960s has corresponded with an increase in public expenditure on sport. The Henley Centre for Forecasting (1986) estimated the level of public expenditure on sport and these are the figures we use here. Following the Henley Centre we split public expenditure into central government expenditure and local government expenditure.

Central government expenditure on sport

The Henley Centre identified two major areas of central government spending on sport:

(i) grants to other government agencies;
(ii) that part of central government grant to local government (formerly the Rate Support Grant and now the Revenue Support Grant) which may be attributed to funding local authority expenditure on sport.

Two particular groups of grants to government agencies are most relevant to sport. The first is the grants-in-aid to the Sports Council, the Scottish Sports Council, the Sports Council of Wales and the Sports Council of Northern Ireland. In 1984–85 these were respectively £28.6 million, £4.1 million, £2.9 million, and £1 million. For the 1988–89 financial year the Sports Council grant had increased to £38.4 million. However, even at this level this only represents a doubling in real terms of the original grant of £3.6 million in 1972. Virtually all this real increase took place in the 1970s.

The lack of any increase in the central government funding for sport is surprising perhaps in the light of comments made earlier about a greater government commitment to sport over this period. The contrast is even sharper when compared to Arts Council funding which stood at £154.7 million in 1988–89. However, unlike the situation in the arts, the majority of subsidies to sport originates in local government programmes rather than in those of central government. Of the Sports Council grant-in-aid itself, about one third is passed on to local authorities to finance capital expenditure. Most of the rest goes as grants to the voluntary sector which will be discussed in more detail below.

The other major funding from central government to sport and recreation comes from the Urban Programme, which assists local authorities with specific urban problems. In 1985–86, £23.9 million of Urban Programme grants was allocated to sport and recreation schemes. By 1987–88, the figure had fallen to £21 million. The administration of the Urban Programme is principally undertaken at local government level and again most of this money is income to local government.

There are several other agencies receiving grants from central government that, although not solely or even mainly involved in sport, do have some responsibility for sport and recreation. These are particularly the agencies involved in countryside recreation: the Countryside Commission, the Countryside Commission for Scotland, the Nature Conservancy Council, the National Parks, and the British Waterways Board. It is impossible to indicate what share of central government grants to these bodies went to sport and recreation.

Table 2.2 – Central government expenditure on sport: 1984–85

	£million
Grants to Sports Councils	37
Grants to Urban Programme	24
Sport-related component of RSG:	
local authority net expenditure on sport	258
local authority net expenditure on education	167
Other	59
Total	545

Source: Henley Centre for Forecasting (1986)

The main area of central government expenditure on sport, however, is through the Revenue Support Grant (RSG), formerly the Rate Support Grant, paid to local authorities. The portion attributed to sport covers two areas of local authority spending: 'net expenditure on sport' and the sports component of education expenditure. The former is easier to estimate since local authority expenditure on this is relatively well documented. The Henley Centre estimated that for 1984–85 the central government grant to cover local authorities net expenditure on sport would be £258 million. The part of local government expenditure on education that relates to sport is much more difficult to gauge and there must be a much wider margin of error attached to the Henley Centre's estimate of £167 million for this component.

Table 2.2 summarises the main areas of central government expenditure on sport for 1984–85.

Local government expenditure on sport

Statistics on local government expenditure on leisure and recreation include items such as expenditure on the arts and on tourism. It is necessary therefore to decide which items relate specifically to sport. The categories that we have taken as sport related are: indoor swimming pools, indoor sports halls and leisure centres (with and without pools), outdoor sports facilities and golf courses. One other category of expenditure – urban parks and open spaces – includes sports facilities (in particular, tennis courts, football pitches, miniature golf, and bowling greens) but is not exclusively sport. We have followed the guidelines of the Audit Commission (1989) and the Henley Centre in including 40 per cent of this expenditure.

Capital expenditure on sports facilities started to rise (both in absolute terms and as a proportion of total capital expenditure of local authorities) in the early 1970s. This corresponded to new investment in indoor facilities in particular. Despite the economic crises of the mid-1970s and the election of the Thatcher government in 1979, capital spending on sport continued to rise in the early 1980s. The Audit Commission (1989) indicated that capital investment in local authority sports facilities was running at more than £100 million a year throughout the 1980s. Table 2.3 looks at capital expenditure by local authorities in England for 1987–88, indicating how much was funded through the Urban Programme. If we take 40 per cent of capital expenditure on parks and open spaces as sport related, then total capital expenditure on sport and recreation in 1987–88 was £212.5 million. Of this figure, 64 per cent is capital expenditure on indoor facilities, sports centres and swimming pools.

Table 2.3 – Capital expenditure of local authorities in England 1987–88

	Total (£million)	of which Urban Programme (£million)
Parks/Open spaces	71.5	8.9
Indoor sports and leisure centres	87.1	4.7
Golf courses	2.6	0.0
Other outside sports and playing fields	22.6	2.2
Swimming pools	49.9	3.1
Other recreation	21.7	2.1

Source: Local Government Financial Statistics (England)

This high level of capital expenditure has implications for revenue expenditure since, once opened, these facilities do not cover their operating expenses. Table 2.4 gives the breakdown of revenue expenditure for 1987–88 together with the income generated by these facilities. The total net revenue expenditure on these facilities (again taking 40 per cent of net expenditure on parks and open spaces) is £639 million, 52 per cent of which is taken up by net expenditure on indoor sports centres and swimming pools.

Table 2.4 – Total revenue expenditure on and income from sport and recreation by local authorities in England and Wales 1987–88

	Expenditure (£,000)	Income (£,000)
Sports and recreation centres	334,701	143,901
Parks and open spaces	516,950	115,431
Golf courses	21,294	18,648
Playing fields and sports grounds	50,055	9,943
Swimming pools	206,038	64,465
Miscellaneous recreation facilities	138,466	35,481

Source: Local Government Financial Statistics (England)

Thus a correspondence of circumstances in the mid-1970s – the creation of the executive Sports Council, the publication of *Provision for Sport*, local government re-organisation, the publication of the White Paper *Sport and Recreation*, increasing focus in public policy on inner-city deprivation, and a focus on sport as welfare – led to local government investment in a new area. The rapid investment in indoor sports centres and new swimming pools at a time of public expenditure cut-backs in the late 1970s and early 1980s is clearly an unusual occurrence.

Although central government funds much of this local authority expenditure indirectly through the RSG (and Urban Programme money), the decisions on the extent of such public leisure provision are made by local government.

The next question to be answered is how this public expenditure is directed towards the two main public policy goals: promoting mass participation and promoting excellence.

Finance for mass participation and for excellence

In the earlier sections of this chapter we have looked at how governments have attempted both to set and to achieve objectives in sport. In this section we will analyse the way in which public expenditure has been directed in pursuance of these objectives. We have already outlined the generel level of government expenditure in sport and recreation in the previous section. Here we are concerned with the distribution of that expenditure over the two major policy areas, mass participation and excellence.

Although there is a wide range of organisations in the public sector involved in sport and recreation, the Sports Council and the local authorities are the bodies most concerned with the objectives of mass participation and excellence. The difficulty is in allocating this expenditure to the two objectives. Luckily that task has been made easier following a study by one of the present authors, (Taylor 1990), who investigated the funding of sporting excellence from all sources. The data for governing bodies are based on an analysis of the development plans, annual reports and accounts of 21 governing bodies of sport, representing fourteen sports, together with qualitative material from interviews with representatives of seventeen of these sports. The data for local authorities are based on a questionnaire survey of all authorities in England and Wales covering the period 1985–86, which achieved a response rate of 83 per cent.

The main estimates concerning expenditure on excellence in sport appear in Table 2.5. There are three major non-government contributions to the funding of excellence in sport: commercial sector sponsorship, voluntary sector support through the expenditure of governing bodies (net of Sports Councils' grants), and the spending of individuals.

Sponsorship dominates financial support for excellence but sponsorship is a rather patchy and random process that leaves some sports and some performers well-supported but others struggling for finance. Often the decision over which sports to sponsor is media-determined, with firms only willing to provide sponsorship if there is guaranteed television coverage. Sponsorship is not a comprehensive form of finance for the élite level of sport given that two sports – motor racing and association football – receive over half of sponsorship money.

Government in some ways attempts to fill the gaps left by sponsorship. One attempt to do this was through the establishment of the Sports Aid Foundation in 1976. This is an independent organisation, set up with the support of the Sports Council, whose aim is to channel sponsorship money to aid the training and preparation of élite performers. It essentially tries to give financial help to those sportsmen and women who cannot find personal sponsorships: that is, it is trying to fill gaps referred to above. Unfortunately from 1976–83 the Sports Aid Foundation only managed to raise £2.5 million, which included an initial grant of nearly £0.5 million from the Sports Council. Table 2.5 shows that in 1985–86 Sports Aid Foundation finance for excellence was still small in quantative terms. However later in 1986 the Minet Group provided the Sports Aid Foundation with £1.5 million specifically for the financing of individuals training for the 1988 Olympics. Although the amount of finance for the Foundation is small, its aims are essentially those of the Sports Council with regard to excellence and is not subject to many of the criticisms that relate to commercial sponsorship in general.

After sponsorship, the next most important item in Table 2.5 is the spending of individuals. This is rather an unusual item and Taylor is the first to attempt an estimate of it. This item relates to the spending of the athlete and his/her family in paying for expenses associated with training and competition. In many ways it is in direct contrast to sponsorship in that sponsored individuals get such expenses paid for by the sponsor. The £21 million expenditure in 1985–86 indicates again the extent to which both sponsorship and government fail to provide support for excellence across the whole spectrum of sport.

The third non-government source of expenditure on excellence is the expenditure of the governing bodies of sport. Taylor found a wide variation in importance given to excellence in governing bodies' programmes. The proportion of gross expenditure devoted to excellence by the 21 governing bodies investigated by Taylor varied from 25 per cent to 100 per cent, the average being 56 per cent. There is also wide variation in the extent to which this expenditure is financed by the Sports Council grant-in-aid to the governing bodies, from nothing (in the case of tennis) to 90 per cent (in the case of wrestling). On average the Sports Council financed a fifth of governing bodies expenditure on excellence. The figure of £15.95 million in Table 2.5 has netted out the Sports Council grants. Governing bodies raise revenue to finance excellence from staging events, television fees, and other 'commercial' activities.

Table 2.5 – Expenditure on excellence in sport 1985–86

		Amounts in £million
Sports Council		7.1
of which *National Centres*	*3.2*	
Governing bodies grants	*3.75*	
Other	*0.15*	
Local authorities		10.0
Governing bodies (net of Sports Council grants)		15.95
Sponsorship		109.5
Sports Aid Foundation		0.465
British Olympic Association		0.269
Individuals		21.0
Total		164.284

Source: Taylor (1990)

The British Olympic Association (BOA) is a separate item in Table 2.5 although in many ways it is similar to a governing body. The BOA is concerned with raising money for the expenses involved in sending British teams to the Olympic Games. As the Table shows the amount of money involved in a non-Olympic year (1985–86) is small.

Compared to the contributions of the commercial sector and the voluntary sector to funding excellence in sport, the public sector's contribution is relatively small. Taylor splits the contribution of both the Sports Council and local authorities into two types: direct supply of facilities and transfer payments.

Less than one-fifth of the Sports Council's grant-in-aid (£29.4 million in 1985–86) goes to the finance of excellence. About half of this is taken up by the finance of the five National Sports Centres (ie direct supply). It is interesting to note that Taylor does not include all expenditure on National Centres by the Sports Council in Table 2.5, but only 36 per cent of it. This is because only a proportion of the users of these 'élite' centres in 1985–86 were in fact concerned with excellence in sport. The majority of users were schools, clubs and casual users – that is, more the type of customer associated with a typical local authority sports centre.

Transfer payments from the Sports Council for excellence purposes are the grants to the national governing bodies of sport and the National Coaching Foundation referred to earlier. Total Sports Council expenditure on excellence in 1985–86 was £7.1 million. The most tentative estimate of Table 2.5 is that relating to local authorities' support for excellence in sport. The estimate of £10 million is based on Taylor's survey of English local authorities. Very few authorities attempted to put a financial valuation on their support for excellence.

In the survey 74 per cent of the responding authorities claimed to be actively supporting excellence in sport, another six per cent offered minor or occasional support, and a further six per cent expressed an intention to develop their sports policy into this area in the near future. There is some evidence from the survey to suggest that while some local authorities have a long history of supporting excellence in sport, for many this policy is a fairly recent development. Any continued shift in expenditure in favour of excellence in sport will have a significant impact on the total public sector financing of such excellence, given the context of £1 billion and more spent by local authorities on leisure services.

Individually local authorities do not usually offer a wide range of means of supporting excellence in sport, but collectively the methods are quite diverse, including grants to individuals, teams and other organisations, concessions at facilities, in-house coaching, provision of specialist facilities, schools or centres of excellence and hosting special events. The most popular method is the transfer payment – 61 per cent of authorities give grants to individuals and teams, 28 per cent give donations to relevant organisations such as the Sports Aid Foundation or local sports councils, and 26 per cent give grants for facilities to 'outside' organisations. Nearly a third of responding local authorities claim at least one recent development in their support for excellence in sport, endorsing the impression that it is a developing area of local authority sports policy.

The public sector therefore seems to play a relatively minor role in financial terms when it comes to excellence, accounting for only 10.4 per cent of total financial support for excellence. The role of the public sector is much greater than this however. As we have seen, the Sports Council uses the grant-aid to governing bodies of sport to influence the policy of the governing bodies and therefore it has some degree of control over the £15.95 million contributed by these bodies. Similarly the Sports Council is actively involved in many of the sponsorship deals and has its own Sports Sponsorship Advisory Service which acts as a broker between sports organisations and potential sponsors. This finance for excellence is a complicated mixture of public, voluntary, and commercial sector activity and the public sector though minor in financial support is the major policy-making force in this mixture.

The same story is also true when we look at the financial resources involved in the promotion of mass participation. Here we expect the public sector to be a much more equal partner with the voluntary and commercial sectors when it comes to the level of finance. Table 2.6 indicates the level of resources involved. These figures have been estimated by the authors from those presented by The Henley Centre for Forecasting (1986).

Table 2.6 – Finance for mass participation 1984–85

	£million
Public sector	
Sports Council	23
Local authorities	901
Voluntary sector	
Voluntary Sports Clubs	1195
Commercial sector	
Company Provision of Sports Clubs	292
Participation Clubs	19
Total	2,411

Source: Own Estimates from The Henley Centre for Forecasting (1986) and Taylor (1990)

The figures in Table 2.6 for the commercial sector only relate to private participation sports clubs that are run for profit and sports facilities provided by companies for their own employees. These are two relatively small items when compared with total commercial sector expenditure on sport estimated by the Henley Centre of £2.34 billion. A large share of this is expenditure on sports equipment, clothing and footwear, and is not really comparable to the other items in Table 2.6.

The estimates for private participation clubs is obtained by estimating total consumers' expenditure on admissions and playing fees and deducting from this payment to the voluntary and public sector clubs. Such an estimation procedure is obviously subject to a large degree of error and the size of the estimate indicates clearly that private clubs take up a relatively small share of sports participation spending.

The other item in the commercial sector directly related to participation in sport is likely to be subject to a wider margin of error. The Henley Centre assumed that employers, on average, spend on sports facilities 0.15 per cent of total income from employment. This is little more than a 'best guess' since there are no data available on company provision of sports facilities, and, for some reason, firms seem reluctant to divulge how much they spend on such facilities.

The Henley Centre's estimate for the voluntary sector is based on a sample of voluntary sports clubs in various sports which was then grossed up using information on the number of clubs in each sport. It shows that the voluntary sector, in financial terms, is the most important sector in provision for participation in sport.

However the public sector is not far behind in providing resources for mass participation. One area of local authority expenditure on sports facilities is not available from published statistics – those facilities provided by local authorities in schools and colleges. The Henley Centre estimated expenditure on this item to be £300 million in 1984–85 by assuming that 60 per cent of the cost of education in schools and colleges to be teachers pay and that 7.5 per cent of teachers' time is taken up with sport and PE. This £300 million is included in the total figure of £901 million for local authorities. The other £601 million refers to the current expenditure of Leisure and Recreation Services Departments in local authorities after deducting the amount spent on excellence.

The £23 million figure for the Sports Council in Table 2.6 represents the government's grant-in-aid to the Sports Council minus that allocated to expenditure on excellence. There are two major items in this figure: capital grants to local authorities and voluntary clubs for the provision of facilities and grants to governing bodies of sport that are concerned with participation rather than excellence.

Conclusions

This chapter has shown how, within a relatively short period of time, there has been a dramatic increase in the extent of government involvement in the sports market. Chapter 1 indicated how there was relatively little change in government policy towards sport and recreation from the middle of the nineteenth century to the middle of the twentieth. Yet from 1960 onwards not only were new government funded institutions such as the Sports Council set up, but also local authorities substantially increased capital investment in new sports facilities. Since all these facilities receive substantial subsidies, increased capital spending on sport leads to increased revenue expenditure.

There has been no shortage of statements of aims and objectives of government policy for sport and recreation over this period. Department of Environment White Papers and Sports Council policy documents have specified a whole series of justifications for this increased level of expenditure and an associated set of objectives to be achieved by it. However, there has been considerable change in the direction of policy over this short time period. Two overall objectives are clear: the promotion of mass participation and the promotion of excellence. The public sector role in relation to the participation objective has moved from sport for all to sport for the recreationally deprived. As our earlier discussion indicated, there seems to have been some confusion over exactly what public policy is aiming at in relation to excellence. Consequently it is not surprising that the bulk of the increased level of public sector resources in sport have been directed at the participation objective.

We have not only looked at public expenditure on sport and recreation in this chapter but also at how the public sector compares with other sectors in its provision of finance for sport. The commercial sector dominates in the provision of finance for excellence. However, the voluntary sector is the most important sector for participation in sport and also plays a crucial role in promoting excellence. Since the voluntary sector receives grants from government and makes extensive use of public facilities the interrelationship between this sector and the public sector needs to be investigated further. This we do in Chapter 7.

Any supplier of sport and recreation opportunities, whether public, commercial, or voluntary, must have a good understanding of consumer behaviour in sport in order to meet specified objectives. For this reason the next chapter attempts an analysis of this consumer behaviour.

3 The demand for sport

It may seem surprising in a book dedicated to the analysis of the role of government in sport to include a chapter on the demand for sport. Surely our attention should be focused on the supply side of the market and the place of government within the structure of supply. Sport, however, is essentially a service industry. As Iso-Ahola (1982) points out:

> it is not simply enough to plan, organise and deliver leisure services. Services in themselves are meaningless. It is the people, service recipients, who attach certain values and purposes to leisure activities. Since their ultimate objective is to improve people's quality of life through leisure services, practitioners must be aware of the reasons for people's engaging in certain leisure activities, what people are likely to derive from participation in these activities, and why.

In order to determine the appropriate role for government and to evaluate the extent to which government has fulfilled that role in sport we must analyse the nature of consumer demand for sport. In this chapter we attempt to put forward such an analysis.

Before we analyse the nature of the demand for sport, it is useful to consider in more detail the problems of understanding consumer behaviour in sport using economic theory alone and the need for a more general social science approach.

Approaches to the analysis of consumer behaviour in sport

As economists, our starting point for the analysis of consumer behaviour in sport is the theory of consumer demand. This has remained virtually unaltered for over a century. It is a theory developed from the nineteenth century economist Alfred Marshall. The consumer is regarded as having a given set of tastes and preferences and, facing a given set of prices of goods and services, allocates his income in such a way as to maximise utility, which results in a spending pattern where the relative marginal utilities of different goods are equated to relative prices. Economic theory concentrates on such 'rational' maximising behaviour.

This approach to the analysis of consumer behaviour has not escaped criticism from within the economics profession. Hosseini (1990) critises the economic approach:

> Neoclassical economic theory has been founded on the assumptions that economic agents are omnisciently rational and that they are always optimising . . . . That is to say that the standard neoclassical theory, at least implicitly, assumes that economic agents should do what they believe right and believe that what they do is right. In this body of thought values and actions are always consistent . . . .
>
> The optimisation hypothesis is based on what should be well-established preferences. For example, we assume that future preferences are exogenous, stable and known with adequate precision to make decisions unambiguous. These assumptions are questionable. When we deal with collective decision-making, individual objectives might be in conflict, or, individual preferences might very often be inconsistent, fuzzy and changing over time. It can also be argued that as human beings, while engaged in decision-making, we often ignore our own fully conscious preferences. Instead of maximising rationally, we often follow rules, traditions, hunches, and advice and actions of others.

Fine (1990) points out how the economic approach prevents a broader analysis of consumer behaviour and shifts the emphasis away from the individual and on to the commodity markets:

> By homogenising and setting aside non-utility maximising behaviour as 'irrational', economics precludes the possibility of an *inter-disciplinary* theory of consumer behaviour and heavily discourages even a *multi-disciplinary* approach. In addition, the economic theory of consumer behaviour focuses attention away from individual acts of exchange. These become of no interest in their own right, since each is meaningless in isolation from the others. Only bundles of commodities give utility, so that the individual acts of obtaining and enjoying them become irrelevant.

Similarly, Kenneth Boulding (1956) has argued: 'it is the behaviour of commodities not the behaviour of men which is the prime focus of interest in economic studies'. He goes on to emphasise that the economist 'is not really interested in the behaviour of men' (quoted in Hosseini (1990)).

In this chapter we do make an attempt to explain the behaviour of men and women. To do this we have to go beyond the boundaries of economics and into areas of psychology. Psychology adopts a more general approach to consumer behaviour than economics. It concentrates much more on the individual consumer than on the commodity and it concentrates much more closely on the process by which a consumer obtains satisfaction (and sometimes dissatisfaction) from consumption. This, we feel, is an essential element of an analysis of the demand for sport. We are not sure whether what follows is economics or psychology, or whether it is economic psychology. We feel that it is probably the latter since it draws on the work of two economists, Tibor Scitovsky and Peter Earl, both of whom have developed approaches to consumer demand that use psychology in the analysis.

Scitovsky's approach first appeared in *The Joyless Economy: An Inquiry into Human Satisfaction and Consumer Dissatisfaction* (1976) and was later extended in Scitovsky (1981) and in *Human Desire and Economic Satisfaction* (1986). Scitovsky used both behaviourist and physiological psychology in his analysis of the basis of consumer satisfaction and most of what follows in the next section is based on his work.

Peter Earl's analysis of consumer behaviour first appeared in *The Economic Imagination: Towards a Behavioural Analysis of Choice* (1983) but a more comprehensive treatment appeared in *Lifestyle Economics: Consumer Behaviour in a Turbulent World* (1986). Earl used personal construct theory from psychology in his analysis but we do not want to concentrate on this aspect in this chapter. Rather it is his concept of 'priorities-based choice heuristics' we wish to employ in our analysis of demand for sport and leisure.

The nature of the demand for sport

Scitovsky criticises neoclassical theory of consumer demand, indicating that at best it can contribute only to a partial analysis of consumer behaviour. He particularly criticises the assumption of a given set of preferences, the model of a rational consumer who knows what he wants and fails to achieve it only for lack of means. For Scitovsky, to understand demand one has to understand the motive force behind behaviour, that is we need to investigate how preferences are formed. To do this his starting point is psychology and in particular the theory and concept of arousal.

Initial psychological behavioural analysis looked at 'stimulus response', that is how organisms respond involuntarily to various physical stimuli. This was later extended to voluntary actions prompted by various drives. However, such drive theory explanations of behaviour imply that an organism is basically inert, unless disturbed by physical deprivation or a disturbance that generates a drive to eliminate the disturbance. Such a theory has a limited application to human beings capable of engaging in various complex activities. The more modern approach to explaining behaviour relates to physiological research into the brain's arousal level.

The level of arousal has a lot to do with general feelings of satisfaction or dissatisfaction. Too much arousal and too little arousal are both unpleasant. Scitovsky uses the example of solitary confinement of prisoners as a case of low arousal and stimulus deprivation leading to pain, nausea, confusion and general feeling of unpleasantness. Similarly, over arousal felt by an executive faced with too much extremely demanding work can lead to stress, fatigue, anxiety and physical illness.

Thus too little and too much stimulation and arousal are both unpleasant. Psychologists argue that there exists an optimum level of total stimulation and arousal which, when reached, gives rise to a sense of comfort and well-being. Below this optimum, a person is likely to feel boredom, above it, he is likely to feel anxiety and tension. If the arousal level falls below the optimum level, or rises above it, these feelings provide an inducement to attempt to bring the arousal level back to the optimum. The greater the divergence of the present position from the optimum, and the longer the duration of this divergence, then the greater the inducement to attempt to return to the optimum level. Thus this theory of optimal arousal provides the motivation for human behaviour.

Scitovsky uses examples of different personality types as an illustration. Introverts are high-arousal personalities and their behaviour tends to be withdrawn. They avoid excitement and their behaviour is characterised by arousal-reducing activities (eg watching television). Extroverts, on the other hand, are low-arousal personalities. They seek excitement and outside stimulation (eg social gatherings, high-risk leisure pursuits, gambling). Scitovsky points to the conflict with the conventional economic approach to consumer behaviour. Economists say that these groups of people have different tastes (which they take as given); in fact, they have different types of personality which goes some way in explaining their different tastes. The optimum level of arousal of the two groups are probably similar, but they start from different points along the scale, which accounts for differences in behaviour.

The theory of optimal arousal as a basis for analysis of behaviour is broader than the economic approach, although there is a considerable overlap. Economists see consumer demand as want satisfaction. If an individual is deprived of food, he experiences discomfort in hunger (ie he becomes over-aroused). Consumption of food relieves the discomfort and lowers his arousal level back towards its optimum level. Pleasure (utility) results from the comfort of returning to an optimum level of arousal from the heightened level caused by hunger. Comfort is the feeling that results from being at the optimal level of arousal; pleasure on the other hand, results from moving towards the optimal level from a non-optimal level. Scitovsky uses the analogy between speed and acceleration (or deceleration) to explain the difference between comfort and pleasure.

When we are deprived of the essential elements of human existence (food, clothing, shelter) then we 'demand' these essentials and receive pleasure from the satisfaction of these demands. However, this is not the only source of pleasure. Pleasure flows from the change in arousal level rather than the state of being at a particular level. Pleasure will also follow from moving from a low level to a higher one: the relieving of boredom. Some activities are so stimulating that they raise arousal levels too high (ie beyond the optimum level), causing anxiety and tension, but pleasure still follows when the activity finishes and arousal levels fall back towards the optimum.

Scitovsky criticises economists for only considering the want satisfaction (lowering too high arousal) aspects of demand and completely ignoring stimulation-seeking behaviour (raising too low arousal). It is this latter aspect that relates his theory to demand for sport:

> The simplest remedy for too low arousal is bodily exercise. Not only is bodily exercise a good weapon against boredom it is also pleasant. It seems most pleasant when it fully engages our skill and powers.... Competitive sports and games are popular because the pleasantness of exercise is maximised by the full exertion of our strength and skills called forth by competition. Higher animals also engage in playful combat and other forms of competitive behaviour. (Scitovsky, 1976).

The basic source of stimulation is experience that is new, unexpected, or surprising. New and surprising experience is always stimulating, but if it is completely outside the bounds of our previous experience it can be so stimulating as to be disturbing. As Scitovsky indicates: 'what is not new enough and surprising enough is boring: what is too new is bewildering. An intermediate degree of newness seems the most pleasing.' What an individual considers 'new' obviously depends on his previous experience. What is stimulating to one person, may be boring to another; not because of differences in tastes, but because of differences of experience. The nursery slope can be terrifying to the person on skis for the first time, and yet boring to the expert.

Danger or threat is the most obvious source of stimulation but we need to broaden out view of what we mean by a threat as Scitovsky explains:

> Anything new, in the sense of anything unexpected is a threat to our

> survival, because we do not know how to deal with it. Each of us, through the accumulation of personal experience, develops a view of the world, starting from day one. And that view is the basis of the strategy we use for living – for surviving. Which would be fine if it were not for the fact that the world changes all the time and so threatens to render our strategy obsolete. For that reason we must continually update our world view, by perceiving new information, processing it, and relating it to our previously accumulated fund of knowledge which it will complete and modify. By doing this we update our strategy of survival.

In this quote, Scitovsky is introducing the concept of 'skilled consumption'. The perceiving and processing of new information is 'skill acquisition' and the more skills acquired then the greater the opportunity for pleasure through stimulation. Enjoyment of novelty requires learning.

Scitovsky uses an example of the difference between classical (serious) music and pop (light) music to illustrate the concept of skilled consumption:

> For example, when I first listen to a complex piece of music with a large information flow, my brain automatically keeps the subjective information flow within the limits of its capacity by blocking out part of the harmonic complexity. Only as repeated hearing reduces the subjective novelty of what I have already heard and so frees part of my brain's information processing capacity so I begin to notice the complexity I have previously missed. This enables one to listen to the same piece of music repeatedly with undiminished or even increased enjoyment, because the increase in subjective redundancy does not diminish the flow of subjectively new information I perceive at successive hearings. Also, the more-than-manageable inflow of information which I receive on first hearing complex music creates a mild frustration or disorientation, whose resolution, and my expectation of whose resolution, is an important part of my enjoyment. Novelty creates a problem, and its enjoyment comes from the resolution of the problem.

Light music rarely has the disturbing aspect referred to above. On the other hand because of the lower information content, it is less durable than serious music. Repetition can make light music boring.

The main question Scitovsky addresses in *The Joyless Economy* is why, in the USA, increasing affluence does not seem to have led to increasing happiness. He argues that a major reason for this is that there has been too much emphasis on the acquisition of production skills and not enough on the acquisition of consumption skills. Consequently, American consumers seek pleasure through want satisfaction rather than stimulation seeking since they do not possess the skills to 'enjoy' the stimulation. However, once the basic demands for material goods have been met, there is less and less opportunity for pleasure through want satisfaction. Hence the overall picture of an affluent, but bored, joyless society.

The overall point of Scitovsky's analysis is that stimulation-seeking is the motivator behind many if not most leisure demands, and is certainly the main motivation for participation in sport. Not all leisure activities require a high degree of consumption skill. Scitovsky makes the point that America's three most popular leisure-time activities – watching television, shopping and driving for pleasure – are low-skill activities.

Thus Scitovsky's approach can be adopted to provide the basis of a theory of demand for sport. As a society becomes more affluent, there is less and less potential for pleasure through want satisfaction (ie wishing to earn money to purchase goods and services that by themselves give pleasure) and a major avenue to pleasure comes through stimulation seeking. Such stimulation can be obtained through interesting and challenging work, again conflicting with the economists' categorisation of work as disutility. However, for many it is through their leisure activities that we would expect to see stimulation-seeking behaviour.

Low-skill leisure activities can be stimulating when tried for the first time, but repetition can quickly make the experience boring. Hence the tendency for the demand for leisure activities in general to be volatile as consumers move in and out of the market. We often see rapid growth in demand for a new leisure activity (eg the cinema in the 1930s) only to see equally rapid decine in demand as the novelty effect wears off and other new leisure experiences emerge (eg television) to widen the spectrum of leisure-time choices facing the consumer.

For activities that provide the potential for skilled consumption, the same leisure activity can continue to be stimulating since, as the consumer's skills develop, the nature of his enjoyment also changes. The competitive sportsperson may move to higher and higher levels of competition and even find that excitement and stimulation increase the more skilled he becomes and the higher the level of competition he enters. Within the broad field of sport, however, demand will be heterogeneous since participants will have different backgrounds, experiences, interests, and skills. What is stimulating to a football participant may be boring or uninteresting to the golfer. The demand for sport is not a homogeneous demand.

A more detailed analysis of the way in which sport generates satisfaction and happiness is Csikszentmihalyi's fascinating study into man at play entitled *Beyond Boredom and Anxiety*. The aim of his study was to explore why people took part in activities that yielded no extrinsic rewards. He referred to such activities as autotelic, which he defined as an activity that required formal and extensive energy output on the part of the actor yet provided few, if any, conventional rewards. Thus, he was interested in why people spent a lot of their time in activities that an industrial society would regard as unproductive.

He attempts to describe the nature of autotelic experience:

> It is easier, at first, to say what the experience is not like. It is not boring, as life outside the activity often is. At the same time, it does not produce anxiety, which often intrudes itself on awareness in 'normal' life. Poised between boredom and worry, the autotelic experience is one of complete involvement of the actor with his activity. There is no time to get bored or to worry about what may or may not happen. A person in such a situation can make full use of whatever skills are required and receives clear feedback to his actions; hence, he belongs to a rational cause-and-effect system in which what he does has realistic and predictable consequences.

Csikszentmihalyi refers to this 'holistic sensation that people feel when they act with total involvement' as flow. He describes the relationship between flow and skills:

> at any given moment in time, people are aware of a finite number of opportunities which challenge them to act, at the same time, they are aware also of their skills – that is, of their capacity to cope with demands imposed by the environment. When a person is bombarded with demands which he or she feels unable to meet, a state of anxiety ensues. When the demands for action are fewer, but still more than what the person feels capable of handling, the state of experience is one of worry. Flow is experienced when people perceive opportunities for action being evenly matched by their capabilities. If, however, skills are greater than the opportunities for using them, boredom will follow. And finally, a person with great skills and few opportunities for applying them will pass from the state of boredom again into that of anxiety. It follows that a flow activity is one which provides optimal challenges in relation to the actor's skills.

This quote adds a greater insight into Scitovsky's concept of skilled consumption, and it also explains why such skilled consumption can generate high levels of consumer satisfaction. Moreover, whereas sport has the potential for providing such flow experiences, Csikszentmihalyi argues that normal life experiences rarely have the ability to provide such enjoyment. This is because in many everyday experiences we do not have the control to make sure that challenges match one's skills. Also, most activities in life are not experiences in the sense that they are 'interactive sequences with a beginning, a middle and an end, which provide a clear cognitive or emotional resolution.' Sport provides both of these characteristics: the ability to equate the degree of challenge with one's skills and clearly an experience in the sense defined above. Csikszentmihalyi summarises the nature of enjoyment for consumers during a flow experience: 'they concentrate their attention on a limited stimulus field, forget personal problems, lose their sense of time and of themselves, feel competent and in control, and have a sense of harmony and union with their surroundings'. Sport is not the only route to flow experiences. However, we would argue that all sport has the potential to provide such experiences. It is this potential that makes sport different from many other types of consumer behaviour.

Thus Csikszentmihalyi's work complements that of Scitovsky in its attempt to investigate the nature of consumer satisfaction and provides a further building block into our analysis of consumer behaviour in sport.

Scitovsky is not the only economist to use psychology in attempting to explain consumer demand. A similar non-mainstream approach to consumer demand is provided by Earl in his latest book *Lifestyle Economics* (1986). Earl views the consumer as a strategic decision-maker. In order to examine how consumers make decisions about strategy Earl employs personal construct theory from psychology. Earl describes the nature of personal construct theory which originated from Kelly (1955):

> The 'personal construct' term originated in Kelly's concern to emphasise that the impressions people form of 'things' are images that they construct for themselves – there is no such thing as an 'objective' universe. Kelly's own view of the universe was that it is such a complex, integrated structure, in which everything ultimately affects everything else, that people can only make sense of it by imagining that it can be separated into distinct events. These events he saw as being imagined theoretically as mental 'templates' which are then tested, with the aid of other mental templates, for their goodness of fit. A person who can construct a variety of rival theories will try to discover which of them has the least bad fit . . . How a person will feel about a particular environment, and how she will try to behave in it, will depend on how she construes the environment – in other words, on how she 'sees things'. People have different personalities, and often find it hard to get on with each other, because they see the world differently.

There is a close analogy here with the previous quote from Scitovsky relating to skilled consumption. Thus both Earl and Scitovsky are using psychology to exercise the nature of consumer satisfaction and dissatisfaction. Scitovsky's analysis is more general in that he is attempting to analyse consumer behaviour in aggregate for the USA. Earl is looking more at the individual decision-making process, in an uncertain world.

Earl's analysis though not directly comparable with Scitovsky's provides more detail which is useful in the development of a theory of the demand for sport, in particular his discussion of what he calls 'priorities-based choice heuristics'. That is, he assumes consumers make decisions according to an ordered list of priorities or alternatively on the basis of an implicit hierarchy of needs. Although the concept of a hierarchy of needs is normally associated with psychologists and, in particular, Maslow, Earl refers to the economist Menger's (1871) use of the concept in his explanation of the Law of Diminishing Marginal Utility. Menger's idea of a hierarchy of needs seems to have been 'swept aside in the flood of mathematical contributions that the marginal utility idea provoked' (Earl, 1986). Certainly it is a concept not popular with economists today since it conflicts with what economists call the 'axiom of nonsatiation'. That is, incorporation of a hierarchy of needs into consumer demand theory allows a consumer to reach a satiation point for lower order wants and needs. This poses problems for conventional economic analysis since it prevents the use of conventional mathematical techniques that are used to analyse consumer choice (or more specifically it prevents a utility function being represented by a continuous differentiable function).

Although Earl explicitly incorporates a hierarchical approach to consumer demand, Scitovsky almost, but not quite, adopts the same approach. He talks about the standard economic classification of goods into necessities and luxuries:

> 'Necessities serve man's biological functions, which is why the demand for them is urgent at first, but limited and quickly saturated. Luxuries is the catch-all category for everything else. There is also a hierarchical difference between the two categories. Most people feel that necessities have or should have priority over luxuries, and that only as the need for necessities gets saturated should the desire for luxuries be catered to. The dividing line between the poor and the not-poor used to be drawn according to whether a person could afford anything beyond the necessities of existence. Poor relief used to provide necessities alone, or just enough money to buy them. (Scitovsky, 1976).

In this quote he is really referring to a crude hierarchy of needs, with lower needs having satiation points which then lead to demands for goods to satisfy higher needs.

The concept of a hierarchy of needs is more common in management, marketing, and behavioural science literature than in economics. In fact, Earl recommends that economists should integrate much more of the marketing literature into the analysis of consumer demand. It automatically follows that marketing information is a crucial input to understanding consumer decisions from Earl's subjective approach. If there is no such thing as an objective universe, we need to investigate how consumers view the universe in order to understand their decisions. If every consumer is unique, then there is no point attempting to analyse consumer decisions, since any theory will only apply to one consumer. However, it is likely that subjective assessments of the universe will overlap to a large extent and lead to recognisable groupings among consumers. Recent developments in marketing have increasingly focussed on identifying such consumer groupings with respect to values. Evidence of this kind on consumer attitudes provide a means of testing the theories of Scitovsky, Earl, and Csikszentmihalyi. But before we move on to look at evidence it is appropriate that we summarise the discussion in this section.

We have argued above that in order to understand consumer behaviour in sport it is necessary to go beyond the confines of conventional consumer demand theory. The reason for this is that the generation of consumer satisfaction in sport is of an essentially different kind than that associated with want satisfaction. It is stimulation-seeking behaviour. It is also the type of activity that has the potential to generate flow. However, whether that potential is realised or not depends on the ability and skill of the individual. Lack of consumption skills, knowing how to enjoy consumption, can prevent the consumer obtaining satisfaction. In the context of sport this does not mean that only people who are good at sport can enjoy it. Consumption skills are not the same as sporting skills, although it is probably true that in acquiring sporting skills the consumer also acquires consumption skills: that is, he learns how to enjoy taking part in sport. However, the jogger who aims for, and achieves, a four-hour marathon may not be regarded as a brilliant runner but has the potential for obtaining the same intrinsic rewards as an élite runner. He simply needs to understand the process by which enjoyment is generated (ie the characteristics of flow experiences discussed above). He needs to be a skilled consumer, not necessarily a skilled sportsman. Lack of consumption skills are a major barrier to obtaining satisfaction in leisure in general and sport in particular.

There is another factor however that is important in understanding consumer behaviour in sport, and that is the concept of consumers making decisions on the basis of a hierarchy of needs. This will be developed further in the next section where we integrate this hierarchical approach into the discussion of consumer attitudes.

Consumer attitudes

Interesting work on consumer attitudes and values in Britain has been done by the Taylor Nelson Monitor (now Applied Futures) and

MacNulty (1985) reports their results. His paper provides empirical support for Scitovsky's and Earl's analysis in the UK (since the Taylor Nelson Monitor research was based on large-scale, in depth, interviews), and MacNulty links Taylor Nelson Monitor results with the hierarchy of needs at an aggregate level.

Taylor Nelson Monitor has been carrying out a regular survey of British social attitudes since 1973. MacNulty reports that their studies indicate that the British population divides into three broad groups on the basis of social attitudes held: Sustenance-Driven, Outer-Directed and Inner-Directed.

Members of the Sustenance-Driven group are motivated by the need for security. For them want-satisfaction is most important since they are concerned with satisfying the basic needs of human existence, and leisure activities are secondary. The Sustenance-Driven are mainly in socioeconomic Groups D and E, with some C2s. They can be of any age, although the largest proportion are either old (and retired) or young (and unemployed).

Outer-Directed people are motivated by the search for esteem and status. They do things so that other people can see them doing them. They are materialistic and judge success by other people's criteria. The conspicuous consumer is a typical Outer-Directed person.

Inner-Directed people are not interested in the opinions of others. They are individualistic and set their own criteria for success. It is stimulating experiences they are searching for, whether it be through work or leisure.

The Outer-Directed and Inner-Directed groups have some factors in common. They occur mainly amongst A B C1 socioeconomic groups with some C2s. They involve people who have money and are willing to spend it, though for different reasons.

The Taylor Nelson Monitor surveys indicate that it is this Inner-Directed group that is increasing as a percentage of the British population. MacNulty predicted that by 1989 this group would account for 38 per cent of the population compared with 34 per cent for the Outer-Directed and 28 per cent for the Sustenance-Driven. Perhaps more importantly their surveys indicate that the Inner-Directed group has only emerged as an identifiable group over the last twenty to 30 years. Stimulation-seeking behaviour seems to be on the increase.

MacNulty comments on the Inner-Directed in a way that identifies members of this group as skilled consumers, with strong focussing on stimulation-seeking and not on want-satisfaction:

> Taken as a whole the Inner-Directed Groups tend to espouse a large number of trends, which suggests that their members have a complex system of values which enable them to consider alternative courses of action, to devise a variety of solutions to their problems, and to make a

> flexible response to the situations they encounter. They can also be expected to exhibit a relatively high tolerance to frustration. Among the many trends expressed by the Inner-Directed population there are several (which have been rising for the past ten years) which relate to autonomous behaviour and low material consumption.

MacNulty discusses the implications of this grouping of consumer attitudes in the context of the hierarchy of needs. Figure 3.1 shows Maslow's (1952, 1970) seven levels of need with self-actualisation at the top and survival at the bottom. In an analysis that could be criticised for an over-simplistic application of the hierarchy of needs, he argues that the attitudes held by the Sustenance-Driven group of consumers are associated with the bottom rungs of the hierarchy of needs and also typified earlier social paradigms (agricultural and industrial in Figure 3.1). Outer-Directed groups are associated with the middle rungs of the hierarchy and the industrial social paradigm whereas Inner-Directed groups are concerned with self-actualisation at the top of the hierarchy and typify the post-industrial social paradigm. Over time, for society as a whole, attitudes change. As discussed in the last section, individuals satisfy more basic needs before they turn their attention to those higher in the hierarchy. A social paradigm is the dominant set of attitudes, values, and beliefs shared by members of society. Hence as attitudes change, there is a paradigm shift. Sustenance-Driven attitudes were dominant in agricultural and early industrial society, and Outer-Directed attitudes became dominant in later industrial society. Inner-Directed attitudes are growing in importance in the post-industrial environment.

MacNulty argues therefore that the future will be one of an Inner-Directed society:

> The economy will be designed to support a society which places value on such things as concern for the ecology and conservation of natural resources, low level of material consumption, work as a means of personal fulfilment (rather than economic necessity), and the creative use of leisure time for individual growth.

One final quote from MacNulty confirms the similarity of the conclusions of his analysis with that of Scitovsky:

> Leisure activities in an Inner-Directed society will be widely varied in keeping with the individualistic character of the population. There will, however, be greater emphasis on the experience and less on the status which might accrue. People who play tennis will do so because they enjoy it, to be seen in the 'right' tennis club will be of increasingly less importance. Many forms of leisure will emphasise self-development which may take the form of educational activities as well as sports such as sailing, camping and climbing which develop confidence and self-reliance. Zero-run games will become of correspondingly less importance.

Figure 3.1 Social paradigms and social value groups

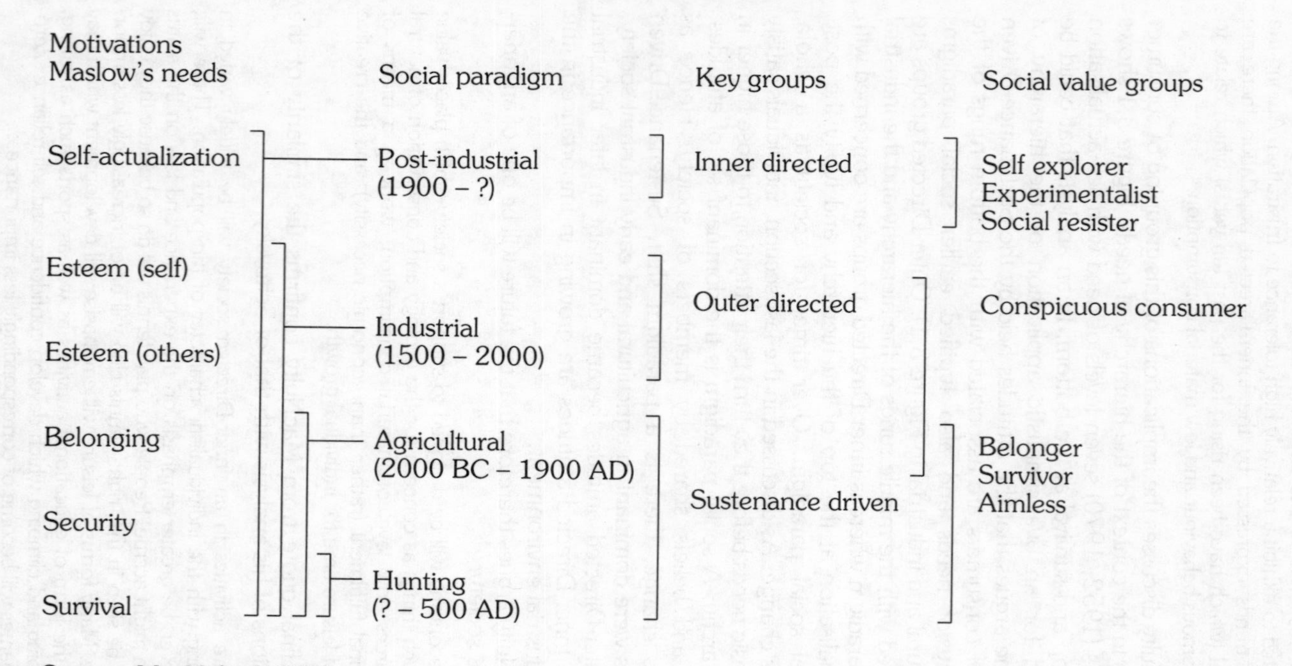

Source: MacNulty (1985)

This discussion of the hierarchy of needs and consumer attitudes takes us a step further in understanding consumer behaviour in sport. Income is an important determinant of consumer behaviour. For people on low incomes attention will be focused on the bottom of the hierarchy of needs. Food, housing, clothing are major priorities. Leisure is likely to be a very low priority for these people. If anything leisure is probably escapism: a way of forgetting the often ugly realities of satisfying even basic needs with limited income. Participation in sport is unlikely to fill this need for escapism although watching sport on television or live (eg football) may well do. In fact, one of the characteristics of the Sustenance-Driven group is that leisure expenditures are home-based.

For many in low-income groups, survival and security are high priority. These make up a substantial proportion of the Sustenance-Driven group of consumers. They are not an important group among sports participants. Csikszentmihalyi suggested that satisfaction of basic needs may be a prerequisite for achieving the enjoyment of flow experience.

For consumers on higher incomes, many of the basic needs will have been satiated and an opportunity will exist to satisfy higher needs and leisure is likely to figure strongly in such discretionary expenditure. Leisure expenditures take an increasing share of total household expenditure as total expenditure increases. However, there will be two distinct groups of leisure consumers in these higher income groups.

The first group will look to leisure as a means of establishing esteem and status. Such consumers will tend to be materialistic. They will still be very interested in purchasing goods and services and looking to want satisfaction for their main pleasure. They will be very concerned at having things and seek status and acceptance from others by showing off their property. Such consumers will be very concerned about appearance. Their leisure activities will reflect this. They will tend to choose activities, that are high status and are the in-thing to do. Thus at the top of the income scale, we are likely to see owning and sailing a yacht as high in the priority list. Car-related leisure pursuits are also likely to be a high priority since such consumers will be very interested in cars as a status symbol. Going out for a meal will be high up on the priority list since knowledge of restaurants and extravagant expenditure in them is an ideal way of displaying financial success and superiority.

As in Veblen's (1899) *The Theory of the Leisure Class*, having extensive leisure time will itself be used as an indicator of the superiority of this group. They will tend to have several different holidays a year: skiing holidays in winter, on the yacht in summer, exotic holidays to far away places in Spring and Autumn. Lower down the income scale, consumers will be more constrained as to the amount of money that can be spent on such discretionary leisure items. However, they will aspire to the 'yuppie' lifestyle and be very concerned to demonstrate to their equals that they are rapidly getting there.

Mason (1981) examined the nature of conspicuous consumption. His analysis shows how qualitatively different it is from the autotelic or flow experience that we discussed in the last section. He indicates that it is a very difficult need to satisfy and conspicuous consumers are in danger of being dissatisfied and frustrated. For instance, if society as a whole gets richer then this general increase in wealth provides no satisfaction to the conspicuous consumer. For him, it is the distance between himself and other consumers that is the basis of his satisfaction. Striving to be in front of a society continually moving forward can be both stressful and frustrating. In many ways, conspicuous consumption has more of the characteristics of work than of leisure. There are even extrinsic rewards to conspicuous consumption: the social prestige that comes from the possession and display of economic superiority.

Conspicuous consumers make up a high proportion of MacNulty's Outer-Directed consumers. They also present to a large extent the archetypical American consumer analysed by Scitovsky.

The other higher income group consumers are the Inner-Directed consumers. These are the stimulation-seeking consumers. They are closest to a new leisure class of a post-industrial era. Within this group we will have strong leisure focusing with consumers having a wide range of leisure activities. Equally we will see people choosing to work very long hours at rewarding jobs and possibly having reduced leisure time as a result.

Acquiring or possessing material possessions is not an end in itself, but merely a means to an end. Material possessions are not wanted for display but for use. In their leisure lifestyles, they will seek excitement and personal development. Education will be important to them in order to provide the production and consumption skills to enjoy the stimulation that can be provided by both work and leisure.

Sports participants will be made up mainly of Outer-Directed and Inner-Directed consumers. We are likely though to see differences in the sports they choose, as well as the motivations that led them to choose them. Sports such as mountain climbing, soccer, fell-running, keep fit/yoga, fishing, rambling, indoor swimming, hockey and self-defence and climbing are likely to be dominated by the Inner-Directed. The Outer-Directed are more likely to figure prominently in such sports as sailing, skiing, motor sports, and air sports. It would be a mistake, however, to suggest that such a division is a tight one. In any sport we are likely to see all types of consumer: Inner-Directed, Outer-Directed, and Sustenance-Driven. They will be participating for different reasons and the nature of their satisfaction will be different.

Over time we are likely to see sports participation dominated by the Inner-Directed consumer not only because they are predicted to become the dominant group of consumers but also, as Csikszentmihalyi has pointed out, because status, power, and money are signs that one is competent and in control but such signs are unnecessary if one feels that control within a life dominated by flow activities.

Demand analysis and government policy for sport

The previous two sections provide the bare bones of a theory of consumer behaviour in leisure in general and sport in particular. The concepts introduced can provide an explanation for some of the leisure behaviour indicated in the historical review in the last chapter and can be linked with government policy initiatives.

In Chapter 1, we reviewed the development of leisure throughout the nineteenth century. During this period, on MacNulty's analysis, the population consisted of just two groups – the Sustenance-Driven and the Outer-Directed. The Sustenance-Driven would have been in the majority, then the new industrial working class. The small Outer-Directed minority controlled the resources: the old aristocracy and the new industrial middle class.

Chapter 1 indicated that in the early part of the 19th century leisure activities of the working class were severely restricted. The aristocracy however were the leisure class, and over the nineteenth century their leisure behaviour was copied by the *nouveau-riche* industrialists. It is interesting that Veblen's (1899) analysis of conspicuous consumption related to the behaviour of similar groups in America in the late nineteenth century.

Veblen's thesis is relevant to understanding leisure in Britain in the nineteenth century. In discussing Veblen, Heilbroner (1972) comments:

> If Marx's view was right, for example, and the proletariat was irreconcilably and diametrically opposed to the capitalist, what prevented the revolution from breaking out at once? Veblen provides an answer. The lower classes are not at swords' points with the upper; they are bound up with them by the intangible but steely bonds of common attitudes. The workers do not seek to displace their managers: they seek to

> emulate them. They themselves acquiesce in the general judgement that the work they do is somehow less 'dignified' than the work of their masters, and their goal is not to rid themselves of a superior class but to climb up to it. In the theory of the leisure class lies the kernel of a theory of social stability.

Hence we saw the 'filtering down' of leisure activities and pursuits during the nineteenth century first from the aristocracy to the middle class and then from both to the working class. Thus in Chapter 2 we saw how the British seaside resorts eventually became the destination for the working class on Bank Holiday day trips whereas initially they were the first holiday destinations of the very rich.

Both the Outer-Directed and the Sustenance-Driven groups were materialistic. The latter, however, were concerned with material goods associated with the basic needs in the hierarchy, survival and security. The Outer-Directed were concerned with obtaining esteem through display and conspicuous consumption. Both groups were mainly concerned with want satisfaction rather than stimulation seeking.

Government leisure policy from the mid-nineteenth century onwards consisted mainly of providing baths, parks and open spaces in inner cities primarily for the working class. Baths were concerned not only with sport and recreation but also with personal hygiene, thus again catering to the lower-order basic needs. We have no data available to assess who were the main beneficiaries of such provision but it seems likely that users would come from the Sustenance-Driven groups rather than the Outer-Directed groups. Social historians tend to confirm this.

Thus this first wave of government investment in leisure was concerned with basic needs: the need for open space in the rapidly expanding industrial conurbations; the need for recreation and laundry facilities for use by industrial workers living in inadequate housing in the early part of the nineteenth century.

The type of facilities provided by government did not change radically from 1860 to 1960. A typical local authority in the early 1960s would have a public park with facilities such as tennis courts, football pitches, bowling greens and lakes for boating and fishing. None of these facilities would be of particularly high quality: tennis participants, for instance, seeking a higher quality would normally join a private club. The emphasis for management in such a park would not be on sport and recreation but on horticulture and park managers usually came from a horticultural background. Similarly most local authorities had few, new, high quality swimming pools. As we indicated in Chapter 2, a large proportion of the stock of swimming pools existing in the early 1960s dated back to Victorian times. Again the emphasis in swimming pool management was on baths management (ie water quality, cleanliness, health and safety).

The second wave of recreational capital investment began in the mid-1960s, when the emphasis was on indoor sports centres and modern swimming pools. In general, these new facilities were of a higher quality than is normally the case in local authority recreation provision. In the case of indoor sports centres, the facility was a new product to the British market. For swimming pools, although many conventional pools were built in the early and mid-1970s, from the later 1970s onwards another new product emerged, the leisure pool. These new facilities were 'luxury' products amongst the portfolio of leisure services provided by local government. It was the construction of these new indoor facilities that led many local authorities to co-ordinate all their various leisure services into one Leisure Services Department. The new facilities were the flagships of these new departments. A new profession, leisure management, emerged with emphasis on the consumer rather than horticulture (parks) or such things as water testing procedures (pools).

This new supply side to public sector leisure provision coincided with an important change in the demand side as MacNulty indicates:

> Until about 25 or 30 years ago the two major classifications outlined above [Sustenance-Driven and Outer-Directed] probably represented a fair picture of society. As we shall see, the major institutions in U.K. society are based on this kind of model. No doubt there were members of the Inner-Directed Groups about, but they were probably so few as to be statistically undetectable. In any case, they appear to have been so unimportant as a group that no one searched for them. Today that situation has changed; and the third, Inner-Directed, classification has assumed significant importance.

The effect of the emergence of this Inner-Directed group, interested in stimulation seeking and self-actualisation, just as government was embarking on a new direction in sports policy will be considered in later chapters of this book. It should not be a surprise for the reader to discover in these chapters that with the changing nature of the demand for sport, meeting policy objectives with regard to certain recreationally deprived 'target groups' has proved elusive. The analysis in this chapter has shown that the people most interested in the stimulation and excitement that sporting experiences provide have, in the last two decades, predominantly been those on higher incomes. These consumers are also more likely to have acquired the relevant consumption skills so important to realising the potential enjoyment in sport.

Conclusions

In this chapter we have attempted to develop a theory of consumer demand for sport which will provide a basis for examining the effects of government intervention in the market for sport and recreation in future chapters.

In developing this theory we have moved beyond the boundaries of conventional consumer demand theory and looked to the small area of literature where economists have attempted to integrate psychology into the study of consumer behaviour. We have also tried to integrate the theory with empirical research into consumer values and attitudes. We believe this approach not only enables us to understand more fully how consumers behave but also is a more suitable basis for evaluating policy initiatives in sport and suggesting improvements to policy.

Two important points emerge from this analysis. The first is that to obtain consumer satisfaction from participation in sport certain skills are required. We are not referring here to sports skills but consumption skills, although there is likely to be a positive correlation between the two. Consumption skills allow the consumer to choose appropriate challenges that adequately engage his abilities and hence create what Csikszentmihalyi has called flow. In acquiring consumption skills the consumer gains recognition of how pleasure and satisfaction are generated through sport. An unskilled consumer may find similar activities create anxiety or are simply boring.

It is certainly the case that for some people, sport will never provide the satisfaction that it does for others. For them, similar flow experiences may be obtained through other leisure experiences such as the arts. Alternatively, or additionally, some people are lucky enough to experience flow through challenging work experience. However, it is equally the case that many consumers are prevented from obtaining consumer satisfaction in sport through lack of consumption skills.

The nature of consumer skill acquisition is such that within sport there is a wide range of skills possessed by consumers. Across sports the skills required are very different. Within any one sport there will be a wide variety of consumer demand ranging from the recreational participant to the national competitor. The demand for sport is a heterogeneous demand.

This importance of consumption skills is also the basis for the second major point that follows from the analysis of this chapter. Iso-Ahola (1982) has referred to the process by which we acquire basic knowledge about leisure and recreation, form fundamental attitudes and values towards them, and learn various skills and motives as 'leisure socialisation'. What the analysis in this chapter has shown is that if government aims to promote excellence and participation in sport it must pay much more attention to sport socialisation. Provision of facilities alone will do nothing to overcome the barriers to participation that lack of consumption skills create. But why should government want to promote participation in sport? It is to this question that we turn in the next chapter.

4 Market failure and government intervention

Why does the government spend money on sport and recreation? This is a question that is fundamental to our discussion, particularly because of the importance placed on intervention in sports markets by central and local government. Consumers' expenditure on sport and recreation accounts for a very small share of total consumers' expenditure on leisure and yet government expenditure on sport and recreation is the largest component of total government expenditure on leisure. In addition, expenditure on sport and recreation has been the fastest growing component of public expenditure on leisure over the last twenty years.

Economic welfare principles provide us with reasons for this government interest in sport. When a private market operates successfully, but still it fails to cater adequately for the full effects of the market on the welfare of society, economists call this a situation of 'market failure'. There are several causes of market failure which are relevant to the market for sport. The main purpose of this chapter is to review the nature of these market failures. In each case the existence of a market failure is a reason for considering government intervention, since intervention has the potential to prevent or compensate for the market failure.

Two broad categories of sports market failure can be distinguished: efficiency-related and equity-related. If sport generates social (collective) benefits over and above the private benefits accruing to the participants, then the market may be efficient for the participants but it is not necessarily efficient for society. An efficient market solution takes account of the value to the participating individuals and the cost of supply, but it fails to take account of any additional social benefits. So the socially desirable output will not be produced by the market, which will underprovide resources to the sport and recreation market.

Individual consumers, through their purchasing behaviour, will not encourage the socially optimal level of production (ie a level that generates not only sufficient private benefits but also optimal social benefits). This is because they can get any social benefits going for nothing, ie they can be 'free riders'. One way to generate the socially optimal level of consumption is to reduce prices, but this is unlikely to be done by private market suppliers in the interests of public welfare! Government, accepting responsibility for social welfare, has a reason to encourage higher production and consumption – by subsidising consumers, subsidising suppliers in the commercial and voluntary sectors, or directly supplying the product at the lower price.

Regarding equity, a distribution of resources and products according to the private market may not accord with what government deems to be a fair distribution – the market in this case is inequitable. Again, government may use this as a reason for either subsidising certain consumers, or suppliers, in order to achieve a more equitable distribution of products, resources and sporting opportunities.

Market failures relevant to sport include health, crime, preservation values, public goods, economic impact and equity considerations. We now review both the theory and evidence of such market failures and the implications for government intervention in sports markets.

Sports participation and health

The 1975 White Paper *Sport and Recreation* indicated that the relationship between sports participation and health was one of the reasons for increasing government interest in promoting sports participation. It pointed to the physical and mental health benefits of exercise:

> For many people physical activity makes an important contribution to physical and mental well-being. There is some evidence to suggest that vigorous physical exercise can reduce the incidence of coronary heart disease which in 1972 accounted for about 27 per cent of the deaths of those over 40.

The evidence on the sports participation/health relationship has been building up consistently over the post-war period. It is in the prevention of coronary heart disease that exercise has been established to have its most significant positive effect on health. Over 30 years ago Morris *et al.* (1953) found that bus conductors (spending most of the day walking up and down stairs and rarely sitting down) were at less risk of having heart attacks than sedentary bus drivers. Probably the most important study of the effect of physical activity as part of work on the risk of coronary heart disease was the San

Francisco longshoremen study (Paffenbarger *et al.*, 1970). The longshoremen were studied over a 22-year period paying particular attention to the different energy demands of the work carried out by cargo handlers and dockworkers, on the one hand, and by supervisory staff on the other. It was established that men expending at least 8,500 kilocalories per week had significantly less risk of heart attack than those using less energy than this per week. The study concluded that if all men in the study had worked at or above the 8500 kilocalories energy level per week then the death rate from heart attack over the study period would have been reduced by nearly 50 per cent.

The obvious question raised is whether it is possible for sedentary workers to obtain such health benefits by physical activity in leisure time. Epidemiological studies seem to indicate that it is. Morris (1973, 1980) followed up his study of London busmen with an analysis of the leisure-time activities of 17,944 middle-aged British civil servants. He found that those who reported regular vigorous physical exercise (mainly through involvement in sport) had less than half the risk of coronary heart disease over the 8-year follow-up period than those who did no vigorous exercise. Paffenbarger *et al.*'s (1986) longitudinal study of 16,936 Harvard alumni involved the construction of an energy expenditure index reflecting total energy expenditure per week, expressed in kilocalories, through sporting activity. They found that death rates (from all causes) declined steadily as energy expended on such activity increased from less than 500 to 3,500 kilocalories per week. Beyond that rate of energy expenditure there was no additional beneficial effect on death rates. The 1986 study looked at death rates from all causes. Earlier papers (Paffenbarger *et al.*, 1969 and 1978) had established the benefits of vigorous leisure-time sports activity on the prevention of coronary heart disease for the Harvard alumni.

Other studies have shown that the reduction of risk of heart attack is not the only health benefit of exercise. Thomas *et al.* (1981) indicate that physical exercise can have a beneficial effect in the prevention and treatment of hypertension, obesity, diabetes mellitus, anxiety, depression and asthma.

In addition to this epidemiological evidence, Gratton and Tice (1989) produced evidence on the beneficial effects of sports participation and health using data from several General Household Surveys and the Health and Lifestyle Survey. Their evidence suggests that sports participants are healthier and lead healthier lifestyles than non-participants. It also suggests that participation in sport is associated with an enriched quality of life since sports participants also take part in a much wider range of non-sport leisure activities than non-participants.

The question arises of whether such health benefits are purely private or social. If the main beneficiary of such benefits is the participant then we do not have a strong case for government intervention on health grounds. There are, however, several aspects to the sports participation and health relationship where government intervention may lead to an increase in social welfare.

One argument relates to the possible difference between the benefits of exercise as perceived by the consumer and the real private benefits. Following Grossman (1972), health economists refer to the health production function where the 'output' of health status is related to a variety of 'inputs', one of which is exercise (the others include diet, housing conditions, work conditions and the health service of doctors and hospitals). Grossman developed a demand for health model where demand depends on the rate of return on health capital, which itself depends on the wage rate and the health production function.

Grossman's model, however, assumes that the individual has perfect knowledge of both the health production function and the rate of return on health capital. In reality, people are uncertain of the impact of exercise on their health capital, but even more uncertain as to the rate of return on health capital. This uncertainty is likely to cause inefficiency in consumer decision-making in the form of underconsumption of 'exercise for health reasons'. This is a specific form of market failure, since the market left to its own devices does not give sufficient knowledge. In the terms of Scitovsky's analysis examined in Chapter 3, there is a lack of consumption skill.

In order to overcome inefficiency due to consumer ignorance, therefore, there is a justification for government intervention to educate consumers on the nature of the benefits from exercise. In Britain this is one of the roles of the Health Education Authority (formerly, the Health Education Council), which has been responsible for several exercise-related promotional campaigns such as the 'Look After Yourself' campaign. The Sports Council also emphasises the health benefits of exercise in its sports promotion campaigns (such as its 'Ever Thought of Sport' initiative).

The effects of ignorance can also be counteracted by offering subsidised exercise opportunities for health reasons. This is a 'merit good' approach – enticing the 'ignorant' consumer to consume greater quantities than they otherwise would have done. However, the ignorance factor is not the only argument for government intervention that relates to the sports participation and health relationship.

Fentem and Bassey (1978 and 1981) identified the main health beneficiaries from sports participation to be those most dependent on health care services. Such services, provided mainly by the government funded National Health Service in Britain, are expensive. If, because of the health benefits of sports participation, health services are released to concentrate on less preventable health problems, there may be efficiency gains. This depends on the relative values of, on the one hand, the cost of prevention via subsidies to sports participation and, on the other hand, the consequent health gains in less preventable problem areas.

Gratton and Tice (1987) have provided further evidence on the importance of this social benefit. Using data from the General Household Survey for 1977 they looked at all those respondents who reported having a chronic illness in the 14 days prior to interview. Table 4.1 shows the percentage of these chronic illness sufferers who have made use of health services (that is outpatients at hospitals, inpatients at hospitals, or GP services) in the twelve months prior to interview, cross-tabulated with sports participation. The table clearly shows that those that take part in sport, though chronically ill, use health services less than non-participants who are also chronically ill. Further cross-tabulations allowing for both age and income show that the sharpest differences between non-participants and participants occur for the older age groups and the lower-income groups, that is those groups most prone to illness and those making the heaviest demand on health services. This evidence indicates that the importance of this benefit has up to now probably been seriously underestimated.

Table 4.1 – Sports participation and use of health services by the chronically ill

	Non-Participant %	Participant %	Total %
No use of NHS services	33.7	41.4	36.00
Some use of NHS services	66.3	58.6	64.00

Note: Sample size = 14,743
Source: General Household Survey, 1977

The implication of this argument is that there is a role for government over and above the educational one. A more efficient means of achieving health policy objectives may be to redistribute resources from health services to direct expenditure on the provision or subsidisation of active recreation facilities, ie prevention rather than cure. There is a temporal problem here in that benefits from any increased participation are likely to take many years to show through in a reduced demand for health services. In the short term, it is unlikely that any increase in public expenditure in sport would lead to any immediate reduction in expenditure on health.

Nevertheless, conventional health care costs have risen dramatically in developed countries, especially under private insurance systems, eg in the USA they account for approximately 12 per cent of the Gross National Product. In the face of such high costs, at least one commentator has suggested that the difficulties of measuring the health care savings arising from increased exercise should not stop government from spending on sport as a substitute for health care, since it is not a marginal problem, but a significant misallocation:

> US analyses suggest that as much as a half of the total burden of medical costs is attributable to preventable forms of disease. Commonly, personal lifestyle is at fault, and often there is evidence an increase of physical activity could contribute to a prevention of the illness in question . . .
>
> . . . Provided that exercise is enhancing health, sport programmes do not necessarily require detailed economic justification. They are at least as legitimate a charge upon government resources as are costly programmes of secondary and tertiary medical care. (Shepherd 1990)

Sport in the Community . . . into the 1990s (Sports Council, 1988) pointed out that government policies designed to maximise these social benefits associated with sports participation may have to be targetted at particular groups:

> At the moment, however, this interest in health is largely middle-class and wider market penetration is likely to take time. There remains great divides in the health of the nation – between rich and poor, men and women, north and south, those in work and the unemployed, and manual and non-manual workers. Recent evidence suggests that these divisions are widening rather than narrowing (Health Education Council, 1987). In particular, women continue to suffer appreciably poorer standards of health than men, especially among the less affluent (Office of Health Economics, 1987). The divisions by social class and geography are similar to variations in sports participation.
>
> There is, therefore, both an opportunity and a challenge for providers of sport and recreation. An increased awareness of health and fitness amongst the more affluent provides considerable opportunity for development, but continuing wide disparities in the health of the nation offer a challenge where sport and recreation could significantly help the Government to achieve its objectives.

This statement is supported by the evidence presented in Gratton and Tice (1989). Figure 4.1 shows a subjective health indicator, the percentage of the sample rating their health as 'good' over the last year, classified by age and income for sports participants and non-participants in 1980. For every category sports participants had a higher percentage than non-participants, suggesting that, whatever their age and income, sports participants in general 'felt better' than non-participants. One of the most significant aspects of Figure 4.1 is that the difference between participants and non-participants increases as we move up the age-groups and down the income groups.

Figure 4.1 – Rating health as 'good' over last year
black for non-participants, white for participants

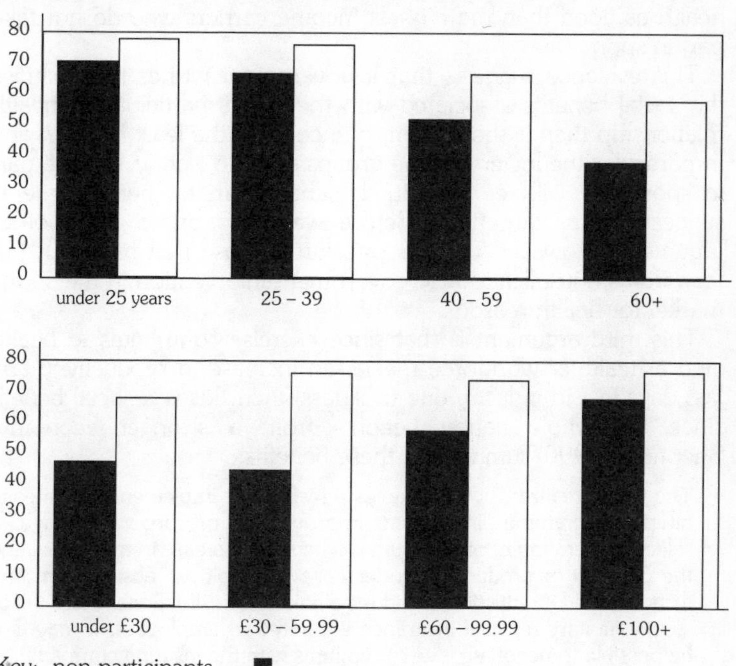

Key: non-participants ■
participants □

Source: Gratton, C. and Tice, A. 'Leisure Participation, Lifestyle and Health' 1987.

The Health Education Council evidence referred to in the quote above has shown that health deteriorates with age, and that better-off people are healthier than poorer people. Shepherd (1990) shows the potential of using exercise in the care of the elderly:

> The provision of social and medical services to the frail elderly has thus become a daunting charge upon national exchequers . . . There is

> good evidence that regular physical activity can induce some extension of the average lifespan . . . Much more important consequences of regular exercise include a strengthening of the cardio-respiratory system and of the skeletal muscles, with an increase of flexibility at the major joints of the body . . . . Exercise programmes thus have the potential to set back and to reduce the need for the costly institutional care of the elderly.

Figure 4.1 shows that for sports participants the decline in health with age, although still there, is less steep; the health differences (on this indicator) between income groups almost disappears for sports participants. In fact after 40 years of age the lowest income earners that take part in sport have a higher percentage rating their health as good than the highest income earners who do not take part in sport.

This evidence suggests that if government wishes to maximise the social benefits associated with the sports participation/health relationship then it should aim to encourage the least healthy, and in particular the lower income groups and the elderly, to take part in sport. We will see later in the chapter that other arguments suggest similar targetting. Before we move on to these other arguments, however, there is one further case that has been put forward as a justification for government intervention in the sports market for health reasons.

This third argument is that since exercise contributes to health (and a healthier workforce means an increase in productivity and less days lost in industry due to illness) then this is a social benefit since the whole nation benefits from a stronger economy. Shepherd (1990) summarises these benefits:

> The gains realized by companies which have implemented work-site fitness programmes include an improvement of corporate image, a selective recruitment of premium workers, an increase in the quality and the quantity of production, a decrease of employee absenteeism and turnover, and a reduction of industrial injuries. In situations where full or supplementary medical insurance is offered to employees, it may also be possible to negotiate lower premiums with the insuring company.

Gratton and Taylor (1987a), show that there is evidence that absenteeism is a major problem in British industry and that over the post-war period, it has been on the increase. Between 1962 and 1982 the number of days of 'certified incapacity for sickness and invalidity' rose by 28 per cent for men and 17 per cent for women. 'Certified incapacity' refers only to those whose illness lasted for three days or more and thus required a doctor's certificate. (Unfortunately this absenteeism data is not available from 1983 onwards because of the introduction of self-certification of illness). This rise in the number of days lost because of illness cannot be explained by changes in employment since, over the same period, male employment fell by 18.4 per cent and female employment rose by 8.8 per cent. Thus the number of days lost for men increased considerably over a period when employment decreased considerably.

Figure 4.2 shows that sports participants are less likely to be 'away from work last week' than non-participants. This is true for every age category and every income category. It seems then that participation in sport is associated with reduced absenteeism. Such reduced absenteeism is a social benefit in that it reduces public expenditure through the statutory sick-pay scheme.

Figure 4.2 – % away from work last week

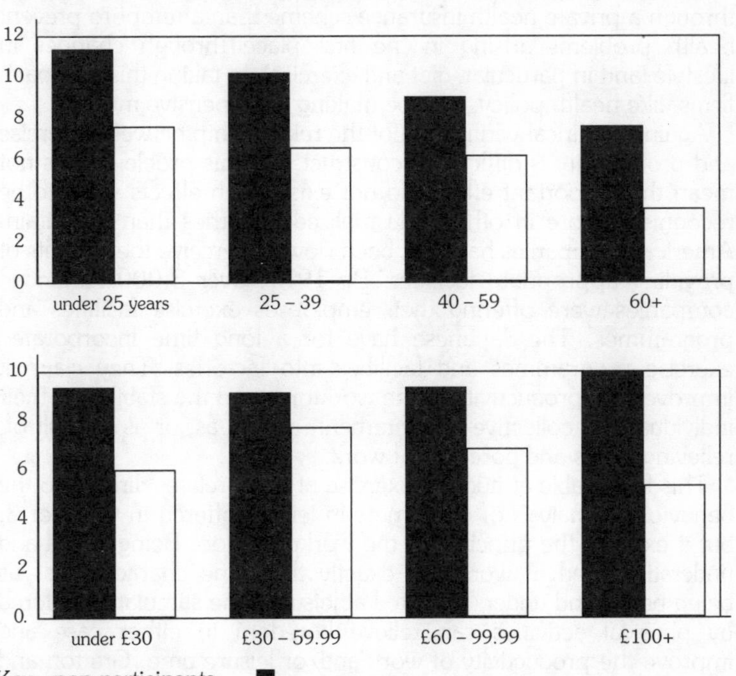

Key: non-participants ■
participants □

Source: Gratton, C. and Tice, A. 'Leisure Participation, Lifestyle and Health' 1987

However, employers are probably the main beneficiaries of any reduction in absenteeism. Not only do they bear a considerable cost burden in terms of occupational sick-pay schemes (particularly for senior staff) but under the new self-certification of illness arrangements it is the employers who carry the main administrative costs of the statutory sick-pay scheme. They pay out the money initially and then recover it from their national insurance remittances to the Department of Health and Social Security. We should expect therefore to see employers providing exercise programmes and facilities for their staff. At the moment, in Britain, there is little evidence that this is happening, with firms offering membership of private health insurance schemes in preference to direct provision of exercise facilities.

It is interesting that British firms, though obviously more aware of the benefits of a fitter, healthier workforce than before, are following the pattern of British health policy over the recent past, with more emphasis on ill-health treatment rather than ill-health prevention. It is thought better to provide high quality health services through a private health insurance scheme than attempt to prevent health problems arising in the first place through changes in lifestyle (and in particular, diet and exercise). In taking this approach firms, like health policy, may be making an expensive mistake.

Again, empirical verification of the relationship between exercise and productivity is difficult to construct, but this problem does not mean that important effects do not exist. Such effects seem to be recognised more in other industrialised countries than in Britain. American companies have not been slow to perceive the benefits of providing appropriate facilities. By 1979, over 3,000 American companies were offering their employees exercise facilities and programmes. The Japanese have for a long time incorporated exercise programmes and facilities into factories. They claim it improves the productivity of the workforce and the stability of their individual and collective temperament, as well as, or as a result of, relieving stress and boredom at work.

This favourable attitude to exercise at work relates directly to the behavioural analysis of consumers in leisure offered in Chapter 3, but it extends the principle to the workplace too. Being bored and understimulated at work has exactly the same characteristics as being bored and understimulated at leisure. The stimulation offered by physical activities can relieve boredom in either case and improve the productivity of work and/or leisure time. Gratton and Tice (1989) use General Household Survey data to show that sports participants in Britain not only take part in a broader range of recreational activities than non-participants, but they also work *longer* hours.

Despite the fact that we might expect this last social benefit arising from the sports participation/health relationship to be provided by the commercial sector, the government could take the 'merit good' approach discussed in the context of consumers, and apply it equally to employers, whose 'ignorance' and underprovision of sporting opportunities contributes to macroeconomic underachievement.

The arguments discussed so far in this section provide a considerable case for government intervention in the sport and recreation market on health grounds. However, up to now we have only considered the positive side of the relationship between sports participation and health. There is also a negative side.

Over the last 20 years there has been an increasing demand for more dangerous recreational activities. The Third Nationwide Outdoor Recreation Plan (US Department of the Interior, 1979) in the USA noted 'the soaring popularity of high-risk activities' amongst the 25 to 34 years age group. The plan indicated that :

> along with increasing risk comes greater numbers of fatalities, particularly in such pursuits as hang-gliding, rock-climbing, off-road and recreation vehicle use, scuba-diving, flying and snow-mobiling. The Metropolitan Life Insurance Company estimates that 10,000 Americans die each year as the result of some planned risk taken for fun or adventure.

In Britain, there is less evidence of 'soaring popularity' of high-risk sports (although the Digest of Sports Statistics (Sports Council, 1986) did indicate that the fastest growing sport in the UK was ballooning!). Perhaps more important to the argument of this section is not so much the occurrence of fatalities connected with the most dangerous sports but rather the occurrence of sports injuries and accidents associated with the most popular sports. It is such injuries that make up the cost side of the balance sheet of the sports participation and health relationship.

This has been an area where there has been a notable lack of empirical evidence. However, for the first time in 1987 the General Household Survey (GHS) included a question which inquired as to 'accidents in the three months prior to interview as a result of which you (or your children) saw a doctor or went to hospital'. Eighteen per cent of accidents leading to a visit to a doctor or hospital happened while doing some kind of sport or physical exercise. Above average percentages of sports accidents were concentrated in the 5–15 and 16–44 age ranges, among men, and among professional groups (ie those groups with the highest propensity to take part in sport). Table 4.2 gives a summary of the results classified by age.

No data exists at the moment on how these accidents are related to individual sports. Also, accidents will not cover all demands on health services related to participation in sport. Many sports injuries would not be reported in response to the question asked in the GHS, although requiring some form of medical treatment. However, the very high proportion of accidents that are related to sport in Table 4.2 indicates that the negative side of the sports participation and health relationship may not be insignificant.

Ideally in order to make sensible policy decisions with respect to government intervention in the sport and recreation market for health reasons, we need to be able to assess the net health benefit of a given level of participation in a given sport taking into account the positive and negative aspects discussed above. We could then consider the possibility of differential subsidies to different sports on the basis of such net benefits. At the moment we simply do not have sufficient information to carry out such calculations or such policies.

Sport and crime

It has been claimed that participation in sport will 'improve life for many who would otherwise be attracted to delinquency and vandalism' (Policy for Inner Cities, Department of the Environment, 1977a). One of the target groups often chosen by sports providers is young people, and both implicitly and explicitly it is often recognised that provision of sporting opportunities for this group will help promote constructive leisure pursuits, at the expense of more negative activities such as crime and vandalism.

If the channelling of energies and effort into constructive leisure pursuits such as sport helps to reduce the likelihood of criminal activity by the individuals concerned, then obviously it is not just these individuals who benefit. Their potential 'victims' also benefit – an 'external' or social benefit which individuals would not pay for, not even the actual 'victims' since they do not realise their parlous state until the crime actually happens. In such circumstances the government may be justified in subsidising and/or supplying sports opportunities, for much the same reason as one of those used above in the context of health and sport – prevention is less costly than cure.

Despite the frequency with which policy makers refer to this relationship between involvement in sport and reduction in anti-social behaviour by, in particular, young adolescents, hard evidence in support of this argument is difficult to come by. There has been no systematic, aggregate work on the size of this benefit in Britain, but there is some rather more *ad hoc* empirical support for it.

The London Borough of Waltham Forest, in the early 1980s, set up a Working Party to examine the problem of vandalism on housing estates. The methods employed included a survey of over

Table 4.2 – Sports accidents by age

	Age						
	0–4	5–15	16–44	45–64	65–74	75–99	Total
Yes, to any accident	88 (4.8%)	172 (4.6%)	553 (5.1%)	176 (3.1%)	66 (2.8%)	64 (4.0%)	1119 (4.3%)
Of which sports accidents	4 (0.2%)	62 (1.7%)	110 (1.0%)	18 (0.3%)	6 (0.3%)	1 (0.1%)	201 (0.8%)
No, to any accident	1745 (95.2%)	3572 (95.4%)	10230 (94.9%)	5550 (96.9%)	2309 (97.2%)	1526 (96.0%)	2493 (95.7%)
Missing values	22	56	18	7	1	4	108
Total	1833	3744	10783	5726	2375	1590	26051

Source: General Household Survey, 1987 (by courtesy of The Sports Council).

350 youngsters on five housing estates. On the question of why vandalism occurs, the Working Party concluded:

> In trying to explain why youngsters 'smash things up' on estates there was a very clear link in the youngsters minds between boredom and vandalism. Whilst other reasons were given ('they do it for fun', 'to prove themselves' and 'expression'), boredom was by far the most common explanation. The strength of this link, together with the youngsters' desire to see better provision . . . supports the Working Party's original brief (to provide recreational opportunities for juveniles living on or around housing estates with a view to reducing vandalism therein). (London Borough of Waltham Forest 1981).

The sentiment behind this finding is entirely consistent with the theory of stimulation-seeking leisure behaviour offered in the previous chapter. In an article explicitly addressing the issue, Scitvosky (1981) suggests:

> an underlying assumption . . . is that different sources of excitement are good substitutes for each other. If true, that points the way to reducing violence and crime by providing socially more acceptable sources of risk, danger and excitement . . . . City officials in the United States are very slowly beginning to recognize man's need to face danger and take risks for excitement's sake, and the absurdity of 'honey and milk toast' activities in urban recreation programs. To quote one official, 'What an indictment against our programs that almost everything children do that is risky and fun is done off the playground'.

Ignorance or inexperience may also be reasons for young people choosing the less desirable route to excitement. Both of these reasons may be seen to demonstrate the specific market failure of a lack of consumption skill.

This sentiment also lies behind the subject of a Home Office report on preventing juvenile crime (Heal and Laycock 1987). This concerns a summer programme of recreational activities (SPACE) for youngsters aged 10 to 16, organised for many years by Staffordshire Police. The report concludes: 'The analyses of the Staffordshire data . . . are consistent with the view that the SPACE scheme had an effect on crime, at least in its earlier years'.

Compared with the August crime figures before the county-wide SPACE scheme began, the figures for shop theft were 17 per cent lower, thefts from motor vehicles 14 per cent lower, and burglary 10 per cent lower. These reductions in crime compare favourably with August crime figures in other counties without such summer recreation programmes. Furthermore, besides the short run objective of reducing juvenile crime by giving youngsters something purposeful to do, the SPACE scheme also has longer term objectives that are crime-relevant, ie:

> reducing the number of developing career criminals; providing an opportunity for the police and young people to meet in non-confrontational situations, may have a positive effect on the attitudes of youngsters to police officers and vice versa. This could reduce the amount of trivial offending and/or the police response to it. A further and important aim of the scheme is an improvement in police/public relations . . . . The work of the police for the young not only affects the youngsters directly but almost certainly would lead to an improvement in police/parent relations. (Heal and Laycock 1987)

Rosenthal (1982) reports a study where 120 juvenile offenders were split into two samples of 60. One set were sent to Outward Bound schools, the other to conventional training schools.

> The results showed positive changes in regard to altruism, alienation, socialisation, manifest aggression, social maladjustment and value orientation for Outward Bound graduates. Significant positive changes also occurred by creating an increased level of aspiration and maturity . A one year follow-up indicated only 20 per cent of the wilderness-adventure group had later lapsed while 42 per cent of the boys in traditional institutions lapsed. (Rosenthal, 1982).

Rosenthal's thesis is that it is not sport but 'risk exercise' (ie physical activity that involves risk) that generates such benefits. He argues that exercise accompanied by this risk factor: 'invigorates one physically and mentally and produces a state of well-being and elation, oft-times bordering on euphoria. All this adds up to a sense of joy and happiness, a renewing of one's courage and vigor, a peace of mind.' (Rosenthal, 1980). He suggests that his work adds: 'a new dimension to the concept of physical fitness, namely a mental adjunct. This is accomplished by the addition of well-calculated risks to the exercise programs.' Clearly this is a specific manifestation of the psychology of leisure choices demonstrated in Chapter 3.

More evidence on the sport-crime relationship is promised by an experimental project, sponsored by the Sports Council. The Solent Sports Counselling Project began life in December 1983 as an experimental, 12-month, pilot project. The aim was to identify first time offenders and young people at risk and encourage them to take part in sport in order to channel their surplus energy into something constructive. After continuing as a Hampshire Probation Service project, funded by the Manpower Services Commission, the Solent project became, in April 1987, one of the Sports Council's National Demonstration Projects (projects designed to show how particular target groups could be attracted into sport).

Two years monitoring of the results of the Solent project led to the following statement:

> In summary, almost half the clients have maintained a trouble-free record since being involved with the project and a further half-dozen clients appear to have reduced their previous rates of offending, although the pattern of their offences remains largely the same, usually petty stealing. In some cases the project has had significant successes in helping to halt long-term criminals with histories of serious crime, in two cases including assault and in one case wounding, endangering life. That fourteen clients have either been re-convicted or definitely face future court appearances is probably not surprising, given the scale of the clients' previous offences. In these cases it can only be hoped that the contact which some of the clients have maintained with the Sports Leaders on an informal basis, and the efforts of their Probation Officers in reminding them of their sporting experiences, may yet have some beneficial impact in the long term. (Sports Council, 1989).

There is some evidence, therefore, that crime and vandalism may be reduced by greater participation in sport. The evidence does not extend, however, to proving that prevention is *less costly* than curing crime, and more work is needed on this cost-benefit problem. Nevertheless, if sport has the potential to generate social benefits through reduction in vandalism and delinquency, then there is a strong case for government intervention to encourage participation in sport. However, such intervention must be targetted at those most likely, otherwise, to engage in such anti-social behaviour, in an effort to compensate for their lack of consumption skills. This argument therefore suggests that government action should probably be directed at young people from low-income, socially deprived backgrounds, living predominantly in inner-city areas.

Of course, it is important to recognise that as well as having the potential to generate external benefits of this type, sport has also achieved notoriety for being associated directly with crime *costs*, particularly in the form of football hooliganism. However, this association is a spurious one for the purposes of this chapter. The distinction between sports participation and sports spectating is a critical one here. The efficiency arguments used to justify government intervention in sports markets are applicable to participation, *not* to spectating.

The nature of utility derived from sports spectating has the potential to be very different to that derived from participation. In terms of the analysis used in this and the previous chapter, the demand for stimulation and excitement via sports participation gives rise to *fulfilment* through physical activity, which results in both private and collective benefits. By contrast the demand for excitement through spectating can give rise to physical *frustrations* that result in hooliganism. As such, spectating is another issue and not relevant to arguments for government subsidy.

Preservation values and sport

This reason for government intervention relates, rather unusually, to benefits to *non-users* from the provision of sporting opportunities and facilities. Walsh (1986) refers to such benefits as indirect consumption:

> Direct consumption refers to the flow of services supporting the experience of on-site use of parks and other recreation sites. Indirect consumption appears to be of two broad types, one a flow and the other a stock. Indirect use refers to the flow of information about these resources and its consumption as indoor recreation. We will refer to the other type of indirect consumption as preservation value, defined as knowing that recreation and environmental resources are protected. Both occur offsite yet depend on the programs of recreation agencies.

The indirect consumption that Walsh refers to above would include, for example, consumers sitting at home watching a television programme (or reading a newspaper article) about sporting activities or resources. These consumers may never take part in such activities but their satisfaction would be reduced if the activities did not take place. An example (though not from the public sector) would be the reported large number of professional football (and cricket) supporters who follow the game through newspapers and television but never attend a live match.

The benefits of such indirect consumption are very difficult to measure. They are also, in the main, private benefits to the individuals concerned, paid for through normal market transactions. Even so, there may be social welfare aspects of relevance here. Recently, satellite television stations have been prevented from purchasing exclusive rights to coverage of major sports events such as Wimbledon and the FA Cup Final. The implication of this action is that such events are 'merit goods' that warrant a broader audience than the satellite stations' service.

The second type of indirect consumption relates mainly to the preservation of sport and recreation opportunities and facilities. Preservation values include option, existence, and bequest demands as suggested by Weisbrod (1964) and Krutilla (1967). Walsh points out the differences between these different aspects of preservation value:

> Option value is defined as the annual payment of a kind of insurance premium to guarantee the possibility of future recreation use (in addition to the expected benefits of direct and indirect use)... Existence value is the willingness to pay for the individual satisfaction of knowing that a recreational or natural resource is protected. Bequest value is defined as the willingness to pay for the satisfaction derived from endowing future generations with these resources.

In each case the values placed on sport and recreation opportunities and facilities are not reflected in many market transactions. Some club organisations may extract payment for these values, through membership fees which some pay for direct consumption but others pay for preservation values. However, the penetration of clubs in the total value of such benefits is likely to be low – most members of sports participation clubs use the opportunity to participate in the clubs' activities, few pay membership subscriptions just for the option of participating, or because of existence or bequest values. As in the general externality case, the presence of option, existence and bequest values requires sport and recreation provision above the level which the private market supplies. The government has a social welfare reason for ensuring greater production through its own supply or through subsidisation of its outdoor and indoor facilities.

There have been various studies in North America attempting to measure the monetary value of such benefits (eg Greenley, Walsh and Young, 1982) and there is some evidence that the main benefits (in terms of willingness to pay) accrue to those who participate in recreation activities. That is, direct users are the ones who are also the major indirect consumers. In which case, it may be possible to internalise such benefits by some sort of extensive membership scheme, such as the National Trust operates in Britain.

Public goods

Some sport and recreation products demonstrate characteristics which qualify them for recognition as 'public goods' (also referred to as 'collective goods'). The principal characteristics attached to such goods are that they are non-rival and non-excludable in consumption. Non-rival means that one person's consumption does not prevent another person from enjoying exactly the same product at the same time. Non-excludable means that no consumer can be prevented from enjoying the product. Under these two conditions private market provision is not worthwhile, so public goods will be underprovided by the private market.

It has been argued that large, natural, resource-based recreation resources, such as forests, lakes and reservoirs, mountains, rivers and coastlines are public goods. The benefits provided to users of such recreation resources are non-rival (until the exceptional case where congestion becomes a problem). Also, such areas are often difficult or expensive to exclude non-payers from. The preservation benefits that accrue to non-users of large outdoor recreation areas also demonstrate non-rivalness and non-excludability. Such areas are not pure public goods but there are certainly elements of collectiveness to the benefits they generate.

Public sector involvement in natural recreation resources of this type can be split into three groups: National Parks; water-based recreation resources; and local and countryside parks. Unlike the USA where provision of National Parks is a major area of government expenditure in recreation, in the UK public expenditure on National Parks is a small area of total government expenditure on leisure. Similarly, although many water-based recreational areas have been publicly owned for many years, recreation is often a minor objective of the water authorities and the British Waterways Board. It is only in the area of local and countryside parks that we see substantial public expenditure and yet, in this area, benefits are often excludable and rival.

International sporting success is a purer form of public good. A quote from the White Paper *Sport and Recreation* (1975) indicates the point: 'Success in international sport has great value for the community not only in terms of raising morale but also by inspiring young people to take an active part in sport'.

Because many of the benefits of international sporting success (eg improved national morale, increased interest in sport) are such that nobody can be prevented from feeling them, they are non-excludable. Because everyone can enjoy these benefits together with no congestion in consumption, they are non-rival. A free market would underprovide such public goods, because there is always the temptation for consumers to become 'free riders', benefiting from the products without paying for them. Government can ensure that adequate provision is made for excellence in sport to be produced, and also ensure that those who benefit from this public good pay, through taxes. The public good effect of sporting excellence has several variants, as illustrated in the *Coe Report* (1985) on British sport's preparation for the Olympics:

(i) Sporting success for Britain makes people proud to be British. Sporting failure or decline has the reverse effect; we blame each other and ourselves and we feel less committed to the national cause.
(ii) The link with prestige abroad is important .... If our teams and individuals are successful, they help the country's image abroad; thus, directly and indirectly, they can help to sell our products and services and earn foreign currency.
(iii) Sporting achievement in the Olympics is also a vital contributor to the Government's and the Sports Council's strategy to boost participation in sport and recreation. The Olympic Games create

> heroes and heroines. These encourage and inspire youngsters – and indeed people of all ages – to participate in sport, to develop and to enjoy themselves.

First, there is the simple utility boost to anyone who enjoys success by national sportspeople. Second, an indiscriminate (non-rival) and universal (non-excludable) economic impact results from excellence in sport; various organisations, such as the Confederation of British Industry, the Trades Union Congress, and the British Council were cited by the Coe Commission as supportive of this view. Third, there is a 'demonstration effect' which will almost certainly beneficially affect the number of people participating in sport, their frequencey of participation and/or possibly the number of years they participate. However, what is not clear is the extent to which such demonstration effects are internationally as opposed to domestically generated: in other words is it just exposure of *any* major event that promotes participation, regardless of who is winning, or does success by *domestic* teams and individuals generate a stronger demonstration effect?

Public good benefits apply at the local level too – regional, national and international sporting successes bring about local public good effects, especially to the home area of the successful sportsperson.

However, whereas it is easy to define *likely* public good benefits arising from sporting success, unfortunately they are also very difficult to measure and so their importance is difficult to assess. Nevertheless, the *ad hoc* evidence and 'expert opinion' suggests that the public good effects of excellence in sport are significant. The Coe Commission produced its report as an appeal for funding for British sport's preparation for the 1990 Olympics – especially support from the Government. The Commission was aware that left to 'the market' there would be insufficient funding, inadequate preparation and therefore underproduction of British successes in the Olympics.

On the basis of the public good arguments alone we would expect to see government involved in the promotion of excellence of sporting achievement and the financial support of élite sportsmen and sportswomen. Of the £164 million expenditure on excellence in 1985–86, ten per cent came from the public sector, as shown in Table 2.5. One part of this expenditure, the subsidisation of National Sports Centres, may be justified on the grounds that such facilities are vital to the production of a public good, excellence.

National Centres can charge élite sportspeople and their clubs for the use of their facilities, but they cannot extract the true value of the resulting excellence from the wider public, who receive the public good benefits. Only the government can 'internalise' these collective benefits by subsidising National Centres through general taxation. Ironically the most recent initiatives concerning National Centres, taken by the Sports Council on behalf of the government, have been designed to eliminate the subsidies given to these facilities. Such initiatives appear to ignore the public good benefits that these Centres help to produce. However, it is possible that excellent users of National Sports Centres will continue to be subsidised, if the reduction in the losses made by the Centres is achieved by making profits from secondary users, the non-excellent.

Another example of the failure of the market to efficiently produce the public good of excellence in sport is sponsorship: 'many of the characteristics of sponsorship are not conducive to effective or efficient production of excellence in sport' (Taylor 1990). The volatility/uncertainty of sponsorship prejudices a continuous production flow of excellence. Furthermore, sponsorship is usually directed towards financing events. Hardly any goes to other inputs at least as important as events in the production process, such as training, coaching, facilities and support services.

Infant industry

The infant industry argument is used to justify government subsidy of the production or sale of a commodity when that commodity is in the early stages of development and faces severe international competition. Excellence in sport might be seen in this light, especially in some emergent sports, and also in view of the immaturity of excellence production processes in British sport compared with, for example the systematised processes of the Eastern bloc and US higher education, or even with more mature 'professional' processes in other competitor nations such as Australia and West Germany. There are several characteristics of an infant industry in the way Britain produces excellence in sport.

Some sports, including judo, volleyball, weightlifting and wrestling in Britain have an *intrinsic commercial disadvantage* in terms of their ability to attract spectators, media interest and/or commercial sponsorship. This disadvantage is rooted in the lack of a history in this country of spectator or media interest in the sports, and also possibly the perceived inappropriateness of the sports for any potential sponsor's 'image'. These sports attract commercial interest in other countries, however, so the intrinsic disadvantage is not necessarily universal, absolute or permanent. Indeed, senior personnel in the English Volleyball Association are well aware of the spectator and media potential in their sport. They are actively promoting high-level invitation tournaments featuring world-class teams, in order to attract such interest as a means of generating a demonstration effect. However, in the meantime volleyball, like other sports with this intrinsic disadvantage, is heavily reliant on the Sports Council for the funding of excellence programmes.

Sports with little immediate potential for generating commercial income from excellence are typically compensated with high excellence grants per member from the Sports Council. Another factor in this favourable *per capita* grant allocation must be the limited ability of these sports to raise their own income from memberships, awards, etc, either because of the limited appeal of such sports for mass participation or the immaturity of their organisational development in this country – a straightforward manifestion of the 'infant industry' justification for public subsidy.

The payment of excellent individuals in sport is not always symptomatic of a mature market. Although some individuals in some sports earn large rewards for their excellence, there is a very retarded system for payments to excellent sportspeople in most sports. Of course this is related to principles of amateurism, which opens up another whole area of discussion. Abstracting necessarily from this debate, one of the results of the British approach to payment of individual excellent sports persons is that many of them make substantial financial contributions to participate and gain very little monetary reward, despite the fact that their excellence often has a market value realisable in commercial events, advertising, publishing, etc.

This hit-and-miss payment of excellent sportspeople is obviously tied in with equity arguments, discussed later in this chapter. But it is also a sign that the market for excellence has a long way to mature.

The provision of training and event facilities for excellence in sport is also a market which is at an early, imperfect stage of development. Competition facilities provide potential for commercial sector provision, for the simple reason that the paying spectator is involved. The most famous spectator facility in Britain is Wembley Stadium, a commercial facility which includes an indoor arena as well as the famous outdoor stadium. Other relevant commercial interests include professional football clubs, county cricket clubs, large tennis venues such as Wimbledon and Queens, and a new generation of commercial indoor arena proposals.

Commercial interest in the development of major event facilities is often hesitant, possibly for good reason (Gratton and Taylor 1987b). The spectator market for major events is largely unproven in Britain. Spectator numbers in this country are dominated by one sport, soccer, which is in long-term decline and continually suffers uncertainties in finance and demand. Other sports have so far been unable to command large attendances (10,000 plus) for more than the one or two, chiefly traditional, major events. Major events facilities require large scale attendances on a *regular* basis, as for instance team franchises in American football and baseball provide for many stadia in the USA. In practice it may well be that indoor arenas in Britain will have as primary targets the more proven markets of exhibitions, entertainments events and conferences, besides the unproven sports events market.

Training facility provision is even less attractive to commercial providers – the main markets, governing bodies, often have very limited resources to pay for the use of such facilities. So it is that the Government is a major provider of both training and competition facilities for excellence in sport. As seen in Chapter 2, the combination of National Sports Centres, provided by the Sports Council, and local authority facilities dominates sports facility supply.

Coaching for excellence in sport has been described as: 'one of the clearest examples in this study of a binding and possibly damaging financial constraint' (Taylor 1990). In the sample of governing bodies investigated for this study, there is substantial evidence of a shortage of national standard coaches in British sport. Representatives from seven of the seventeen governing bodies interviewed indicated a shortage of coaches at the top level. Two sports indicated that development of centres of excellence was hindered by a lack of suitable coaches. Further evidence of problems in the financing of coaching at the excellence level is evidence of emigration by top British coaches to foreign jobs but little or no evidence of immigration by top foreign coaches into British sport. One of the fundamental causes of such evidence is relatively low pay for top coaches in British sport. When employed full-time the salaries for national coaches are low by international standards. When employed by the hour coaches, like individual participants, sometimes have to lose pay and/or holiday entitlement.

Clearly the market for top coaches can also be seen as immature in development terms. One of the major reasons for Sports Council grant-in-aid to governing bodies is for coaching resources, in an attempt to overcome this deficiency. Also the National Coaching Foundation receives public funding and local authorities are in the forefront of employment of sports coaches for both excellence and mass participation coaching.

One other input into the production of excellence in sport demonstrates immaturity in development – support services, eg medical and physiotherapy. It seems odd to suggest this when both of these services are well established commercial professions. However, in serving the production of excellence in sport, most medical and physiotherapy positions are 'honorary'. Although there are spin-offs in terms of personal kudos and, in the case of physiotherapists, promotion of private businesses, there are still signs of shortage. As with individual participants and coaches, physiotherapists, many of whom are self-employed, will lose earnings as a result of their work for governing bodies. The influence of finance on the situation is illustrated by the case of the British Cycling Federation, which used some of its Olympic Review grant to develop physiotherapy and fitness testing support services that it had previously not budgeted for.

Fitness testing, when undertaken, has traditionally been acquired at low cost in higher education establishments, although in the changing financial climate of this sector such services may become more expensive in future. Access to medical services by excellent sportspeople is often gained by unofficial, privileged short cuts arranged by appropriate staff. Some governing bodies seem happy with such a tradition, but most are agreed that we lag considerably behind some of our major competitor nations in this important area, whilst one or two describe the situation as 'diabolical'. The Sports Council is clearly dissatisfied with this position:

> The need has never been greater for British sportspeople, especially but not only top level performers, to have access to adequate medical and scientific support when and where they need it. Yet medicine remains an area of contention, beset by a traditionally muddled British approach. (*Into the '90s*, Sports Council, 1988).

Sport and economic development

The final argument for government intervention on efficiency grounds is a relatively new argument. In the 1980s the public sector has been involved in sport (and in the arts) for economic development reasons. A city or region develops new sporting facilities partly to change the image of the area and attract tourists. The aim is to stimulate the local economy through the multiplier effects of the tourist expenditure. Conspicuous examples include the bids of Birmingham and Manchester to host the Olympic Games and the successful bid by Sheffield to host the 1991 World Student Games.

In the 1960s regional unemployment was tackled by microeconomic regional policies aimed at attracting manufacturing firms to depressed areas. This became increasingly difficult throughout the

1970s due to the decline in total employment in manufacturing industry in Britain. Also the focus of interest switched from the regional level to urban areas. The nature of the urban problem was such that attracting manufacturing industry into inner cities was not really a feasible solution. Rather, cities needed to be revitalised through investment in infrastructure and in facilities that would attract tourists. New job creation was to be in the new rising service industries.

Spatial imbalance, where one area of the country is overheating while another area suffers recession and unemployment, is an inefficient use of resources, since national output would be higher if the unemployed resources in the depressed region could be put to work in the prosperous region. Such spatial market failure is due to market imperfections, in particular the immobility of factors.

Government intervention in the leisure market for such reasons comes in the form of government grants, targeted at tourism and leisure projects, through the Tourism Development Grants Scheme and the English Tourist Board's grant in aid. Leisure and tourism is a major component of government expenditure under the Urban Programme and the Urban Development grant scheme. It was also the focus of a significant number of Manpower Services Commission (MSC) Community Programme projects, until the MSC was reorganised as the Training Commission in 1987.

Increasingly sport and recreation projects are integrated into such leisure developments. In a few instances, sport is the main focus of the project. Invariably projects such as hosting a major Games are not simply government initiatives (ie local, national or EEC), but rather involve a partnership arrangement between public, private and voluntary sectors with the input ratios of each varying considerably from project to project. Thus Sheffield's investment is public sector led. Manchester's proposed investment was commercial sector led. The important point though is that all such projects involve some government funding, and this is a new type of government intervention in the sport and recreation market. It is regional (or urban) policy re-emerging in a different form and the rationale for it stems from the original regional policy initiative in the 1930s.

Equity in sport

The efficiency arguments reviewed above all suggest that government intervenes in the market for sport and recreation because a market allocation would underprovide resources to this market, since the market ignores the collective nature of the consumption benefits of sport. All the efficiency arguments are based on the same premise: it is possible to increase social welfare by altering the market allocation. Equity is not so much concerned with the total level of social welfare attained but rather with how that total is distributed over members of society. The equity argument for government intervention in the sport and recreation market is an argument for a more equal distribution of the benefits generated through sports participation.

Perhaps the most obvious manifestation of the equity objective is the 'Sport for All' slogan used initially by the Sports Council, but subsequently adopted by many local authorities as a reason for the provision of subsidised sports facilities. Regarding excellence in sport, one of the most fundamental reasons for government intervention is to ensure 'equality of opportunity', such that nobody is denied by financial constraints the opportunity to realise their potential for excellent performance.

One example cited as a market failure of an equity type in the excellence market is sponsorship: 'sponsorship is ineffective in its distribution, being very hit and miss' with respect to both sports and individuals within sports' (Taylor 1990). Some sports suffering from intrinsic commercial disadvantage do not attract sufficient commercial sponsorship revenues to ensure continued production of their excellence public good. Even within sports which do attract substantial sponsorship revenues, certain individuals are likely to miss out – especially the up-and-coming who are just below the top of their sport.

The equity argument has always been a problem for economists because it involves essentially normative arguments and value judgements, which are difficult to support or verify by appeal to the facts. 'Sport for all', for example, may be interpreted in a variety of ways, from literally 'sport for all people' to sport for a few 'recreationally disadvantaged' groups, depending on the equity value judgement of the policy maker. The concept causing problems here is that of 'vertical equity', which concerns the choice of different policies for consumers of different types and circumstances. In order that equity is achieved in matters such as access and opportunity in sports participation, value judgements are needed to specify what equity means.

Vertical equity can be interpreted to mean any one of a number of policies, depending on the values adopted. *Utilitarian* equity aims to achieve the greatest utility for the greatest number. *Rawlsian* equity seeks to maximise the benefits to the most disadvantaged. A *natural endowment* approach to equity would direct policy towards the gifted, who are better able to benefit from the the policy. A *needs* approach would direct policy towards those with greatest need, as identified either relative to others or in relation to a specified social minimum. Equity has been interpreted literally as *equality:* equal provision for all, regardless of factors such as income and access. Finally equity according to *deserving* would attempt to distribute benefits according to whatever criteria of deserving are adopted, which could vary from one extreme (eg inability to pay) to another (the amount actually paid indirectly through taxes for public services). Needless to say, not all of these policies are compatible with each other, since they are based on different value judgements.

The nature of equity issues in the sport and recreation market has not been fully considered by economists, either in theoretical or empirical work. However, equity has been discussed widely in the related area of health (see Culyer 1976 and 1980 and McGuire, Henderson and Mooney 1988), and this provides a useful comparison for a discussion of equity in sport.

Equity considerations are essentially to do with the distribution of income. The argument is that willingness to pay is not an acceptable criterion for certain goods and services, since many groups in society do not have the ability to pay due to the existing distribution of income. Many 'right-wing' economists have argued that if the aim is to redistribute income then this is best achieved by cash transfers rather than by interference with the market mechanism. They show that utility will be higher for a consumer benefiting from a cash redistribution rather than a redistribution in kind. They argue that redistribution in kind is paternalistic and assumes that individual consumers are not the best judge of their own welfare. However, this analysis is based on the assumption of independent utility functions, ie one person's utility is independent of other people's consumption and utilities. Much of the attack on such conclusions has been based on the argument that utility functions are in fact *interdependent.*

Culyer (1976) argues that redistribution in kind can be justified on the basis of the existence of 'caring' externalities. Culyer (1976) discussed the 'caring' externality in terms of an individual's health. People are not concerned by the ill-health of others simply because of the selfish reason that they themselves might become infected.

Rather: 'individuals are affected by others' health status for the simple reason that most of them care' (Culyer 1976). In Culyer (1980), the equity dimension is specifically discussed in the context of health care. McGuire, Henderson and Mooney (1988) argue:

> This in principle changes the perspective markedly. It may be more helpful to change the perspective to that of health care as a merit good

> ie a good which some 'elite' decides will be socially under-consumed if left to the willingness to pay of individual sovereign consumers.

This change of emphasis from a caring externality to the concept of a merit good makes a link with sport and exercise since, as was indicated in the early part of this chapter, both health care and exercise are inputs to the health production function. If health care is a merit good, then so too is exercise.

Although this discussion of externalities and merit goods may blur the distinction between efficiency and equity, it clarifies the nature of the equity objective. It also provides a link between the equity objective and the concept of need. Culyer (1980) points out the difference between need and demand:

> Whichever view one takes of need, we should note that they each involve a judgement being made independently of the receiving individual's preferences. It is this that makes a need based on caring preferences different from demand, for a demand is a want for some good or service backed by a willingness to sacrifice resources for it. Where demand and need come together is when one individual wants something for someone else and is prepared to sacrifice resources for it. Need is thus an external demand. It represents one party's view of what another should have.

Thus need is directly related to the concept of merit goods and hence is intrinsically tied up with the discussion of equity. However, whereas there is a broad consensus on the existence of housing, education and health needs, the concept of recreational need is relatively new. Dower, Rapoport, Strelitz and Kew (1981) examined the nature of leisure and recreational needs and argued that leisure provision in general catered to expressed demand rather than need, and as a result many groups were recreationally deprived.

In summary, in the context of the sport and recreation market the equity argument is concerned with participation in sport by those who would be excluded on the grounds of ability to pay. The rationale for government intervention is that certain individuals in society, who may or may not participate themselves, receive an increase in welfare from the participation of specific target groups. The target groups on this basis would specifically be those on low incomes but a similar argument could be made for ethnic minorities, the elderly and the unemployed, where low income is often compounded by other barriers to participation. They might also include excellent sportspeople to the extent that they are felt to have special needs and the market fails to adequately reward many of them for the sacrifices they make. In other words, equity is an important basis for the selection of target groups for sports policy.

Conclusions

In this chapter we have reviewed a variety of arguments in support of government intervention in the market for sport and recreation. It is not necessarily the case that separate policies have to be developed for each of the reasons for intervention. There is a coincidence of objective in many of these reasons, for example encouragement of participation through the demonstration effect of excellence in sport will service health and crime-related objectives; protecting the infant industry of producing excellence in sport will also ensure the production of an important public good in sport; and targeting groups such as low-income and elderly people for equity reasons will coincide with appropriate targeting for health externality reasons.

Efficiency arguments for government intervention lead to similar conclusions as the equity arguments: that is, in order to produce a socially optimum level of collective benefits from sport, public expenditure should be targeted at specific groups. If sports participation by adolescents reduces vandalism and delinquency then such social benefits are only generated if public provision encourages adolescents to take part in sport. A similar targeting, though to different groups, follows from the argument based on the sports participation/health relationship. Health status declines with age and is lower for low-income groups than for high-income groups. Similarly, whether caring for those with recreational disadvantages takes the form of a value judgement, an externality or a merit good, equity requires targeting of groups such as the elderly and those on low incomes. Social benefits generated through government intervention in the sports market are likely therefore to be greatest if low-income groups and older age groups are attracted into sports participation through such intervention.

On the grounds of both efficiency and equity therefore, in order to show that government policy had been at least partly successful it would be necessary to show that public subsidies to sport and recreation had benefitted the least well-off and particular target groups relevant to the market failure objectives.

5 Government failure and the sports market

If government were to attempt to correct for market failures, how would it go about it? Is it capable of effectively and efficiently compensating for the inadequacies of the market mechanism? These questions lie at the heart of current initiatives in the way government intervenes in sports markets. They also call on a well established literature in political economy which expresses grave concerns about government's ability to compensate for market failure. As Weisbrod (1978) suggests:

> Just as there are theoretic reasons to believe that private, profit-oriented institutions will fail to allocate resources efficiently (or equitably) under specified conditions, so too, there are reasons to believe that government institutions 'fail' under certain conditions. . . . . . there are clearly limits to what government institutions can accomplish.

In this chapter we explore the nature of such concern over government intervention in the context of sports markets. This critique is founded on the motives of government, the information at its disposal and the nature of the services it is attempting to provide. In order to give this critique a reference point, we begin with an examination of the way we would *like* government to intervene. This rational model is rather stylised and idealistic, but this is a common approach in economics – start with the ideal and then build in realistic contraints . . . . We follow the ideal with an alternative, behavioural view of the way government behaves, and we review evidence which criticises the way in which government intervention in sports markets is manifested. Policy implications from this approach to government failure conclude the discussion.

Throughout this chapter the term 'government' is used in its broadest sense to signify any form of government intervention, including central or local government, government agencies, 'quangos', etc. The models rely on theories of individual choice as well as analysis of the characteristics and behaviour of public sector organisations, since decisions concerning government interventions are likely to be determined as much by individuals as by truly collective decision making.

A rational model of government

In the idealist theory of market failure and consequent government policy, there are important implicit assumptions about the nature of government intervention. First, government's motives are assumed to be impartial, objective and geared towards the 'public purpose', ie no vested interests. Moreover, the most demanding objective is held to be relevant – *maximising* social welfare – nothing less will do. Second, government is assumed to have all the information necessary to intervene effectively, or at least better market information than individual market participants (consumers and suppliers). Third, government is supposed to be representative of society's group preferences – ie majority opinion. Fourth, intervention by government is assumed to be cost-effective, meaning that objectives are achieved at minimum cost to the taxpayer.

The first of these assumptions implies a unity of purpose throughout the public sector in its intervention in sports markets. Moreover, the 'maximising social welfare' objective directs the theory, and by implication the policy too, towards *marginal* conditions. In other words, another one pound's worth of intervention is worthwhile as long as more than one pound's worth of social benefit results, and intervention stops when the marginal cost of intervention exceeds the marginal benefit.

The second of the assumptions give rise to the term 'unbounded rationality' – an expression of the all-seeing requirement of government intervention in the neoclassical approach to welfare economics. In order to correct for the market failures identified in the previous chapter, and *maximise* social welfare, government would have to be able to identify the problem, measure the scale and direction of the problem, estimate the most cost-effective means of compensating for the problem, and implement this policy. To follow this sequence of intervention procedures requires an enormous amount of detailed information, most of it external to the operations of government. Even the relevant information *internal* to government, about the effectiveness and costs of its intervention policies, is a demanding requirement. Moreover, as indicated in the previous paragraph, the information is required not just at the aggregate and average levels, but also at the *margin*, eg what is the marginal health or crime benefit arising from government subsidy of sports opportunities?

The third assumption implies that democracy works . . .!

Government is quite simply given a licence to represent society on all issues and is presumed able to identify society's *collective* preferences. Only on this basis can it intervene consistently on society's behalf. Collective choices involve a complex matrix of individual preferences and different policy issues, with a lot of interdependency. Sports policy is a good example since, for example, subsidising the supply of sporting opportunities has, as we have discussed in the previous chapter, a number of cross-policy implications, eg for health, crime and economic impact.

The fourth assumption rests on the other three. If government has clear, consistent, measurable objectives, if it has the necessary information to intervene rationally to correct for market failures, and if it is an accurate representative of social welfare attitudes and value judgements, then and only then will it be in a position to intervene cost-effectively. However, this assumption takes the intervention one stage further – it is assumed to be effective in achieving the objectives, and conducted at minimum cost. In the neoclassical welfare economics model this means being *technically* efficient – the optimum output being achieved for the least cost inputs – and *allocatively* efficient – reaching the 'right' markets at the 'right' prices.

These fundamental assumptions about the nature of government, at the heart of the rational model, have behavioural implications which are important to understanding the way government intervenes in practice. Indeed, much of the stimulus to *improve* government intervention, as provided by bodies such as the Audit Commission, is based on behavioural aspirations firmly rooted in the rational model. For an insight into the behaviour required of the rational model the reader is recommended to read Jackson (1982), to whom we are indebted for the following analysis.

Rational government intervention based on the assumptions listed above has several key characteristics:

> techniques and routines are established which should help a completely rational decision maker to arrive at a best decision. One of the implications of the maximisation premise is that alternatives must be compared with one another. That is, search for the maximal requires testing and evaluating alternatives. If comparisons are not made, then the decision maker cannot be said to be maximising anything. The general approach assumes a highly structured situation . . . (Jackson 1982)

The structured process to which Jackson refers involves problem indentification, the search for and choice of a solution, implementation of appropriate policies and monitoring of the effects.

This structured process of decision-making relies on optimising and information processing techniques such as operations research, forecasting, project appraisal and performance appraisal. Management information is at the heart of the process – it enables problems to be identified, it assists the search for and choice of a feasible solution, and it is the main means of identifying to what extent the solution is working in practice. Supplementing formal management information are other sets of less formal information, which are both internal to the organisation (eg. managers' judgements, workers' views and problems) and external (eg customer complaints and behaviour, voters' attitudes, media coverage).

It is also likely that decision-making in government involves structured and informal processes of consultation both within and outside the organisation. Within the organisation the most obvious consultation line is between politicians and administrators (members and officers at the local authority level). Outside the decision-making government organisation, consultation is necessary with other parties such as customers, voters and other government agencies.

The outcome of this network of characteristics, behaviours, techniques and processes is *rational decision-making*:

> when the economist uses the concept of rationality and applies it to the making of choices or decisions, he wishes it to mean more than intelligence or sensibility. In particular, the economist regards a rational choice as one which is deliberate, internally consistent and which maximises the decision-maker's objective function. Thus rational decision-making is purposeful and goal-directed (Jackson 1982).

This rational model of government decision-making is a direct parallel to neoclassical consumer theory. This consumer theory has been heavily criticised, as we have discussed in Chapter 3. Similarly, the rational model of organisational behaviour has been attacked from a number of directions. It is from such criticisms that the next section takes its shape.

A behavioural model of government

Scepticism with the assumptions and requirements of the rational model above is nothing new in economics literature. As far back as the 1950s economists challenged the unbounded altruism of this approach, and posed alternative concepts and models of behaviour, processes and outcomes of decision-making in *any* organisation, not just government. Economists critical of the neoclassical approach to organisations have been variously categorised, including the labels 'institutionalists', 'behaviouralists', 'liberalists' and in the 'New Right' school of thought. Rather than attempt to distinguish between such approaches, we present a composite alternative view founded on a critique of the elements of the rational model.

This behavioural model draws on both individual and collective choice theories, most of which are not public sector specific but apply to any organisations. However, we illustrate the model by reference to appraisals of government provision of sport. One irony in this alternative model is that it is still a *rational* approach, but instead of being unconstrained it is rational within substantial constraints, particularly of information.

Motives and objectives

The main criticisms of the neoclassical approach to the motives of government are that it assumes neutrality and maximising behaviour. Taking neutrality, the assumption that government decision-makers are so public spirited that they have no personal objectives or motivations (or at least if they do they are consistent with the social welfare objectives) is criticised as being naive in the extreme. The term 'economic eunuchs' has been used to describe the unreality of bureaucrats in the neoclassical welfare economics approach. The alternative approach to the motives of both politicians and administrators is to assume that they are likely to have personal objectives which are not only inconsistent with social welfare objectives, but also are probably more important to them.

Concerning politicians, the most common analytical approach is to assume that survival is the primary objective. This may, of course, be seen as dependent on fulfilling social welfare objectives. However, this begs the question of whether or not voters are interested in or conscious of the full range of social welfare considerations that polticians concern themselves with. It also presupposes that politicians are aware of the detailed requirements of the diverse range of individual preferences, or can identify collective preferences, an issue which we examine further below.

Administrators are said by theories of bureaucracy to have utility functions which incorporate much more than altruistic objectives. The size of the bureau, its budget, job conditions and security, a 'quiet life', power, prestige, pay – all these and more have been postulated as being important objectives to bureaucrats. Perhaps the most well known model is that of Niskanen (1971), who simplifies the motivation of bureaucrats thus:

> Among the several variables that may enter the bureaucrat's utility function are the following: salary, requisites of the office, public reputation, power, patronage, output of the bureau, ease of making changes,

> and ease of managing the bureau. All of these variables except the last two, I contend, are a positive monotonic function of the total budget of the bureau during the bureaucrat's tenure in office.

Clearly, if Niskanen is right about the objectives of administrators, then there is little likelihood of them acting in a way consistent with the rational model above. They would not seek a socially desirable optimum production of public services, but rather they would seek to overproduce in comparison with this optimum.

Under the Niskanen model bureaucrats are not necessarily technically efficient – they may well have a tight control on unit costs. But the pursuit of maximum budgets leads to allocative inefficiency through overproduction. A more gloomy view is that such an approach almost certainly leads to technical inefficiency as well, because the absence of a profit motive or any other objective which necessitates control of costs will cause a waste of resources. Also, maximising budgets may well manifest itself in extended lines of communication as the bureau expands, causing the outcomes to suffer as costs rise.

Administrators have more technical information than their political masters about the demand for and supply of their services such as sports facilities. They therefore have the potential for using this 'asymetric information' to their own advantage in setting objectives to suit their motives. Local authorities often have near-monopoly powers in the supply of sports services, and they have been characterised in the past as having more-or-less 'open budgets' with which to subsidise the operation of their services. If facilities make a loss, which is normally the case, then this loss is made up from general revenues. Rarely have local authorities specified clear and specific financial objectives for individual facilities or services.

The motives of an organisation should be apparent in the objectives it sets. Several investigations into the operation of local authority leisure facilities have reached the conclusion that objectives are poorly specified:

> One fundamental observation arising from our survey is the need for aims and objectives to be identified for each leisure centre . . . . Many of the centres we visited do have stated operating objectives but these are occasionally contradictory and often vague (Pannell Kerr Forster for the Audit Inspectorate, 1983).
>
> Objectives are rarely quantified (Audit Commission 1989).
>
> Many authorities do not have a clear idea of what their role in sport and recreation should be and have not reconciled their social and financial objectives (Audit Commission 1989).

Often objectives take the form of generalised aims such as 'sport for all' and 'serving the community', which are not specific enough to ensure the purposeful, goal-directed decision-making of the rational model. This may, of course, be deliberate, since it avoids accountability and allows other non-sport objectives, such as those identified above, to be pursued without apparently prejudicing the sports objectives.

Another subject of intense debate is whether or not politicians and administrators *maximise* anything at all. An alternative view, introduced by Simon (1957) and developed by Cyert and March (1963) is that individual goals are more realistically determined by aspiration levels that are not the highest possible, but a realistic and satisfactory minimum. Aiming for a satisfactory rather than a maximum outcome is termed 'satisficing' and is more in keeping with the study of aspiration levels in psychology. If 'satisficing' is the norm then notions of optimality take on characteristics of 'grey areas' rather than definable outcomes.

It has been suggested that it is in the interests of both politicians and bureaucrats that objectives are as vague as possible, since satisficing is easier under such conditions. In this sense the evidence of investigations such as those of Pannell Kerr Forster for the Audit Inspectorate (1983) and the Audit Commission (1989) demonstrates the satisficing behaviour of local authority leisure service managers.

Information

In contrast to the 'perfect information' requirement of unbounded rationality, Simon (1957) proposed that *'bounded rationality'* was far more appropriate to decision-making processes. In a highly complex world comprehensive, objective information is unlikely. Instead, uncertainty rules and information is inadequate at best and biased at worst. Advertising is often used as an example when considering consumers' decision-making.

The problem for government decision-makers is worse. Although they may attempt to generate objective information through statistical agencies, they are also faced with biased information, eg from the media, from pressure groups, and even from other parts of government. The process of structured consultation is identified above as necessary for a rational approach to the acquisition of information and the formation of collective views. In local authority sports services there is evidence to suggest that this process of consultation is patchy: 'Although customers are vital to the success of any leisure centre, we have observed little consultation with them as to the level of satisfaction achieved' (Pannell Kerr Forster for the Audit Inspectorate, 1983). It has also been suggested that consultation is misdirected in local authority leisure provision. Managers of facilities, for example, often complain of too much consultation or interference in day-to-day decision-making by political members. The consequences of this for efficiency are discussed below.

Even if it were possible in principle to generate complex information about the state of the world, politicians and bureaucrats are likely to impose their own constraints on the quantity of information they choose to base decisions on. Self-imposed bounding is a manifestation of both the 'satisficing' objective and the limits to the politicians' and bureaucrats' information-processing capacity. The self-imposed bounding of decision-making in the public sector is most apparent in the lack of performance appraisal, the final stage in the process of decision-making identified as appropriate for the rational model above.

The private commercial sector, driven by financial objectives, has developed an array of ratio indicators by which to analyse performance. Government, by contrast, may have a battery of economy-wide or society-wide indicators but it has not developed an array of objective performance indicators which relate directly to the efficiency of individual government organisations – service level performance monitoring is still at a fairly rudimentary stage. As the Audit Commission concluded:

> success or failure in meeting objectives (is) rarely measured or monitored.
>
> Only a minority of authorities can demonstrate their achievements in terms of numbers of people participating in sport or increases in participation . . . .
>
> There are also widespread deficiencies in the way in which authorities monitor the costs and use of the facilities they provide. Most collect usage data but they do not always provide members with it. This prevents members monitoring the achievement of social objectives, and hence hinders the development of well thought out policies . . . . Few authorities attempt to examine performance . . . This reflects the widespread lack of quantified financial objectives . . . . Overall, many authorities do not therefore know what they are achieving with the money they spend (Audit Commission 1989).

In the particular context of excellence in sport, local authorities are noted by Taylor (1990) as being lax in monitoring the recipients of grant aid. Only thirteen per cent of authorities supporting excellence asked for systematic reports on progress and, more seriously: 'a third or more of the authorities supporting excellence in sport do not appear to monitor the beneficiaries of their support'.

In addition it would appear that local authorities have little of the information demanded of the 'rational model' approach to decision-making in such vital areas as pricing and programming:

> There appears to have been little quantitative analysis to identify the relative significance of the many factors and variables which interact in the pricing – utilisation equation (Pannell Kerr Forster for the Audit Inspectorate, 1983).
>
> Most authorities implicitly assume that low prices encourage use and are essential to meet social objectives but the real relationship between price and use is not often examined (Audit Commission 1989).
>
> Centres frequently do not have sufficient information about user profiles and patterns to be responsive in programming policies. More significantly, information about the public not using leisure facilities, and the reasons for this, is almost non-existent (Pannell Kerr Forster for the Audit Inspectorate, 1983).
>
> There is generally little market research into the characteristics and origin of centre users, and their satisfaction with the leisure services provided (Pannell Kerr Forster for the Audit Inspectorate, 1983).

Such shortfalls in management information may be deliberate or it may be an inevitable consequence of vague objectives and mixed motives. It also results from the lack of a precise, quantitative relationship between inputs and outputs in many public services. This is not the fault of the bureaucrats, it is the problem of defining outputs in a service such as sport. And even if this problem could be overcome, there is great difficulty in specifying the relationships between outputs and inputs. In other words, accurate information on the issues identified in the investigations quoted above is not always easy.

Government is making decisions on behalf of millions of consumers and the information government decision-makers have on these consumers' needs is likely to be a lot poorer than the individuals have themselves. Jackson (1982) suggests that this problem lies at the heart of government failure: 'Allocative inefficiency is almost inherent in public monopoly and arises from the problems involved in demand articulation'. This is not only a representation problem, as discussed in the next section, but also an information problem. It echoes and reinforces the underlying sentiment of Chapter 3, that consumer preferences are complex and changing, and hence very difficult to identify.

It is argued by liberalists that government can never aspire to have as much information as individual market participants, so it is these that should be driving resource allocation decisions, not government. This argument ignores the failure of individual market participants to include such things as externalities and public goods in their trading behaviour. Even so, it is said that on these collective matters government information is far from adequate enough to determine optimal policy decisions. The lack of information on the value of the links between sport and health, or sport and crime, are good examples of missing information.

Bounded rationality means that all decision-makers, including those from government, are constrained in their quest, if it exists, for optimal decisions. This does not imply that rationality disappears as information constraints tighten. It does, however, lead to different behaviour and processes than those reviewed in the rational model above. One such process, well documented in bureaucracy literature, is 'incrementalism'. In its simplest form this suggests that bureaucrats only ever make marginal adjustments to their budgets (and, by implication, their policies), for the reason that they have not got sufficient information or motivation to do anything else. Add to this poor information the 'satisficing' behaviour of government decision-makers, the politician's objective of security and the bureaucrat's objective of a quiet life, and incremental changes are a rational response.

Representation and collective choice

The claim that government is a fair reflection of society's group preferences, resting as it does on principles of democratic processes, has also come in for attack. The problems for collective choice analysts include the fact that governments are only ever voted in periodically, often by a minority of the total voting population, and on the basis of take-it-or-leave-it packages of policies. In the UK voting takes place on average every three years or so for central government, long enough for circumstances and preferences to change considerably. The UK 'first past the post' method of majority voting ensures that any government bar landslide victors has the voting support of less than half the eligible population.

But for minority concerns such as sport, the most significant of all the criticisms of the representation issue is that voting is for whole packages presented by the political parties, of which sports policy is at best a very small element. Consequently it is entirely feasible that the sports policy adopted by an incumbent government is at odds with social preferences for that particular issue, if voting the government into power was determined by other policy preferences with higher public profile, such as the economy, defence, law and order, etc.

One simple example of a mismatch between decision-makers and consumers on an issue of policy detail is reported by the Bureau of Outdoor Recreation (1979) in the USA. Whilst local authority administrators preferred to offer recreation facilities at no direct charge to customers (ie paying instead through local taxes), on the grounds that this made the facilities accessible to disadvantaged groups, a survey revealed that a majority in the same disadvantaged groups would have preferred to have seen direct charges.

There is little opportunity, through the voting system, for collective preferences to be expressed about particular policy areas. Furthermore, any voting system is quantitative, not qualitative – there is no opportunity to express individual *strength* of preference. Opponents of government intervention claim that expressions of demand in the market mechanism are far more sophisticated than the best-designed majority voting system.

On a more theoretical level, Arrow (1951 and 1963) has shown that it is impossible to devise a collective choice mechanism which would allow government decisions to reflect these individual preferences, without breaking one or more basic requirements of such a social ordering. This impossibility holds even if politicians and bureaucrats aim to maximise social welfare, and have accurate information about individual preferences. The conclusion of Arrow's 'Impossibility Theorem' is that the only means of translating individual preferences into social preferences are by dictatorial rather than democratic means.

Efficiency and equity

Continuing on the critique of assumptions on which the principles of government intervention are founded, it has been claimed that when governments do intervene they do so inefficiently. We have seen earlier how an examination of the motives of government decision-makers can lead to the conclusion that neither technical nor allocative efficiency will result from their decisions.

Perhaps the most damaging accusation levelled at local authority sports provision is that it is allocatively inefficient and inequitable because it fails to achieve what many interpret as the real intention behind the 'sport for all' slogan. This is improving participation in sport by recreationally and socially disadvantaged groups. The Audit Commission is of this view:

> authorities assume that low prices and blanket subsidies encourage use and help ensure social objectives are met. But, sports participation is biased towards people with a professional and managerial background who benefit disproportionately from low prices.
>
> Across the board subsidies may therefore have a reverse effect from a redistributional perspective. Many poorer people are, through their rates, paying to subsidise the pastimes of the rich (Audit Commission 1989).

This is supported by evidence from Veal (1981). Putting together the results from user surveys in 48 leisure centres, Veal concludes that professional and managerial classes make up 24 per cent of users, but are only fourteen per cent of the population, whilst semi-skilled and unskilled manual groups make up thirteen per cent of users and 27 per cent of the population. Similarly, people over 45 years of age make up 47 per cent of the population and only eight per cent of users. Cowling, Fitzjohn and Tungatt (1983) in a similar survey of sports centre user surveys concluded that: 'the majority of indoor sports players are from social classes, A, B and C1 (essentially non-manual)'.

Such evidence represents both inequity and allocative inefficiency. It must be said, though, that both pieces of evidence above are from surveys taken largely in the 1970s. Local authorities would claim that the identification of target groups and the use of positive discrimination in their favour through pricing, programming outreach work, etc, have improved considerably in the 1980s. To the extent that this is so, inequity and inefficiency will have been reduced.

Another allocative efficiency issue concerns the adjustments in policies and decisions that are necessary in a dynamic situation. It has been suggested that because the rational model is largely of a 'comparative statics' nature, comparing 'before' and 'after' situations, it pays scant attention to the costs of dynamic adjustment. These 'transactions costs', it has been claimed, are likely to be much higher in government organisations than in private organisations, because of bureaucratic structures and processes of decision-making.

The transactions costs criticism affects not only allocative efficiency, but also another efficiency concept – 'X' inefficiency. This was devised by Liebenstein (1966) to explain that even if the right technical requirements for efficient production were in place, and even if sufficient market information existed to ensure allocative efficiency, it was still likely that the outcome would be inefficient. The reason is that the *internal* efficiency of organisations may not be up to the optimising task. 'X' inefficiency results from a lack of, or conflict in, personal motivations within the organisation, from inadequately specified labour contracts, and from a lack of measurement and control of performance.

One example of 'X' inefficiency is the too-often conflicting situation that politicians and administrators find themselves in. This is particularly the case in local authority leisure management:

> objectives often appear undefined and uncertain at Committee level. In many instances Members seem to prefer to focus on pricing issues and other operational matters, rather than on policies and standards. As a consequence, managers feel that their responsibility and authority are being eroded, and as a result suffer professional frustration through

> (often well-intentioned) undue control of day-to-day detail by Members (Pannell Kerr Forster for the Audit Inspectorate, 1983).
>
> Local authority decision-making processes can be cumbersome and inflexible, and probably cause commercial opportunities to be missed by requiring sports centre management to follow too many detailed procedures (Coopers & Lybrand for the Department of the Environment 1981).

The 'X' inefficiency charge has been levelled at government organisations more than at private firms. This is because government is seen as more likely to be suffering from a lack of unity of purpose. The lack of specific objectives feeds through to a lack of specificity in labour contracts and a lack of monitoring of performance in achieving objectives at both organisation and individual levels. In a private firm the profit motive may be sufficient to ensure monitoring and control of performance. In the public sector there is no profit motive. The lack of monetary incentives to reward good performance is often cited as a major contributor to poor morale in public sector workforces; this lack is also likely to undermine the efficient operation of the institution.

Without competition, with no possibility of bankruptcy, with few prices to indicate relative costs of production, without specific objectives or measurable outputs, with 'satisficing' behaviour and personal objectives in conflict with a socially optimal production of public services, it is not surprising that accusations of internal 'X' inefficiency abound (often in the form of 'red tape' problems) in reference to the public sector.

Monopolies and freedoms

In addition to the behavioural aspects reviewed above, stemming from criticisms of the ideal 'rational' model, further accusations of 'government failure' emanate from both efficiency arguments and a defence of economic freedoms. On efficiency grounds, critics of government claim that some of the worst monopoly problems in the economy are posed not by private companies, but by government. Private monopolies, according to the 'Austrian' school of economic thought, enjoy only *temporary* dominance, in markets which are essentially contestable in the long run. Furthermore, the temporary abnormal profit can be seen as a reward for beneficial innovation.

On the other hand, government monopolies are created not by enterprise and innovation but by laws, and they are often sustained by the same laws preventing competition. Government barriers to entry are seen as more effective in the long term than the barriers erected by private monopolies, such as patents, advertising, product differentiation and scale of production – all of which can be eroded by the process of competition over time.

The argument against government barriers to entry is usually used to attack legal monopolies, trade barriers, and exclusive trading rights granted by government. There is no reason why the same argument cannot be used against permanent government subsidisation of supply, a policy that has ensured government dominance in the supply of certain sporting products, such as parks, outdoor pitches, swimming pools and sports centres. Of course, these monopoly positions are local and do not make abnormal profit (they rarely make *any* profit!). Yet, for the reasons put forward in the behavioural model above, it is easy to claim that these local government monopolies have suffered from inefficiencies because of the lack of competition.

Regarding economic freedoms, the attack on government intervention is founded on the principle of consumer sovereignty. This principle gives individuals the freedom to choose how to spend their income and the market will respond to these expressed preferences by supplying an appropriate collection of goods and services. Consumer choice is only one aspect of the freedom of the market system. Individuals also have the right to choose how much income to earn (and, by implication, how much leisure to take too) by supplying their factor services to firms. All decision-making is decentralised; individuals make their own market decisions.

Government intervention interferes with this process and centralises decision-making. Government taxation constrains the freedom of the consumer, deprives them of income and hands over the decision on how it is spent to the government. In fact government may be intervening in the cause of what are known as 'positive freedoms' eg such as freedom from poverty, freedom from exploitation. But liberalist economists prefer 'negative freedoms': the absence of government restrictions. Even government subsidisation of sporting products, and the resulting domination of certain supplies, can be seen as a distortion of choice and not consistent with negative freedoms.

Policy implications

The behavioural model of government failure above attempts to disprove the theory that government can intervene in markets effectively (achieving clear objectives) or efficiently (doing so at minimum cost). It is not surprising that the major policy implications of this theory are to reduce the *direct* supply of government services and substitute, where the market is not appropriate, alternative mechanisms. However, the objective is not necessarily to abolish government intervention altogether in markets such as sport, although this is one policy option. The behavioural model does not deny that there may be market failures, nor does it imply that equity is necessarily well served by the market mechanism.

Rather than use government supply as the policy response, the behavioural approach seeks less centralised means of correcting for market failures and equity problems. The objectives of these alternatives are to make sure that consumer sovereignty is protected as far as possible, and that competition acts as a control device to ensure that government services are efficient. We briefly review these policy alternatives, leaving extended discussion of two of them until later chapters.

The most extreme policy solution to perceived inefficiencies in the supply of government services is privatisation, ie the transferring of ownership of assets from the government to the private market. This policy implies that the adverse consequence of market failure are less than the adverse consequences of government failure. However, privatisation has not been proposed for any of the sports services offered by government in Britain. This is partly because many of these services would not sustain a profit if privatised, and this may be seen as a reflection of the strength of market failures.

At the other extreme of policy alternatives, inefficiency in government can be counteracted by the introduction of more incentives and greater control. This would not necessitate a change in the type of government intervention, but it would need different procedures. Performance-related pay is a concept which is beginning to encroach on local authority leisure services. This radical change in payment systems requires accurate monitoring of both service level and individual performance. In principle it offers an incentive to staff to improve these interdependent levels of performance. In practice it requires overturning a highly institutionalised pay system and structure which has the support of the major trade unions in local authorities. Furthermore, increasing monitoring and control mean increasing administration cost, so these have to be assessed against any efficiency gains.

A third policy alternative, another which does not abolish but rather changes the nature of government intervention, takes the form of vouchers. Instead of directly subsidising facilities, which offers no incentive to facility managers to be efficient, the subsidies are given to target groups of consumers, who may then exercise their consumer sovereignty in using the vouchers (or not). When they use the vouchers, they pass over the subsidy to the service they choose, each voucher being redeemable with the government. If they do not use the vouchers then the service does not deserve or *get* the subsidy. This gives the service an incentive at least to be effective and cater to the needs of the consumers.

Under a voucher system of subsidies, of course, the service need no longer be provided directly by government, since vouchers may be used at any outlet providing the product for which the voucher is valid. Ironically many 'passport to leisure' schemes in Britain have proved this point, by extending their validity beyond local authority services to commercial leisure facilities. Vouchers are a more direct means of ensuring that the subsidies go to those identified as target groups. By comparison, as the Audit Commission (1989) is concerned to point out, facility subsidies go to whoever uses the facility, which means the benefits of the subsidies extend well beyond the target groups.

The main problems with substituting voucher schemes for direct provision of government leisure services are ones of calculation, distribution and cost. Detailed calculations are required to estimate the value of vouchers to distribute, particularly if, as is likely, discrimination is used such that more 'deserving' target groups receive higher value vouchers. This raises explicitly the problem of 'vertical equity' – how to discriminate fairly between consumers of different circumstances. Facility subsidies do not have to be explicit about vertical equity, although price discrimination between different users is a similar problem which many local authorities have addressed in their leisure services.

The choice of target groups is itself fraught with problems, as local authority leisure services know too well. For sports services some groups are obvious and identifiable, such as the unemployed, the elderly, the disabled and mothers with young children. Others are more debatable and less identifiable, eg excellent sportspeople, low-wage earners, students, the pre-retired, youths.

It has also been suggested that voucher schemes are costly to administer. With respect to sports subsidisation, however, no empirical evidence exists to compare the costs of subsidising facilities with the cost of subsidising consumers. Such evidence would have to standardise, of course, for the number of successful visits made by target group users as a result of the different subsidies.

Another policy alternative to direct, subsidised government supply of sports services, given that these services have elements of collectiveness to them, would be to rely on private clubs, a form of organisation common, of course, to sport. This policy would include the subsidisation of private sports clubs where the externalities, public good benefits, etc. are felt to warrant it. One problem with this alternative is that clubs have to enforce exclusion in order to succeed. This is difficult if a high degree of collectiveness exists. Furthermore, where exclusion is possible it is often on the basis of price, which excludes many of the target groups conventionally selected for attention by government sports provision. We explore the club alternative to government supply further in Chapter 7.

Finally, to introduce more competition into a situation of government monopolistic supply, contracting can be used. Government may retain ownership and policy control over sports services and facilities, but to prevent complacency in their operation contracts can be awarded for the management of them. These contracts would be competed for by private and possibly public sector organisations and it is this competition that in theory gives the contract winners the incentive to be efficient. Given the current compulsory competitive tendering legislation affecting sports provision by local authorities in Britain, and moves to put the management of National Centres onto a similar contracting basis, this important policy option is explored fully in Chapter 8.

Conclusions

It must be stressed that the general tenor of this chapter is essentially biased. It portrays government as failing in the responsibilities given to it by the previous chapter. It results in government failure posing as many if not more problems than market failure. However, it is not possible empirically to 'weigh' the arguments presented in this chapter with those of the previous chapter; the evidence just does not exist. So we conclude rather inconclusively (!) with a few overall considerations of relevance to the debate.

This chapter, as critical as it is of government intervention in sports markets, may *not* be used to infer that 'less would be best' with respect to this intervention. If government intervened less in these markets then market failures would re-emerge. Moreover, because of the precedent set by long-term intervention by government, the market failures would be all the greater and the costs of adjusting to a purer market system would be very high. If there is any substance to the market failure arguments of the previous chapter, then policy changes should concentrate on *changing* the nature of government intervention to make it more effective and efficient, rather than getting rid of it altogether. This need not require any reductions in government subsidy, but will probably involve more 'market-based instruments'. One example of this approach is compulsory competitive tendering for the management of local authority leisure facilities. Local authorities still have the power to decide on the levels of subsidy to give to leisure facilities, even though competition is being introduced by means of the tendering process.

It is too simplistic to suggest that government intervention in sports markets should be cut on the grounds that the effects of government failure are plain for all to see, whilst the effects of market failure are less easy to identify. Even if this were the case, which is debatable, just because you cannot put a value on something does not mean that it has not got a value! The intangibility of collective benefits is the very reason why the market will not cater for them, and it is government that has traditionally accepted the responsibility for them. One possible alternative would be that the private voluntary sector could take on more of the responsibility for collective benefits. We will examine this alternative further in Chapter 7.

There are counterarguments to the behavioural model which take three broad forms. First, the neoclassical, rational approach can be adapted to cater for 'real world' constraints and behaviours, such as information constraints and transactions costs. Second, if the end result predicted by the rational model is realistic, then it does not matter if the processes have been ignored by the model. Behaviouralists tend to concentrate on processes, whilst the neoclassical approach tends to concentrate on outcomes. Third, some evidence denies the behaviouralist view, for example the very much *non*-incremental, radical increases in indoor sports provision by local authorities in the 1970s and 1980s that are evaluated in the next chapter.

It is also worth pointing out that *all* types of organisation have been charged with being 'X' inefficient, not just government institutions. Moreover, this criticism extends to small as well as to large organisations. Government is a 'soft target' for this criticism for the simple reason that it has more public accountability. Where is the private sector equivalent of the Audit Commission?

One last irony remains to be highlighted. In the face of evidence of government failure there are two distinct approaches to the problem. One, until recently to be found largely in text books and learned journals, is to radically change the scope and nature of government in markets such as sport. The other approach, to be found in the very documents that testify to government failure (eg the Audit Commission, 1989, Pannell Kerr Forster for the Audit Inspectorate, 1983) is to recommend improvements in the *existing* mechanisms of government supply.

The irony of this second approach is that the reason for it is taken from a *behavioural* analysis of government failure, whilst the response to it is taken very much from the *rational* model. There remains a belief, implicit in many critiques of government services, that there is the potential *within the existing service framework* to improve the effectiveness and efficiency of government intervention by moving towards the rational approach. Behaviouralists might claim that such an approach is logically inconsistent with the proven behavioural characteristics of both politicians and bureaucrats. However, one of the main criticisms of the behaviouralist approach is that it doesn't lead to very clearcut policy recommendations. For example, should we accept behavioural constraints and work within them, or attempt to break them down?

To take these inconclusive conclusions to their logical outcome, it may be that some recommendations fit *both* the models presented in this chapter. One possible example is to improve management information, another may be to use market based instruments rather than direct government supply. Both these possibilities will be discussed further in the context of contracting in Chapter 8.

6 Evaluation of government expenditure on sport

Ideally an evaluation of the effectiveness and efficiency of government policy with respect to sport and recreation would follow the principle of programme evaluation outlined in Driver and Rosenthal (1981) and summarised in Figure 6.1. Inputs (ie resources used up in supplying recreation opportunities) should be quantitatively related to outputs (defined as the direct products of management actions). For sport and recreation, use of these outputs and the negative and positive impacts (which are the social benefits referred to in Chapter 4) of producing and consuming these outputs should also be measured and linked to inputs. Such evaluations are only just starting to be considered in the well developed applied economics areas of health and education. It would be highly ambitious to attempt such an exercise in sport and recreation given the small amount of economic research that has so far been generated in this area.

Figure 6.1 – Basic components and processes of the outdoor recreation program evaluation framework

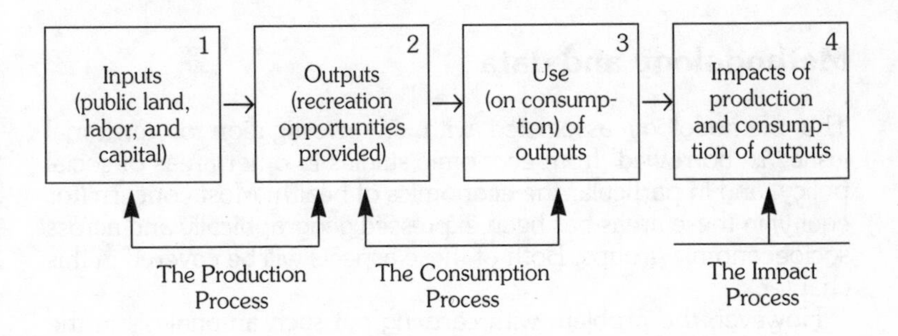

Source: Driver and Rosenthal (1981)

The two previous chapters have provided a great deal of apparently conflicting theory and evidence about the way in which government intervenes in a market such as sport. To resolve the conflict requires a balance sheet approach to the pros (arising from market failure) and the cons (arising from government failure), with valuations attached to each side of the balance sheet. However laudable such an approach is in principle, it is impossible to present in practice – the detailed evidence required just does not exist. Therefore, in this evaluation chapter we step back from the 'micro' details of the preceding chapters and attempt to evaluate the effects of government intervention on the sports participation market at a more general 'macro' level. This evaluation concentrates on mass participation rather than specific markets such as excellence in sport. It is possible to conduct a quantitative evaluation of participation, but very difficult to do the same for excellence. However, a more qualitative evaluation of government intervention in the excellence market is integral to Chapters 7 and 8.

One of the issues central to both the efficiency and equity of government intervention in sport is the targeting of particular groups of the population. Many of the normal target groups in sports policy are socially disadvantaged and it is such groups that yield external benefits associated with health and crime. Efficient subsidisation requires that subsidies to sport should benefit those in greatest need. This is an objective consistent with the 'need' approach to equity identified in Chapter 4, and possibly with 'Rawlsian' equity too. In this chapter we examine the targeting issue at an aggregate level through a detailed analysis of the territorial justice of government expenditure on sport. The second part of the chapter attempts to assess the effects of the most radical, recent change in government expenditure on sport – the increase in spending on leisure centres and swimming pools over the last twenty years.

Methodology and data

The methodology associated with an investigation of territorial justice is 'borrowed' from economic studies in other areas of social policy, and in particular the economics of health. Most concern (for equity) in these areas has been expressed geographically and across socioeconomic groups. Both of these aspects will be covered in this chapter.

However, the problem with carrying out such an analysis in the area of sport is the inadequacy of the data at national level. This chapter makes use of the two main data sources available to leisure researchers, the Chartered Institute of Public Finance and Accountancy's (CIPFA) Leisure and Recreation Statistics Estimates and the General Household Survey data.

The next section uses the CIPFA data to examine the territorial justice of sport subsidies. The CIPFA data record net expenditure (ie subsidies) on various sport and recreation facilities and programmes across all local authorities in England and Wales. As the title of the CIPFA publications indicates, the data are estimates of expenditure not out-turns.

The specific data used in this chapter are the 1981–82 data, since these correspond in time with various need indicators that have been derived from the 1981 Census. Also, the major investment in new indoor facilities took place between 1971 and 1981, and therefore the 1981 data give a timely reflection of the pattern of expenditure and resultant effects after the new investment had taken place.

The following two sections make use of the main source of data on sports participation, the General Household Survey which, although carried out annually, only collects information on leisure participation at (normally) three-yearly intervals. Although this is cross-section data, related to behaviour at a particular point in time, it is now possible to obtain information about trends in participation since it provides data on sports participation for 1973, 1977, 1980, 1983 and 1986 (although for some sports the 1973 data is not comparable with other years because of differences in survey methodology). The first of these two sections uses this data to analyse the effects of new local government investment in swimming pools on the swimming market. The second of the two does the same thing for sports centres.

Territorial justice and public subsidies to sport and recreation

The pioneering work into the concept of territorial justice was carried out by Bleddyn Davies (1968) who defined territorial justice as: 'an area distribution of provision of services such that each area's standard is proportional to the total needs for the services of its population'. He went on to indicate how we could assess the extent to which territorial justice had been achieved:

> If resources were allocated to each according to the needs of the particular area we should get a perfect positive correlation between standards of provision and an index measuring the relative needs of each area for the service: the relative inequality of the standard indices being the same as that of the index of relative needs (Davies 1968).

However Davies also suggests that territorial justice in this sense may not be enough:

> In some situations it is not sufficient to distribute resources in such a way that would secure territorial justice, to ensure that people in equal needs would be equally likely to receive them. Social survey evidence implies that this is insufficient for achieving a correlation of consumption with needs, since different social groups are not equally good at seizing the opportunities available to them.

Non-price barriers are likely to constrain access by lower income groups, even to free services such as the NHS. The lack of private transport, inescapable domestic responsibilities, and inflexible, elongated work time can all prevent certain target groups from taking up opportunities presented by government. At the same time, people *not* facing such constraints are in a much better position to exploit such opportunities. So just to accept the responsibility of non-market allocation is not enough.

Thus we see that a necessary condition for territorial justice is an unequal distribution of resources where the inequality matches that of recreational need. However this is not sufficient. For territorial justice to have been achieved we must also show that this inequality in the distribution of resources results in those most in need being in receipt of these resources. This point will not be lost on many local authorities that, having made special provision to improve sports participation opportunities for the unemployed, have then been frustrated by a low take up.

Thus the process of assessing the effectiveness of government policy involves first of all looking at how the distribution of resources is related to the distribution of recreational need and secondly the extent to which the most 'needy' actually receive the resources directed at them. Only the first point will be discussed in this section; the second point will be discussed in later sections of the chapter.

There is certainly no doubt that subsidies are allocated unevenly. Gratton (1984) pointed to the tremendous variability in the level of new expenditure on sport and recreation facilities by local authorities. Table 6.1 gives the estimated net expenditure per head on sport and recreation for the English and Welsh authorities in 1981–82.

The figures show that subsidies were highest in London, followed by Wales, then the Metropolitan Authorities of England, with the lowest subsidies being in the Non-Metropolitan English authorities. The pattern differed between subsidies to indoor and outdoor sport and recreation, however, with Wales having the highest subsidies to indoor recreation but only the third highest to outdoor.

Table 6.1 – Estimated net expenditure per head on sport and recreation 1981–82

Area	Indoor (£)	Outdoor (£)	Total (£)
London	5.48	10.26	15.74
Metropolitan	4.89	6.34	11.23
Non-Metropolitan England	3.31	3.98	7.29
Non-Metropolitan Wales	5.59	6.12	11.71

Source: CIPFA (1981)

The only consistency is that non-Metropolitan English authorities had the lowest subsidies for both indoor and outdoor recreation, but even here there was considerable variation. For English and Welsh counties there is a range of 0.85 to 9.05 for indoor recreation, and from 1.95 to 11.60 for outdoor. Mid-Glamorgan (17.46 per head) and Gwent (17.25 per head) stand out clearly as the highest total spenders in 1981–82; while the Isle of Wight (4.07 per head) and Oxfordshire (4.12 per head) were clearly the lowest. At district level the variation is much greater still, with perhaps the most interesting comparison being that between the indoor expenditure of Cherwell in Oxfordshire (0.53 per head) with that of Torfaen in Gwent (14.30 per head). That is, Torfaen's expenditure per head on indoor facilities was 27 times greater than that of Cherwell!

The question is do these regional variations in subsidy have any association with the differential recreational 'needs' of the regional populations? To answer this question, we must tackle the problem of measuring recreational need.

The concept of recreational need is closely related to other areas of deprivation. As Dower *et al.* (1981) point out:

> The aim of 'Leisure for all' and the sense that it has not yet been achieved, led to the concept of recreational deprivation or disadvantage . . . some official reports have shown, or implied, that recreational disadvantage tends to coincide with social deprivation.

Dower *et al.* therefore measured recreational need by standard indicators of social deprivation. They support this correspondence of recreational need with general social needs by quoting from the House of Lords Select Committee (1973):

> many inner urban areas have lagged behind other parts of the community in recreational provision . . . because of the nature of their environment, they are under special difficulties in making up ground which they

> have lost . . . Among the characteristics of the areas may be a shortage of open space, exaggerated by poor housing conditions, and a dearth of alternative facilities to compensate for the shortcomings of the urban environment.

Further support comes from the Greater London Council (1975) in its review of recreational deprivation: 'The most needy areas from the point of view of recreation tend also to be those which are socially deprived'. This correspondence of social deprivation with recreational need is further supported by social survey evidence which shows that recreation participation is positively related to income, occupational status, educational achievement, car ownership, and employment status.

Gratton (1984) used three recreational 'need' indicators obtained from the 1981 Census – the number of unskilled manual workers per 1000 population in their area, the percentage of households in the area owning one car, and the percentage owning two cars. This study correlated these indicators with subsidisation of sport and recreation by local authorities. The consistency of the results is perhaps surprising. Every correlation coefficient has the sign we would expect if subsidies were distributed efficiently: all car-ownership/expenditure correlations are negative and all manual workers/expenditure correlations are positive. The evidence suggests that the territorial distribution of subsidies is consistent with resources being directed to the most needy areas.

It is possible to expand the empirical analysis used by Gratton (1984), using more sophisticated statistical indicators showing urban deprivation, derived from the 1981 Census and available from the Department of the Environment's Inner Cities Directorate. The indicators developed by the Inner Cities Directorate measure a variety of housing, economic and social elements of deprivation and disadvantage. These indicators are derived at county and district level for all local authorities in England and Wales.

The basis for the urban deprivation indicators comprises the following eight indicators.

(i) percentage unemployed persons;
(ii) percentage overcrowded households;
(iii) percentage single parent households;
(iv) percentage of households lacking exclusive use of basic amenities;
(v) percentage pensioners living alone;
(vi) percentage population change;
(vii) standardised mortality rate;

(viii) percentage of residents living in households where the head of household was born in New Commonwealth or Pakistan.

In addition to providing data on all these indicators, a 'standardised Z-score' approach, based on the normal distribution, has been adopted to provide a single index of deprivation.[1] In this method each indicator is scaled so that areas with above average performance on the indicator have a positive score and those with below average deprivation have a negative score: the size of the score depends on the extent to which an area is above or below average. A high score implies a relatively high level of deprivation and a low score a relatively low level of deprivation.

A range of simple weights is assigned, by the Inner Cities Directorate, to different indicators (and Z-scores calculated accordingly) to bias them towards, alternatively, the social, the economic, or the housing aspects. In the tables that follow only the 'Economic Z-Score' is used, since this is considered to be the most closely associated with recreation deprivation. The 'Economic Z-Score' gives a weight of four to the unemployment Z-Scores and one to the Z-Scores for overcrowding, amenities, ethnics, single parents and pensioners.

To these indicators we have added a 'Recreation Need' index, using the percentage of households with no car and the percentage with head of household in an unskilled manual occupation. This Recreation Need index consists of:

Unemployment Z-Score + Single Parent Households Z-Score + Percentage of No Car Z-Score + Percentage of Unskilled Manual Z-Score

Three alternative indicators are used to represent the occupational data: percentage of unskilled manual, percentage of unskilled and semi-skilled manual, and percentage unskilled, semi-skilled and skilled manual.

The various indicators and indices have been correlated with net revenue expenditure on sports centres, swimming pools, outside pitches and parks and open spaces. The former two were added together to give indoor facilities and the latter two outdoor facilities. Total Expenditure in all four was also correlated with the 'need' indicators. The results appear in Tables 6.2 to 6.6. As in the Gratton (1984) results, positive signs for the correlation coefficients in the tables indicate that resources are being directed to the areas of greatest need.

For non-Metropolitan Districts (Table 6.2) nearly all the correlation coefficients are positive and significant. Taking just the indicators that most relate to recreational need (the Economic Z-Score,

Table 6.2 – Non-metropolitan districts (N = 289)

	Sports centres	Swimming pools	Outside pitches	Parks and open spaces	Indoor facilities	Outdoor facilities	Total expenditure
Unemployment	0.06	0.286	0.128	0.246	0.23	0.26	0.30
Overcrowding	0.116	0.282	0.02	0.248	0.284	0.241	0.308
Single parent families	0.066	0.213	0.163	0.274	0.194	0.299	0.295
Lacking basic amenities	–0.117	0.113	–0.066	0.139	–0.04	0.117	0.053
Ethnic	0.028	0.049	–0.033	0.097	0.056	0.085	0.084
Economic Z-score	0.022	0.242	0.136	0.310	0.17	0.326	0.3
No car	0.134	0.44	0.215	0.587	0.399	0.609	0.604
Unskilled manual	0.102	0.44	0.194	0.389	0.368	0.415	0.464
Unskilled + semi-skilled manual	0.233	0.428	0.150	0.426	0.482	0.440	0.542
Unskilled + semi-skilled + skilled manual	0.275	0.371	0.132	0.371	0.487	0.384	0.509

Note: r significant at 5% level if >0.10.

Table 6.3 – London districts (N = 30)

	Sports centres	Swimming pools	Outside pitches	Parks and open spaces	Indoor facilities	Outdoor facilities	Total expenditure
Unemployment	0.514	0.559	0.248	0.582	0.743	0.620	0.732
Overcrowding	0.390	0.389	0.235	0.348	0.539	0.381	0.487
Single parent families	0.584	0.412	0.229	0.558	0.684	0.593	0.689
Lacking basic amenities	0.317	0.393	0.144	0.337	0.492	0.359	0.452
Ethnic	0.383	0.284	0.232	0.253	0.458	0.285	0.389
Economic Z-score	0.488	0.511	0.285	0.536	0.691	0.578	0.683
No car	0.508	0.511	0.19	0.612	0.705	0.643	0.731
Unskilled manual	0.472	0.528	0.135	0.794	0.693	0.821	0.841
Unskilled + semi-skilled manual	0.363	0.577	0.244	0.711	0.655	0.75	0.778
Unskilled + semi-skilled + skilled manual	0.215	0.461	0.278	0.583	0.474	0.624	0.616

Note: r significant at 5% if >0.35.

Table 6.4 – Metropolitan districts (N = 36)

	Sports centres	Swimming pools	Outside pitches	Parks and open spaces	Indoor facilities	Outdoor facilities	Total expenditure
Unemployment	0.215	0.331	–0.011	0.071	0.418	0.065	0.274
Overcrowding	0.097	0.335	0.045	–0.048	0.324	–0.031	0.166
Single parent families	0.090	0.279	0.014	0.061	0.277	0.065	0.193
Lacking basic amenities	–0.213	0.223	–0.037	0.215	–0.013	0.197	0.104
Ethnic	–0.23	0.011	–0.078	–0.257	–0.181	–0.28	–0.26
Economic Z-score	0.061	0.371	0.037	0.028	0.321	0.041	0.205
No car	0.207	0.697	0.196	0.348	0.678	0.411	0.616
Unskilled manual	0.168	0.614	0.331	0.310	0.585	0.423	0.571
Unskilled + semi-skilled manual	0.022	0.440	0.175	0.132	0.338	0.193	0.301
Unskilled + semi-skilled + skilled manual	0.014	0.339	0.102	0.007	0.259	0.044	0.171

Note: r significant at 5% if r >0.3.

Table 6.5 – Welsh districts (N = 35)

	Sports centres	Swimming pools	Outside pitches	Parks and open spaces	Indoor facilities	Outdoor facilities	Total expenditure
Unemployment	0.619	−0.133	0.225	0.495	0.566	0.546	0.686
Overcrowding	0.434	0.018	0.223	0.370	0.440	0.435	0.540
Single parent families	0.549	0.003	0.353	0.394	0.549	0.522	0.661
Lacking basic amenities	0.093	0.059	−0.057	0.440	0.115	0.356	0.291
Ethnic	−0.039	0.151	0.079	0.091	0.019	0.12	0.086
Economic Z-score	0.602	−0.069	0.183	0.518	0.575	0.544	0.69
No car	0.483	0.015	0.235	0.714	0.488	0.741	0.759
Unskilled manual	0.435	0.027	0.162	0.288	0.444	0.334	0.480
Unskilled + semi-skilled manual	0.468	−0.032	0.205	0.606	0.455	0.632	0.671
Unskilled + semi-skilled + skilled manual	0.447	−0.015	0.222	0.605	0.429	0.640	0.660

Note: r significant at 5% if r >0.3.

No Car, and the Manual workers classification) they are all positive and only one (Economic Z-Score with sports centres subsidy) is not significant at the five per cent level.

There is a clear pattern in that subsidies on sports centres and outside pitches show lower correlations with these indicators than subsidies for swimming pools and parks and open spaces. The correlations of the indicators with subsidies for sports centres is particularly important because these facilities hardly existed before 1970 and it is the investment in these facilities in particular that should express the direction of policy. Swimming pools, outside pitches, and parks and open spaces have a much longer history. It is interesting then to notice that these new facilities have not been directed to areas of deprivation to the same extent as the older facilities. However it is still true to say that non-Metropolitan Districts with higher levels of deprivation spend more on sport and recreation facilities than those with low levels of deprivation.

London Districts (Table 6.3) are similar in that all the signs are positive and most are significant. The exception is 'Outside Pitches' which has no significant correlations even though they are all positive. This may be due to the difficulty of finding land for pitches in London, particularly for inner city authorities which are often the most deprived. In contrast to the findings for outside pitches, the correlations for subsidies on 'Sports Centres' in London are high relative to those for non-Metropolitan districts. It does seem that authorities with high levels of deprivation have attempted to alleviate the problems associated with this by providing indoor recreation facilities, since these can normally be built even in areas where space is relatively scarce.

Table 6.4 (Metropolitan Districts) shows a similar pattern to London in that most of the correlation coefficients for subsidies to outdoor facilities are not significantly different from zero (and several of them are negative). It is also similar to Table 6.2 in that there are relatively small correlations between subsidies to sports centres and need indicators. In fact, none of these correlation coefficients are significant. It is only swimming pools that provide significant positive correlation coefficients for Metropolitan Districts.

Table 6.5 (Welsh Districts) shows just the opposite to the Metropolitan evidence as far as indoor facilities are concerned: sports centres have high, significant correlations, swimming pools have correlations that are not significant. For outdoor facilities outside pitches have low correlations that are not significant but parks and open spaces in general have high, significant correlations.

Table 6.6 is a useful summary table showing the correlations of the 'Recreation Need' indicator with subsidies on the various type of facilities. All the patterns picked out above are clearly visible in this table.

Table 6.6 – Correlations of recreation need index and net revenue expenditure

	Sports centres	Swimming pools	Outside pitches	Parks and open spaces
Non-metropolitan districts	0.115	0.439	0.223	0.477
London districts	0.539	0.529	0.209*	0.249*
Metropolitan districts	0.20*	0.565	0.156*	0.232*
Welsh districts	0.634	–0.027*	0.297*	0.575

Note: Significant at 5% level except where marked by *.

The overall conclusion is that there is some evidence that local authorities faced with high levels of recreation need spend more on recreation facilities than those areas faced by lower levels of recreation need. This is indicated by the preponderance of positive signs in all the tables. However, the discussion above indicates that the pattern of the relationships seems to be rather uneven and certainly not as strong as we might expect.

On the other hand, the evidence for territorial justice in the distribution of recreation resources is much better than other studies have revealed for health, education and social services. In these cases the correlation coefficients were mostly the opposite to that expected.

It is important to stress that directing resources where they are most needed does not guarantee efficiency or effectiveness. An uneven distribution of subsidies that matches the uneven distribution of recreational need is only a necessary condition for effective policy: it is not sufficient. We need also to look at the *beneficiaries* of these subsidies. The next two sections attempt to assess who has benefited from the large increase in investment in swimming pools and sports centres over the last twenty years.

The market for indoor swimming

The aim of this section is to examine what has happened in the market for indoor swimming over the recent period that the public sector supply situation has changed considerably. Swimming is an ideal market in many ways for examining changes over the last twenty years. On the supply side it is the only facility for which adequate data exist on the existence of facilities. In 1982 the Sports Council carried out a full survey of all swimming pools in England which allowed a detailed database to be constructed (Sports Council 1983). On the demand side, if we ignore darts and snooker, it is by far the biggest indoor sport in Britain as far as numbers of regular participants is concerned. If we ignore walking, it is the most popular active recreation in Britain. Nearly all of this demand is catered for in publicly provided indoor pools.

Swimming pools have been part of the public sector investment boom in sport in the last twenty years. The supply of pools has increased rapidly and at the same time the quality of the swimming pool stock has risen. Evidence from the last section indicates that with the exception of Welsh Districts there is a significant correlation between net expenditure on swimming pools and recreation need. So there appears to be some territorial justice in the distribution of the recent public expenditure on swimming pool provision. In this section, after looking in more detail at how the supply side of swimming has developed, we examine the effects on the demand for swimming of this new supply situation.

The supply side of the swimming market

The historical development of swimming pool provision in England shows an uneven profile (for geographical details, See Appendix I). The first major investment boom occurred in the 1870–1914 period, mostly in and around large urban areas. By 1914 over 500 swimming baths were open to the public in England. Of these pre-1914 pools, 201 were still open in 1977. In the inter-war period investment in swimming pools continued but at a reduced rate – some 250 were built, nearly all of which were still open in 1977.

The period 1946 to 1959 saw a virtual halt to new swimming pool development – only two indoor pools were opened in this period. One major reason is suggested by the Sports Council (1983), to explain this: investment expenditure by local authorities during this period required loan sanctions from the appropriate central government department, and during post-war reconstruction loan sanction was generally not given for swimming pool construction. Housing, education and infrastructure were much higher in the public investment priority list.

Thus by 1960 England's capital stock of swimming pools was an ageing one with a significant number dating back to the Victorian era. In the 1960s there was an easing of loan sanctions for swimming pools and 166 new indoor swimming pools were built between 1960 and 1969. However, it was post-1970 that had the largest growth yet in swimming pool provision, as we have already noted in Chapter 2: 394 new pools were opened between 1970 and 1977. After a slowdown from 1977 to 1982, another 144 new pools opened between 1983 and 1988.

Swimming is also one of the most highly subsidised recreation activities. In 1987–88 swimming pools only recovered just over 31 per cent of their total expenditure in income from sales, fees and charges (see Table 2.4). This is a substantial increase in cost recovery from 1979–80 when it was only twelve per cent. Thus although it is highly subsidised, the rate of subsidy has been falling. Nevertheless, the *total* subsidy given to swimming has increased in real terms over the last twenty years, since the effect of new provision has outweighed the improvement in average cost recovery.

However, as we have noted before, increasing supply only indicates more *opportunity* for participation. It is a necessary but not sufficient condition for generating the collective and equity benefits from public expenditure on sport. To see if these benefits have actually occurred, we need to examine the demand for swimming over this period of expanded public investment and subsidisation.

The demand for indoor swimming

The best source of information on the demand for indoor swimming is the General Household Survey. The General Household Survey asks adult respondents (aged sixteen and over) what activities they participated in four weeks prior to interview. This gives a participation rate for each activity. They also ask in how many days during the last four weeks the respondent participated in those activities. Thus we also have data in frequency of participation.

In our analysis we use 1986 data. The participation rate (the percentage swimming at least once in the four weeks prior to interview) for adults in indoor swimming in 1986 was 9.5 per cent. The female participation rate was higher than that of males: 9.9 per cent compared with 9.0 per cent for males.

Table 6.7 gives a detailed breakdown of participation rates by age and sex. The table shows clearly that in only one age category (30–44) does the male participation rate exceed that for females in 1986. The biggest difference between males and females in 1986 occurs in the 16–19 age bracket but participation rates for women are also substantially higher than for males in the 20–24 and 25–29 age ranges.

Table 6.7 – Adult participation in indoor swimming, 1977 and 1986, by age and sex

	% Participation in 4 weeks prior to interview						
Age	Males		Females		Total		% Increase 1977–1986
	1977	*1986*	*1977*	*1986*	*1977*	*1986*	
16–19	10	13.8	11	19.3	10	16.5	65
20–24	7	14.3	8	17.8	1	16.1	100
25–29	9	13.2	7	18.6	8	16.1	100
30–44	9	13.4	6	13.2	7	13.3	90
45–59	2	5.1	2	6.2	2	5.7	185
60–69	1	3.7	1	3.7	1	3.7	270
70+	Ø	0.6	Ø	0.8	Ø	0.7	na
All ages	5	9.0	4	9.9	4.5	9.5	90

Note: Ø indicates participation < 0.5 per cent.
Source: General Household Survey 1986.

Participation drops dramatically after 45, but the highest growth in participation rates between 1977 and 1986 are in two of the oldest age groups, 45–59 and 60–69.

The figures on participation can be used, together with figures on frequency of participation to give national indicators of swimming demand. The overall adult participation rate of 9.5 per cent for 1986 implies that 4.15 million adults in Great Britain swim regularly (ie at least once a month). The average frequency of participation for these participants was 3.4 times per four-week period according to the 1986 General Household Survey. This means that an adult participant swims on average a bit less than once a week. Since there are thirteen four-week periods in a year then the total number of adult swims in Great Britain in 1986 was calculated to be 183.4 million. The various stages in this calculation are given in Table 6.8, which includes comparisons with 1977.

The Sports Council (1986) estimated that the ratio of junior swims (ie swims by those aged less than sixteen) to adult swims was 3:1. However, their information for this estimate was based on two surveys: one carried out in the late 1960s, surveyed those aged nine and over; the other, carried out in the late 1970s, looked at those aged under eight. It seems reasonable to expect that this ratio has dropped in the 1980s for two reasons. Firstly there has been a reduction in the number of children in the Great Britain population aged under sixteen. This age group now makes up a smaller percentage of the total population than it did in 1980. Secondly, there has been a sharp increase in participation by adult swimmers (see below).

Table 6.8 – The demand for indoor swimming by adults, 1977 and 1986 (Great Britain)

	1977	1986
Adult population	41.5m	43.7m
% participation in 4-week period	4.5%	9.5%
Number swimming in 4-week period	1.87m	4.15m
Frequency in 4 weeks	2.8	3.4
Swims in 4 weeks	5.24m	14.11m
Annual swims (x13)	68.12m	183.4m
Averaged over whole population to give frequency per annum	1.6	4.2

Two local swimming surveys carried out by the North West Sports Council tend to support this hypothesis. In Tameside, Greater Manchester, the ratio of junior swims (<15 years) to adult swims fell from 3.4:1 in 1971 to 2.3:1 in 1981. In the Wirral, the ratio of junior swims (<16) to adult swims fell from 3.5:1 in 1967 to 1.8:1 in 1982 (Data supplied by Mike Fitzjohn, Senior Research Officer at the North West Sports Council).

Consequently in order to estimate the total indoor swimming market we have used a 2:1 ratio of junior to adult swims. This gives a total annual Great Britain market of 550.2 million swims a year or on average, 10.2 swims per individual in the population per year (this is sometimes called the 'attendance factor'). A similar exercise carried out for 1977 gives a total market of 204.4 million swims a year. On this basis then the total number of swims has increased by a multiple of 2.6 over this nine-year period.

This is confirmed by Table 6.9 which shows a doubling in the adult participation rate between 1977 and 1986. The rise has been faster for women than for men so that now the women's participation rate is greater than the males by one percentage point whereas in 1977, the male rate exceeded the females by the same margin. Also the frequency of participation has gone up over the same period from 2.8 (per four-week period) to 3.4. Twice as many adults in 1986 were swimming than in 1977 and those that were going swimming were doing so more often.

Table 6.9 – Adult participation in indoor swimming, by sex, 1977 to 1986 (Great Britain)

	% Participation in 4 weeks prior to interview			
	1977	1980	1983	1986
Males	5	6	7	9
Females	4	6	7	10

Source: General Household Survey, 1977, 1980, 1983, 1986.

Rapid growth is not unusual in sports markets. For instance the press release for the introduction of the Sports Council's *A Digest of Sports Statistics* in 1986 pointed to ballooning as the fastest growing sport in Britain with a fifteen-fold increase between 1970 and 1984. In such a case as this there is a simple reason for rapid growth – the very small participation base from which the growth emanates.

What is remarkable about the growth of the swimming market is that even in 1977 it was already the most popular indoor active participant sport (excluding darts and snooker). To have such growth in a sport which already had a significant number of participants makes this growth a major feature of the sports market of the 1980s. It seems that most of this growth has been in the recreational swimming sector of the market since the admittedly rather patchy evidence available shows no spectacular growth in the number of swimming clubs. There is no information available on the number of *members* of clubs affiliated to the Amateur Swimming Association but the actual number of clubs affiliated rose only slightly from 1619 in 1975 to 1683 in 1985 (Sports Council, 1986).

The explanation for this spectacular growth in the swimming market must lie to some extent in the change in public sector provision. That is, there is a major supply-generated demand effect. If the sole objective was to increase participation, this has been achieved by the expansion in provision.

However, it is not only quantity of swimming pools that has increased. During this period of expansion, two forces were operating to create a substantial increase in quality. New conventional pools were replacing old Victorian pools. A whole generation of swimmers, roughly corresponding to the 45 years and older groups in Table 6.7, missed out on swimming in a 'new' pool as a child. Gradually, post 1960, a new generation has grown up with a 'modern' swimming experience and this has filtered down into subsequent age groups. Thus, the reason there is a dramatic fall-off in participation after the age of 45 in Table 6.7 may be not so much to do with people giving up swimming as they got older, but rather to do with the fact these older age groups were never regular swimmers in the first place. If this hypothesis is correct then the implication is that swimming demand will continue to expand as the younger age groups with high participation rates continue to swim as they get older.

A second change in quality occurred in the form of a new product, the leisure pool, which emphasised the fun element in swimming. Thirty-five of the pools that opened between 1982 and 1988 were leisure pools (approximately 25 per cent of all pools built in this period). Only about twelve leisure pools were operating prior to 1982. The emergence of the leisure pool has led to two clear market segments in the swimming market: 'swimming for fun' and 'swimming for fitness'. The opening of a leisure pool in an area has often led to an increase in both markets with the serious swimmer finding that the quality of their swimming environment in a conventional pool has increased due to the 'siphoning off' of the fun swimmers to the leisure pool.

Both types of new swimming pool, conventional and leisure, are appropriate to the changing nature of demand analysed in Chapter 3. Older provision catered for basic needs, for example cleanliness, whilst modern pools cater for higher order needs, in particular self-actualisation through health and the stimulation-seeking behaviour that is satisfied by leisure pools.

Another catagorisation of target groups of importance to the efficiency and equity of public sector provision is socioeconomic. Table 6.10 shows the socioeconomic group mix of swimmers for 1977, 1983 and 1986. Although the participation rates are highest in the professional and employer/manager categories, it is the semi-skilled manual category that shows the greatest *increase* in participation rates. The unskilled, however, continue to have low participation rates, despite the increased public sector provision.

As well as examining participation *rates* it is instructive to look at the actual *numbers* of people participating from different groups. Since the GHS sample is broadly representative of the population structure, the participation numbers taken from this sample are also representative. Table 6.11 shows the numbers of adults in the GHS sample from different age and socioeconomic groups who swim

Table 6.10 – Participation in indoor swimming by socioeconomic groups, 1977–1986

<table>
<tr><th></th><th>1977</th><th>1983</th><th>1986</th><th>% Increase 1977–1986</th></tr>
<tr><td>Professional</td><td>9</td><td>12</td><td>16</td><td>77</td></tr>
<tr><td>Employer/Manager</td><td>6</td><td>9</td><td>11</td><td>83</td></tr>
<tr><td>Intermediate non-manual</td><td>7</td><td>11</td><td rowspan="2">12</td><td rowspan="2">100</td></tr>
<tr><td>Junior non-manual</td><td>5</td><td>10</td></tr>
<tr><td>Skilled manual</td><td>4</td><td>5</td><td>7</td><td>75</td></tr>
<tr><td>Semi-skilled manual</td><td>1</td><td>4</td><td>7</td><td>600</td></tr>
<tr><td>Unskilled manual</td><td>2</td><td>3</td><td>3</td><td>50</td></tr>
</table>

Note: 1980 figures by socioeconomic group were not published.
Source: General Household Surveys 1977, 1983, 1986.

regularly (ie at least once a month). Regular adult swimmers are more likely to be over 30 years of age rather than under 30 and this is the case for both 1977 and 1986. The median age of adult swimmers was 31 years in 1977 and 33 years in 1986. Regular swimmers in 1986 are also concentrated in the intermediate and junior non-manual, skilled and semi-skilled manual categories. However, the smallest number of swimmers comes from the unskilled manual category.

So what can we conclude about the effectiveness of government intervention in generating the collective benefits and equity identified in Chapter 4? As regards equity, the conclusion must be that the benefits of swimming provision and subsidies are distributed unevenly, with those in the middle socioeconomic groups achieving the greatest benefits. The extent of the inequity, however, is less than is often assumed.

With respect to allocative efficiency arguments the conclusion is partly influenced by the uneven incidence of benefits just reported. This is because we suggested in Chapter 4 that to be efficient, benefits of government intervention should disproportionately favour certain target groups, notably the lower socioeconomic groups and the elderly. As we have seen above this does not appear to have happened – participation rates are higher for the higher socioeconomic groups and younger ages.

However, a conclusion that government has failed in achieving both equity and efficiency through its swimming provision would be missing two important considerations. First the proper reference point for current participation patterns is *not* their representative-

Table 6.11 – Numbers swimming regularly (at least once a month) in GHS sample, by age and socio-economic group; 1977 and 1986

	1977	1986
16–19 years	167	220
20–24 years	152	269
25–29 years	177	283
30–44 years	402	681
45–59 years	110	235
60–69 years	33	106
70+ years	–	26
Median age	31 yrs	33 yrs
Professional	58	99
Employer/Manager	118	258
Intermediate and junior non-manual	384	713
Skilled manual	210	283
Semi-skilled manual	51	274
Unskilled manual	34	35

Source: General Household Survey 1986.

ness with respect to the importance of the target groups in the population. Rather, it should be the participation that would have occurred by these target groups in the absence of the government intervention. The evidence above demonstrates that even though participation by the lower socioeconomic groups and elderly groups is not representative of their importance in the population, it *is* markedly better than it was before the recent wave of public investment.

Table 6.7 demonstrates that the fastest growth in participation rates between 1977 and 1986 was among the elderly. Table 6.10 shows that the growth in participation rate for the semi-skilled was the highest of any socioeconomic group in the same period, but unfortunately the bottom group, the unskilled manuals, showed the lowest growth in this period. Table 6.11 shows good representation by older participants in the *numbers* of regular swimmers.

Secondly, with specific reference to the elderly, we have noted above how there is probably a 'generation gap' in swimming, with the present older people never having participated much, and certainly not in the new, higher quality pools. If this is the main reason for their low participation, then we will have to wait twenty years for the full effects of the new provision to feed through to substantially improved participation by the elderly. In this time the more aware and higher participation people aged 25 to 45 will feed through to the older age bands.

In addition to the distribution of swimming participation, it is important to point out that a general increase in swimming participation may well generate substantial collective benefits. This relates back to the arguments concerning sport and health, discussed in the first section of Chapter 4. Whilst accepting that certain target groups may be more important than others in this respect, it is nevertheless the case that any general increase in sport will reduce the likehood of preventable diseases being taken to health care services, and increase the probability of lower absenteeism and higher productivity at work. Swimming is particularly relevant to this line of reasoning, as the Amateur Swimming Association (ASA) state: 'For all people, swimming is an enjoyable way of keeping fit. It improves stamina and stimulates the circulatory and respiratory systems, thereby promoting a feeling of general well-being' (ASA 1987).

Our conclusion is therefore that government intervention in the swimming market has had a positive effect on both equity and efficiency. This cannot be quantified in value terms, but the public welfare consequences of the dramatic supply-led effect of government intervention on swimming participation must not be dismissed simply because we cannot put monetary values on them.

The market for sports centres

Sports centres are similar to swimming pools in that they too went through a boom in public investment in the 1970s and 1980s. Unfortunately, for three reasons, it is not as easy to carry out a similar analysis for sports centres to that in the last section. Firstly, there is no national database for sports centres yet, to match that for swimming pools. Secondly, whereas swimming is a homogeneous activity there is a variety of sports and other activities that take place in leisure centres. Finally, whereas indoor swimming in Britain invariably takes place in a publicly provided pool, for sports that take place in indoor centres there are normally alternative facilities provided by both the voluntary and commercial sectors. Hence it is not as easy to tie demand figures in with changes in public sector provision.

The supply of sports centres

Between 1970–71 and 1980–81 sports centre provision in England grew from twelve to 461. During the 1980s, despite local government cutbacks, this expansion continued. In *Sport in the Community – The Next Ten Years* (1982) the Sports Council established a target of an additional 800 indoor sports halls which it wished to see provided by 1988, and indicated that at least 150 of these should be in areas of social and sporting need. In that document, the Council argued that it was not necessary to build large new facilities, and that there was a case for much more small scale centres often converted from old buildings. The advantages of such facilities would be their local nature and the cheapness of provision.

In fact, less than 50 per cent of the Sports Council target was achieved. According to the 1988 figures, 347 halls had come into public use over the five-year period 1983–1988. Most of these, 282, were of the large (four badminton courts or more) purpose-built variety and local authority financed. Figure 6.2 shows the regional distribution of these new halls. Although investment in sports centres may seem modest compared to Sports Council targets, the 347 new sports centres which opened between 1983 and 1988 represented a 75 per cent increase in provision.

The conclusion must be that, as with swimming pools, the investment in sports centres has radically changed the supply side of public sector indoor sports facilities. Again, though, provision is not enough to guarantee efficiency and equity in government intervention. We need to examine the effects of this supply change on the demand for such facilities.

The demand for sports centres

Because there is no homogeneous activity that takes place in sports centres it is difficult to identify the effects on demand of the increased provision. We can identify four major sports that take place in public sector centres and these are badminton, squash, keep fit/yoga and gymnastics/athletics/weightlifting (NB these are GHS-coded activities that relate to indoor sports centres). Keep fit/yoga data is likely to be dominated by keep fit and gymnastics/indoor athletics/weightlifting data is likely to be dominated by weightlifting.

Unfortunately many of these sports take place in commercial and voluntary sector facilities as well as in public sector facilities and there is no data that allows a breakdown of the relative share of

Figure 6.2 – Additional sports halls brought into public use, 1983–1988

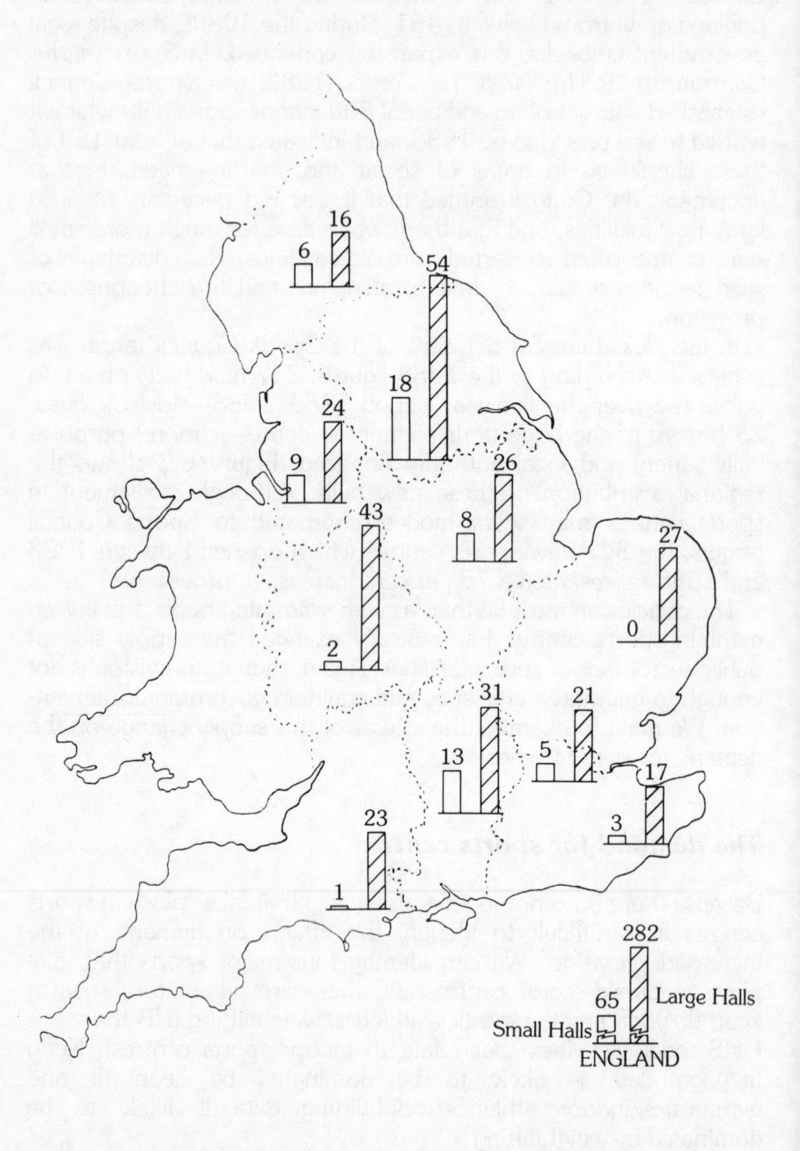

Note: Sports Council Regions.
Source: The Sports Council (unpublished), regional facilities data.

each market provided for by the different sectors. Even so it is worthwhile to look at overall participation data for these indoor sports over the period that public sector provision for them was expanding at a rapid rate. Unfortunately, consistent GHS data covers the period 1977–1986: not quite the full period of supply expansion noted in the section above, but still relevant.

The General Household Survey data for these sports is shown in Tables 6.12 and 6.13. Table 6.12 reports the four-week participation rates from 1977 to 1986. Although the two major sports in 1977, badminton and squash, have stayed fairly flat in demand terms, there has been rapid expansion in keep fit/yoga and gymnastics/athletics/weightlifting.

Table 6.12 – Demand for sports centre sports, 1977–1986

	Adult participation rate (%)			
Sport	1977	1980	1983	1986
Badminton	2	2	2	2
Squash	2	2	3	2
Keep Fit/Yoga	1	2	3	3
Gymnastics/ Indoor Athletics/ Weighlifting	Ø	1	1	2

Note: Ø indicates participation < 0.5 per cent.
Source: General Household Survey, 1986.

Table 6.13 – Frequency of participation in sports centre sports, 1977–86

	Average frequency of participation per adult per year			
Sport	1977	1980	1983	1986
Badminton	1.0	1.2	1.0	0.9
Squash	1.1	1.3	1.4	1.3
Keep Fit/Yoga	0.7	1.1	2.2	2.7
Gymnastics/ Indoor Athletics/ Weighlifting	0.3	0.5	0.8	2.1

Source: General Household Survey, 1986.

This is shown more clearly in Table 6.13 which reports the average frequency of participation per adult per year which is a measure of the total number of occasions of participation in an activity per year divided by the whole sample. It therefore incorporates measures of both participation and frequency. Table 6.13 shows that on this measure keep fit/yoga and gymnastics etc. are much more significant indoor activities than badminton and squash. Not only do as many or more adults take part in these activities, they do so more frequently. In fact, gymnastics etc has the highest four-week frequency of participation of any sport, indoor or outdoor, with the average participant taking part on nine days in a four-week period. Keep fit/yoga has a four-week frequency of six days compared with three for badminton and four for squash. Thus the average participant in gymnastics etc participates on average over twice a week, compared with less than once a week for badminton.

Tables 6.14 and 6.15 show the age/sex and the socioeconomic group breakdowns for these sports. These profiles have not altered significantly since 1977, so only 1986 data is reported in this table. There is mixed evidence here for an analysis of efficiency and equity from government supply, as judged by the targeting of lower socioeconomic groups and older people. On the positive side, there is a contrast in the socioeconomic make-up of the 'new' popular activities of keep fit/yoga and gymnastics/indoor athletics/weightlifting compared with the more conventional indoor sports of badminton and squash. Participation rates are much more similar across socioeconomic groups for the 'new' activities. In contrast, badminton and squash have much higher participation rates by professionals and other non-manual groups than for skilled, semi-skilled and unskilled manual groups. Table 6.14 shows the domination of women in keep fit/yoga as well as substantial participation in this activity in the over-45 groups.

On the negative side, the socioeconomic profile of participation rates in badminton and squash has not altered significantly in the period 1977–1983, despite the expansion of government supply. Furthermore, the age profile of participation rates in these two sports is neither representative of the age profile of the population, nor has it changed much as government supply has expanded. Younger people have much higher participation rates than older groups in all the sports reported in Table 6.14.

However, as with swimming, although participation *rates* may be higher in the younger age groups and higher socioeconomic groups, it is certainly not the case that the greatest *numbers* of participants come from these groups. As Table 6.16 shows, badminton and keep fit/yoga have more 'over 30' than 'under 30'

Table 6.14 – Participation in sports centre sports by age and sex, 1986

	Participation rates %							
	Badminton		Squash		Keep Fit/ Yoga		Gymnastics/ Indoor Athletics/ Weightlifting	
Age	Men	Women	Men	Women	Men*	Women	Men	Women
16 –19	5	4	6	4	–	6	9	4
20 – 24	4	2	6	3	–	10	8	2
25 – 29	3	3	9	3	–	9	5	2
30 – 44	3	3	5	1	–	8	3	1
45 – 59	1	1	2	Ø	–	4	1	Ø
60 – 69	Ø	Ø	Ø	0	–	2	0	Ø
70+	0	Ø	0	0	–	1	Ø	0
Total	2	2	4	1	1	5	3	1

Notes: Ø indicates participation at < 0.5 per cent;
*Figures for male participation in keep fit/yoga broken down by age not reported in 1986 GHS.

Source: General Household Survey, 1986.

Table 6.15 – Participation in sports centre sports by socioeconomic group, 1986

	Participation Rates (%)			
	Badminton	Squash	Keep Fit/ Yoga	Gymnastics/ Indoor Athletics/ Weightlifting
Socioeconomic group				
Professional	5	9	2	3
Employers and Managers	2	4	2	2
Intermediate and junior non-manual	3	3	6	2
Skilled manual	1	2	1	2
Semi-skilled manual	1	1	3	2
Unskilled manual	1	0	2	1

Source: General Household Survey, 1986.

participants in the representative GHS sample, and median ages of 32 and 34 respectively. Nearly as many squash and gymnastics/ indoor athletics/weightlifting participants in the GHS sample are over 30 years of age as under 30 – these sports having participant median ages of 29 and 26 respectively. Furthermore, the median ages of participants in badminton and squash is one or two years older in 1986 than it was in 1977.

Table 6.17 shows that by far the highest number of participants in the GHS sample in these sports come from the intermediate and junior non-manual group. It is also the case that the manual groups together have more participant numbers than the professional and employers and managers groups together.

The conclusion for sports centres is therefore less positive than that for swimming pools. The evidence indicates that the new investment in sports centres has only partially created a supply-generated demand – in the 'newer' activities of keep fit/yoga and gymnastics/indoor athletics/weightlifting. These two major growth activities also show relatively even distribution of participation rates over socioeconomic groups and, for keep fit/yoga, good take-up by the older age groups and women. It may be that it is these newer activities that are more in tune with the changing values of leisure consumers reported in Chapter 3, in that they have less class

Table 6.16 – Numbers of participants in GHS sample, 1986, by age

	16–19	20–24	25–29	30–44	45–59	60–69	70+	Median age
Badminton	55	67	53	157	39	–	–	32
Squash	69	84	106	157	39	–	–	29
Keep fit/Yoga	55	101	89	262	78	26	–	34
Gym/athletics/ weights	83	84	71	105	39	–	–	26

Source: General Household Survey 1986.

Table 6.17 – Number of participants in GHS sample, 1986, by socioeconomic group

	Professional	Employers and managers	Inter-mediate & junior non-manual	Skilled manual	Semi-skilled manual	Unskilled manual
Badminton	31	47	178	40	39	12
Squash	56	94	178	81	39	0
Keep Fit/Yoga	12	47	356	40	117	24
Gymnastics/ Indoor Athletics/ Weightlifting	19	47	119	81	78	12

Source: General Household Survey 1986.

connotations and might be seen to be more appropriate to the increasing numbers of inner-directed consumers. On the other hand squash and badminton may, through their traditional images, be more attractive to outer-directed consumers.

The major beneficiaries of public sector subsidies to sports centres are not the older groups in the population, nor the unskilled manual groups at the lower end of the income distribution. It is rather the young to middle-aged groups, and the middle order of the socioeconomic categories that are the greatest beneficiaries. Thus there is some inequity in the distribution of such subsidies. Furthermore, it must be remembered that the evidence used in this section is only for a restricted range of activities. It is probably the case, as reported by Veal (1981), the Audit Commission (1989) and others cited in the previous chapter, that the main beneficiaries of public provision of sports centres will be young, male, middle-class and white, rather than the recreationally disadvantaged.

Conclusions

In this chapter we have shown that there is some evidence, though not conclusive, to suggest that public sector expenditure, on swimming pools particularly and on sports centres to a lesser extent, is related to recreational need. However, evidence on participation in swimming and sports centre sports indicates that the main beneficiaries of subsidies to such facilities do not seem to have been the recreationally or socioeconomically disadvantaged.

This equity problem is compounded by the changing leisure values of consumers noted in Chapter 3. An historical legacy of provision is possibly still causing a mismatch between supply and demand. If sports provision is in any way conditioned by the thought that it is basic, lower order needs that are being satisfied by such provision, this is a throw-back to the early days of government intervention, on grounds of cleanliness, fitness for work, etc. It is also entirely inappropriate for the emergent inner-directed consumers seeking self-actualisation and stimulation. These consumers are seeking high quality provision and price does not appear to be a significant barrier.

A policy trap exists for any government agency interested in recreationally disadvantaged target groups. It is caused by these changing consumer values and takes the form that providing 'basic' facilities is unlikely to attract either the growth in inner-directed demand driven by higher order needs, or significant increases in demand from the sustenance driven, part of whom are the recreationally disadvantaged, who have lower order priorities. Any higher quality government provision will appeal more to the inner-directed and outer-directed consumers than the traditional target groups, the disadvantaged. The problem is that local authority sport may well have been largely operating on an out-of-date social paradigm, providing for basic needs when sport is intrinsically a higher order need. Hence subsidies directed at keeping prices generally low are misdirected, since the most common customers are more interested in quality than price.

Despite such questions relating primarily to the equity of public provision, there are collective efficiency benefits which are more difficult to measure in the context of public provision. We have shown in this chapter that the increased expenditure on indoor facilities is probably the single most important factor in increasing participation in swimming and some other indoor sports. There are likely collective health and quality of life benefits from such increased participation which, unfortunately, nobody has attempted to value.

The conclusion to this chapter must be similar to the Audit Commission's *Sport for Whom?* (1989): the lack of equity in the distribution of the benefits from public sector sports provision questions the validity of such a high degree of public subsidisation. However, one of the problems with this chapter and the whole subject area is the lack of empirical evidence on the achievement of social objectives and the benefits that are generated through such achievement. As the discussion in Chapter 4 indicated, the nature of the collective benefits generated through increased participation in sport is such as to make them very difficult to measure. Consequently, what evidence that does exist is evidence that is easy to measure: who is using sports centres and swimming pools. That evidence shows the regressive nature of blanket subsidies, although the redistribution is not so much from poor to rich as from poor to middle-income groups.

Given the potential importance of collective benefits in terms of health, quality of life, and crime prevention, there is a need for much more research on the value of such effects. As indicated in the introduction to this chapter, ideally evaluation should look at the impacts of public provision rather than the outputs. Unfortunately that stage has not yet been reached in the field of public sector sports provision. Without such evidence, any efficiency benefits tend to be forgotten in the clamour about the lack of equity in usage.

Note

[1] Z-Score $= \frac{Xi - \bar{X}}{Sx}$

where $\bar{X}$ is the mean of Xi;
Xi is the relevant deprivation indicator;
Sx is the standard deviation of the Xi.

7 The context of government intervention

In Chapter 4, we looked at the inadequacies of the commercial sector in meeting the demand for collective-good aspects of sport. In Chapter 5, we showed that government also may fail to meet this demand completely and Chapter 6 indicated clearly that there is certainly evidence of government failure in public sector intervention in the sports market in Britain. The discussion in these chapters has, however, implicitly assumed that all goods and services must be provided either by the commercial sector or by government. It ignores the importance of a third sector, the voluntary sector, a sector with particular importance in sport.

In this chapter we first of all look at the nature of voluntary sector activity in sport; secondly we analyse the economic rationale for the existence of this sector, and finally we discuss the nature of the interrelationships between the commercial, government and voluntary sectors in the sports market.

The voluntary sector in sport

In sport in Britain, voluntary sector activity is very significant. Most sports are organised on a club basis. This is almost certainly the case for team sports and is the most common form of organisation for individual sports. The clubs make up the base of the pyramid of voluntary sector organisations in sport. Most of the income to the club will come from membership subscriptions. The expenditure of the club will be concentrated on the organisation of the sport for the members. The people doing the work of organising will typically also be participants, or former participants, providing voluntary labour without payment.

Many clubs will affiliate to the sports governing body. The governing body regulates and administers the sport. Normally the main objectives of the governing body are to, within its own sport, promote excellence and participation: that is, the same as the

Sports Council's objectives for sport as a whole. The governing body is normally responsible for organising national and international competitions and events, selecting and training national squads, and organising coaching at the élite level, and for the sport as a whole. Not surprisingly, given the similarity of objectives, the Sports Council is closely involved with the governing bodies and provides finance for certain of their functions.

In an ideal world, every participant would be a member of a club, every club would affiliate to the single governing body for that sport, and it would be possible to present a detailed analysis of sport through statistics on participation, club membership and governing body affiliations. Unfortunately, and perhaps not surprisingly, one of the major features of the voluntary sector is its variety and although there are some sports that operate on the basis of the above model, there are many that do not.

In some sports, many participants join neither club nor governing body. Facilities may be provided by the commercial, public, or voluntary sector and the participant simply pays a charge for each occasion of participation. This is the pattern in two of the biggest participation sports as revealed in the General Household Survey data on participation, swimming and walking, although for the latter there is normally no admission charge in Britain. In the 1986 General Household Survey, walking (over two miles, for recreational purposes) had an adult participation rate of 22 per cent. Indoor swimming, as already discussed in Chapter 6, had an adult participation rate of 10 per cent. These are by far the largest participant, physical activity, sports. Yet no walking or swimming organisations appear in Table 7.1 (The Ten Largest Governing Bodies of Sport, 1985) or Table 7.2 (The Ten Fastest Growing Sports Bodies, 1975–1985), both Tables appearing in the Sports Council's (1986) *Digest of Sports Statistics*. Both these sports are informally organised. Less than 0.5 per cent of walkers are members of the Ramblers Association, although the latter did increase individual membership form 32,000 in 1975 to 58,000 in 1985, a rise of over 80 per cent. There is no information available on individual membership of the Amateur Swimming Association and the number of clubs affiliated has remained fairly static (1619 in 1975; 1683 in 1985) over a period of rapidly expanding participation in the sport.

There are other sports, such as hang gliding, where a very high proportion of participants will join the governing body of the sport. It is estimated that over 80 per cent of regular hang gliders are members of the British Hang Gliding Association. On the other hand, hang gliding does not exactly fit the model outlined above since only about half of these members will be a member of a club.

This indicates another aspect of voluntary sector organisation in sport. A participant may be a member of a club that is affiliated to a governing body or he or she may be an individual member of the governing body, without joining a club, or in addition to joining a club (that itself may or may not affiliate to the governing body).

Table 7.1 – The ten largest governing bodies of sport, 1985

Governing body	Affiliations	
	Members (000s)	Clubs
English Golf Union	445	1325
National Federation of Anglers	333	4310
Lawn Tennis Association	230	2443
Camping and Caravanning Club	174	—
Ladies Golf Union*	154	1866
English Bowls Association	120	2682
Badminton Association of England	104	5058
English Ladies Golfing Association*	91	1162
Scottish Bowls Association	88	874
British Association for Shooting & Conservation	75	358

Note: *1984 figures.
Source: *A Digest of Sports Statistics* (Sports Council, 1986).

As if this is not confusing enough, there is a further complicating factor. Our discussion above has implicitly assumed that each sport has only one governing body. Appendix II shows, sport by sport, the various governing bodies that were approached in the preparation of the Digest of Sports Statistics. The single governing body in sport is very much the exception. In one way Appendix II makes the situation look more complicated than it is. Often as well as a Great Britain governing body, there will be separate bodies for Scotland, Wales, England and Northern Ireland. For many sports, the main purpose of these separate bodies will be team selection and organisations for the Commonwealth Games, one of few major international competitions remaining where England, Scotland, Wales, and Northern Ireland send separate teams. In another way, however, Appendix II underrepresents the level of complication. There is only one entry under 'Martial Arts', the Martial Arts Commission. The Commission itself is composed of 14 national governing bodies, including 4 for Karate, and others representing Kung Fu, Jiu Jitsu, Aikido, Kendo, Shorinji Kempo, and Thai and Korean Martial Arts. Judo is not included in the Commission and is organised by the British Judo Association (BJA), with separate organisations for Scotland, Wales, and Northern Ireland. The BJA also has responsibility for the sport in England.

Table 7.2 – The ten fastest growing sports bodies, 1975–85

CLUBS Sport (Organisation)	Increase %	 (no.)
Movement, Dance & Fitness (MMM)*	401	(771)
Roller Hockey (NRHAGB)	338	(54)
Shooting (UCPSA)	260	(70)
Weight-lifting (NIAWLA)	250	(5)
Volleyball (EVA)	164	(137)
Netball (WNA)	251	(93)
Shooting (CPSA)*	142	(505)
Netball (AENA)	137	(1629)
Bowls (WIBA)	133	(4)
Bowls (SBA)	117	(75)

MEMBERS Sport (Organisation)	Increase %	 (no.)
Movement, Dance & Fitness (SBTA)+	1173	(2345)
Weight-lifting (NIAWLA)	818	(90)
Roller Hockey (NRHAGB)	500	(1000)
Parachuting (BPA)	467	(42000)
Volleyball (EVA)	355	(7806)
Shooting (UCPSA)	350	(3500)
Movement, Dance & Fitness (MMM)*	333	(10000)
Fives (EFA)	316	(380)
Parachuting (SSPA)	233	(7000)
Bowls (WLIBA)	208	(743)

Notes: * 1984 figures;
+ 1976 figures;
See Appendix II for the full names of the organisations.
Source: *A Digest of Sports Statistics* (Sports Council, 1986).

These examples serve to indicate that the voluntary sector in sport is a very diverse sector. The current organisational structure for any sport is a result of a range of influences: historical factors, different disciplines within the sport, different interests and policies in different regions, demands of international bodies, and organisational developments related to interactions with the Sports Councils, upon whom many depend for funding. It is perhaps not surprising then that the interaction of such factors leads to different organisational structures in different sports.

Historical factors are particularly important in explaining the diversity of governing bodies of sport. Although some sports clubs and governing bodies date back to the eighteenth century (the Royal and Ancient Golf Club of St. Andrews was formed in 1754; the Marylebone Cricket Club was formed in 1787), for most of the traditional sports in Britain, the governing bodies were formed in the nineteenth century. For instance, the Football Association was founded in 1863, the Grand National Archery Society in 1861, the Amateur Athletic Association in 1880, the Badminton Association in 1893, the Amateur Boxing Association in 1880, the Lawn Tennis Association in 1888, the Amateur Rowing Association in 1882, the Rugby Football Union in 1871, and the National Rifle Association in 1860.

It is possible to see how complications have arisen over time in the organisation of a sport by looking at how the relationship between the last of the examples above, the National Rifle Association (NRA), and the sport of shooting has developed since the founding of the Association in 1860. The National Rifle Association represented all forms of rifle and pistol shooting up until the end of the nineteenth century. In 1901, the National Small-bore Rifle Association (NSRA) was formed because it was felt that the National Rifle Association inadequately represented the interests of small-bore shooters. Since many pistol shooters shoot both full-bore and small-bore pistols (it is less common for rifle shooters to shoot both disciplines) this split in the organisation meant that these shooters would probably have to join two governing bodies if they wished to take part in national competitions. In 1979, the National Pistol Association (NPA) was formed. The NPA deals with all pistol disciplines and was formed because of dissatisfaction amongst some members with the way that pistol shooting was organised and represented in both the NRA and NSRA. It remains the case that pistol shooters appear as members of the NPA, the NRA, and the NSRA. Some may only join one of them, some join two, and some join all three. Others do not join any of them and simply join a club.

Add to this the Clay Pigeon Shooting Association (CPSA), which is a separate governing body responsible for another shooting discipline (shotgun), and the fact that all the disciplines have equivalent governing bodies in Wales, Scotland, and Northern Ireland, we see that over the 130 years since the single body, the NRA, was formed, the organisation of the sport has become increasingly more fragmented with over 20 governing bodies associated with the sport of shooting. Mainly because of these complications and, with the encouragement of the Sports Council, most of these governing bodies are now represented on the Great Britain Target Shooting Federation, formed in 1988, in a move to coordinate the organisation of shooting in Great Britain.

A further complication in the study of the voluntary sector in sport is the lack of statistical data relating to the sector. Appendix II indicates all the organisations that were contacted during the preparation of the *Digest of Sports Statistics*. It also indicates those that did not respond. This was a substantial number and for many of these organisations, little is known about the size of membership (both club and individual) and the type of organisational structure.

This diverse nature of the voluntary sector in sport raises the question of whether such diversity is appropriate for the efficient organisation and administration of sport. In order to begin to answer this question we have to look firstly at the rationale for the voluntary sector and secondly at the interaction between this sector and the commercial and public sectors.

Economic rationale for the voluntary sector

Weisbrod (1978, 1988) provides an economic rationale for the existence of the voluntary sector. He sees the voluntary sector as essentially fulfilling the same role as government namely, providing collective goods. There is a need for this sector since, as we have seen in Chapter 5, government fails to correct for all private market failures. Weisbrod argues that two of the reasons discussed in Chapter 5 are particularly relevant to the stimulation of voluntary sector activity. Government itself lacks adequate information on consumer demands and also government officials often follow their own personal objectives rather than acting on the basis of abstract concepts of allocative efficiency and distributional objectives.

Weisbrod (1988) adds another dimension to government failure, providing one possible explanation of why attempts at redistribution in kind may have failed:

> In a democratic society, government must make its services available to everyone who meets certain conditions – the 'equal access' constraint.

> Inevitably, some people who benefit from government services are unintended beneficiaries: they are included only because of the cost of excluding them. At the same time, some who do not obtain the services are excluded unintentionally, victims of the high costs of targeting the consumer population more accurately . . . In some cases a more decentralised, non-governmental institutional mechanism, such as a non-profit, may have better access to diverse, localised information, thereby overcoming some of the problems of over- and under-utilisation.

The above quote is related to a central theme of Weisbrod's argument. Government may be an efficient provider of collective goods if demand for such goods is homogeneous. In circumstances where there are diverse demands, the voluntary sector is likely to be the more efficient provider. He argues:

> when a collective good is collective for only some persons – in the sense that the good enters positively the utility functions of only those persons – the potential for organising collective good activity outside of government, in voluntary non-profit organisations, appears more likely (Weisbrod, 1978).

In effect, Weisbrod is saying that there has to be a wide degree of consensus on the collective nature of a good before government enters the market. For minority interests government is likely to fail to provide collective benefits:

> the undersatisfied demand for collective-type goods is a government 'failure' analogous to private market failures. That is, the combined willingness of part of the population to pay for an additional collective-type goods exceeds the incremental cost of providing them and yet government, responding to majoritarian interests, does not provide them (Weisbrod, 1988).

Government fails to obtain relevant information on consumer demand when demand is heterogeneous and fragmented, even when the nature of the good concerned is collective. There are several reasons for this.

Firstly there is a motivation problem. The behaviourist model indicates that politicians are likely to be more concerned with the objective of maximising their chances of re-election than meeting an abstract social welfare objective. Where there is a majority demand for a collective good then the two objectives are likely to lead to the same action, provision of the good. However, for minority interest collective goods, the re-election objective is not necessarily fulfilled by provision.

Secondly, there is an information problem. For majority interests, there is less likely to be a problem in politicians perceiving the demand for the collective good. For minority interests, it is much more difficult to establish the strength of demand.

Jackson (1982) adds another dimension to this information problem:

> It is a well known result in public sector economics that the rational individual, who realising that the decision to produce the collective good is unlikely to turn on his preferences, will take up a strategic position in which he distorts his preferences in order to pay less for the public good, thereby acting as a free-rider. Not only does the problem of the free-rider impede the the use of benefit taxes or prices for public services, but (taken to its logical conclusion) if everyone was to act as a free-rider then the information which this process produces for the decision maker will in itself lead to inefficiency, since the information is not a true reflection of individual preferences.

Thus the difficulties the politician has in discovering the preferences for minority-interest collective goods is compounded by this aspect in the motivation of the consumer to hide those preferences. Add to this the inefficiencies in the implementation of the decisions of the politician through the bureaucratic process it is perhaps not surprising that there is a significant part of consumer demand for collective goods that goes unmet by both the commercial sector and government. The voluntary sector fills the gap.

This argument is specifically relevant to sport because Chapter 3 indicated that the nature of the demand for sport is such that demand is likely to be fragmented. Data on participation rates from the General Household Survey shows that demand for any particular sport is a minority demand.

Weisbrod discusses the wide spectrum of types of non-profit organisation. At one end, are what may more appropriately be called 'clubs'. Buchanan (1965) has analysed the economic formation of clubs. The benefits of such organisations accrue only to the members of the club; in fact, Buchanan saw the objective of such a club as the maximisation of the net benefit of the typical member.

At the other end of the spectrum 'collective-type non-profits, such as providers of medical research and aid to the poor, produce public-type services that bring widely shared benefits' (Weisbrod 1988). These organisations are more like mini-governments. Government does not provide such collective benefits because of their minority nature or because of information inadequacies. Such organisations are, however, likely to be publicly subsidised and receive a large part of their income in the form of contributions, gifts, or grants. Weisbrod suggests a 'collectiveness index' to measure the percentage of an organisations income that comes from these sources. An organisation that provides mainly private goods and services to its own members (ie clubs) would be expected to have a 'collectiveness index' close to zero. At the opposite extreme, any non-profit providing purely collective goods (ie all the benefits accruing to individuals who did not pay for them) would have a collectiveness index approaching 100. Thus we have a whole variety of voluntary sector organisations.

It seems that many sports clubs (eg amateur football clubs, athletics clubs, etc) would be at the 'private good' end of Weisbrod's spectrum of voluntary sector organisations. Weisbrod argues that this type of non-profit is most similar to the commercial sector. Most of the income comes from membership dues and from sales. There is little or no public subsidy since few if any benefits are generated to non-members: the collectiveness index therefore should be very low. There is some limited data available with which to test this hypothesis.

The Henley Centre for Forecasting estimated the total income of the voluntary sector in sport and in an Appendix to their report they provide data on income of sports clubs for seven sports: football, rugby, athletics, cricket, tennis, golf and bowls. Table 7.3 shows the major breakdown of the income to sports clubs. It should be emphasised that the sample of sports club accounts on which these estimates were made was very limited, and was drawn from those voluntary clubs that had submitted applications to the Sports Council for grants or loans. Since many such grants are related to facilities, the sample might have been biased towards those clubs possessing their own grounds and/or club houses. Certainly this is likely to be the case for rugby and cricket and hence may explain the predominance of bar profits in the income to these sports.

Despite this possibility of bias, the message from Table 7.3 is quite clear. Grants, gifts, and donations is almost non-existent as a source of regular income for sports clubs. Only football has a non-zero item under this heading and then it only accounts for one per cent of income. The majority of sports club income comes from two sources: membership subscriptions and fees, and bar profits. The other sources include income from other social events, and raffles and gaming. Since it is normally the members themselves who drink in the club bar, use the gaming machines, and attend social events, the majority of the income from sports clubs is likely to come from members.

If we consider the typical rugby club or cricket club (amateur) then it should not be too surprising to see such a picture. The benefits provided by the club are exclusive to its members. The major benefits provided are to the players. Their participation in their chosen sport is made easier and considerably cheaper by the organisation provided by mainly volunteer labour. Weisbrod (1988) discusses at length the role of volunteer labour in the voluntary sector and examines why people are willing to work for nothing in this sector. This leads him into the economics of altruism literature.

Table 7.3 – Sports clubs sources of income (1985)

	Football	Rugby	Athletics	Cricket	Tennis	Golf	Bowls
Subscriptions and fees	6	16	50	9	90	56	31
Raffles and gaming	11	1	0	10	0	4	13
Bar	52	70	0	72	0	36	39
Other social	18	7	50	5	10	0	17
Grants/donations	1	0	0	0	0	0	0
Other	12	6	0	4	0	2	0
Total	100	100	100	100	100	100	100

Source: Henley Centre for Forecasting (1986).

Although there is an element of altruistic giving in the volunteer labour provided to sports clubs, most of this labour is provided by the players themselves (the main beneficiaries), former players (and hence former beneficiaries), relatives of the players (hence indirect consumers of the benefits), or volunteers who receive positive utility through their involvement in the sport (more details are given later in the chapter). There will always be an incentive for a player to receive the benefits without making a contribution and leave the club as soon as he or she ceases to play. This is the familiar 'free-rider' problem. However, sports clubs are also social organisations and social pressure can be an important deterrent to free-rider behaviour.

This volunteer labour is a substantial resource in the voluntary sector and distinguishes this sector from both the public and commercial sectors, both of whom must pay market rates for their labour. Table 7.3 shows that a substantial proportion of sports club income comes from a commercial activity that is in direct competition with the commercial sector, the selling of alcohol and other drinks (ie income from the bar), thus the sporting activity of the club is cross subsidised from commercial operations. One of the reasons sports clubs can successfully do this is that they can often sell their drinks at lower prices than the commercial sector due to lower costs. One of the main reasons for these lower costs is the supply of volunteer labour.

Thus the product provided by the typical sports club is essentially a private product. People participate in the club for reasons of self-interest rather than altruism. The motivation of club members is not to generate the collective benefits of sport discussed in Chapter 4, but rather to maximise benefits for club members. The fact that some of the collective benefits are incidentally generated (eg the health benefits and possibly the occasional generation of an élite performer) may mean that the club is treated favourably by government (eg subsidised charges for ground rental; Sports Council subsidy for facilities). But normally we do not see direct government involvement at this level of sport in Britain.

However, when we rise up the hierarchy of sport we see much more government involvement at the level of the governing bodies of sport.

Government and the voluntary sector in sport

Governing bodies of sport are different than sports clubs in that they have a specific commitment to excellence that is rarely the case in clubs. As we have argued in Chapter 4, international sporting success is the most collective of all benefits provided in sport, being close to a pure public good. Since governing bodies are at least partly involved in the production of this good we would expect this to be reflected in a higher value for the collectiveness index.

Butson (1983) provides data on a sample of 242 governing bodies of sport (108 in England, 69 in Wales and 65 in Scotland) from which we can derive a value for the collectiveness index. Table 7.4 shows the income to these bodies in 1979–80.

Table 7.4 – Governing bodies of sport: income and expenditure 1979–80

Income	£,000	% of Total
Sports Council grant	3,506	18
Other subsidies	431	2
Sponsorship	602	3
Donations	1,615	8
Membership	2,472	12
Investments	881	4
Coaching	749	4
Events	7,783	39
Other	2,014	10
Total	20,063	100

Note: Sample = 242 governing bodies of sport.
Source: Butson (1983).

Some twenty per cent of income is a direct subsidy from government sources, most of which is grants from the Sports Council. Another eight per cent comes from donations, giving a collectiveness index of 28 per cent from grants, gifts and donations.

Despite the fact we have a much higher collectiveness index for governing bodies Table 7.4 shows that nearly 70 per cent of income to this sample of sports organisations was generated from within the organisation, some of it from membership fees but most of it, 39 per cent of all income, coming from the staging of events. Again, this is more or less straightforward commercial activity, but a different type of commercial activity than that used by sports clubs to generate income.

Further information on the income and expenditure of governing bodies in sport is given in Taylor (1990), where 21 governing bodies were investigated (see Table 7.5). This study goes beyond Butson in that it attempts to split the income and expenditure programmes of governing bodies into excellence and non-excellence programmes. The proportion of gross expenditure devoted to excellence ranged from 25 per cent to 100 per cent, with an average of 56 per cent. On average, twenty per cent of this expenditure on excellence programmes came from the Sports Council, although for individual sports this varied from nothing in the case of tennis to 90 per cent in the case of wrestling. Not all grants given to governing bodies are for excellence purposes. Estimates by the Grants Unit at the Sports Council suggest that at least 51 per cent of the total grant allocation to governing bodies was for excellence programmes in 1985–86 (the year of the study).

Table 7.5 – Sports and governing bodies sample

Sport	Governing bodies
Athletics	Amateur Athletic Association
	Women's Amateur Athletics Association
	British Amateur Athletics Board
Badminton	Badminton Association of England
Cycling	British Cycling Federation
Gymnastics	British Amateur Gymnastics Association
Hockey	Hockey Association
	All England Women's Hockey Association
Judo	British Judo Association
Netball	All England Netball Association
Skiing	English Ski Council
	British Ski Foundation
Squash	Squash Rackets Association
	Women's Squash Rackets Association
Swimming	Amateur Swimming Association
	Amateur Swimming Federation of GB
Tennis	Lawn Tennis Association
Volleyball	English Volleyball Association
Weightlifting	British Amateur Weightlifting Association
Wrestling	English Olympic Wrestling Association
	British Amateur Wrestling Association

Table 7.6 gives the breakdown of the sources of finance for excellence. The reason for the variation in Sports Council funding of excellence has less to do with the nature of the 'product'

provided by the governing body (ie the degree of collectiveness) but rather the potential for other sources of income. Sports Council grant for excellence is at its greatest in sports considered to have intrinsic commercial disadvantage eg judo, weightlifting, and wrestling (see Chapter 4). Generally, the more a sport is able to generate income from events, media and sponsorship, the less dependent it is on Sports Council's grants. The exceptions to this pattern, and therefore on the face of it less easy to justify, are badminton, cycling, skiing, and swimming. These have relatively high dependence on Sports Council grants but do not have intrinsic commercial disadvantages.

Table 7.6 – Governing bodies' revenue sources for excellence Programmes

	% of Revenue						
Governing bodies	Sports Council	Events	Sponsors (+ SAF)	TV	Individuals	Cross-subsidy from other programmes	Other
AAA			100				
WAAA	15	4	35	30			16
BAAB	2	6	11	74			7
BAE	36	40	15	5			4
BCF	67		13			20	
BAGA	24		66			10	
HA	50		27			23	
AEWHA	29	46	17	2			6
BJA	75	8	17				
AENA	41	28				28	3
BSF	50		40				10
ESC	44		11		45		
SRA	6	28	66				
WSRA	28	72					
ASA	51	36		13			
LTA			100				
EVA	54				37	9	
BAWLA	85	1	14				
EOWA	90	10					

Source: Annual reports and Sports Council reports.

Badminton, in fairness, was an unusual case in the study because at the time it was establishing, with Sports Council help, its own national centre at Milton Keynes. Skiing might be seen as one of the most contentious cases, since although it is a conspicuous sport in terms of media attention and public interest, Britain suffers from a permanent comparative disadvantage in the production of international standard skiers, for obvious geographical reasons. Although this might be seen as a reason for special subsidy to overcome natural comparative disadvantage, economic theory would only justify this if the product was essential and not available through trade. International excellence by British skiers is improbable and much of the public interest in this sport is likely to be non-partisan – in other words *we import* the public good and demonstration benefits from foreign stars, rather than seek them from British stars.

Table 7.7 presents Sports Council assistance to governing bodies for excellence programmes in a manner that reflects again the 'club' aspect to sports organisations – ie excellence grant per member. This might also be seen as one indicator of equity in the distribution of grants for excellence between sports. There are, of course, other indicators of equity and other criteria for grant-in-aid awards – the latter will be discussed below. In the meantime, Table 7.7 shows a considerable variance in the excellence grant-in-aid per member.

Whereas Table 7.6 shows Sports Council excellence grants in relation to total excellence income, Table 7.7 shows these grants in cash terms per member. Out of the sports identified above as not having intrinsic commercial disadvantage, but benefitting from relatively high dependency on Sports Council assistance for their excellence programmes, cycling and skiing emerge as high excellence-grant-per-member sports. Because of their reasonably high membership numbers, the amounts for badminton and swimming are fairly modest in comparison with the highest figures in Table 7.7. Another sport, gymnastics, emerges as having a high excellence grant per member, although it does not have any intrinsic commercial disadvantage and its proportional dependency on the grant is not high. The large excellence grant per member in gymnastics is simply indicative of the large absolute size of the excellence programmes of the British Amateur Gymnastics Association.

At the other extreme, the sports with little immediate potential for generating commercial income from excellence are typically compensated with high excellence grants per member, ie judo, volleyball, weightlifting and wrestling. Another factor in this favourable per capita grant allocation must be the limited ability of these sports to raise their own income from memberships, awards, etc, either because of the limited appeal of such sports for mass participation or the immaturity of their development in this country. Strong government support for a sport with immature development is a straightforward manifestation of the 'infant industry' justification for public subsidy outlined in Chapter 4.

Table 7.7 – Grants per member

Sport	Sports Council Excellence Grant per member (£)
Athletics	0.21
Badminton	0.97
Cycling	6.54
Gymnastics	4.07
Hockey – men	1.18
– women	1.63
Judo	5.52
Netball	0.68
Skiing	4.92
Squash – men	0.14
– women	0.08
Swimming	0.30
Tennis	0.16
Volleyball	4.23
Weightlifting	3.51
Wrestling	7.77

Sources: Annual reports, Sports Council reports, *A Digest of Sports Statistics* (Sports Council 1986).

As indicated in Chapter 2, the system by which grants are awarded to governing bodies by the Sports Council changed in 1985. Prior to 1985 governing bodies received annual grants for five years with little monitoring of the effectiveness or efficiency of the spending of the grants. Since 1985 applications by governing bodies for grants must take the form of three- to five- year development plans. The aim here is to persuade the voluntary sector to specify objectives and targets that fall in line with the Sports Councils corporate plan.

This is undoubtedly a move towards more central control over the provisions of the public good, sporting excellence. The argument for this is that sporting excellence is a homogeneous product and centralisation ensures that minimum standards of efficiency and economy are achieved. It should help to prevent well meaning but incompetent governing bodies' administrators from inefficiently using public funds.

On the other hand, proponents of decentralisation would suggest that central authorities like the Sports Council just do not have sufficient information about the precise, detailed requirements of the production process to make efficient decisions. This view echoes that of some governing body representatives that they know far more about the requirements for excellence in their particular sports than it is possible for the Sports Council to know, so the Council should just hand over the money and let them, as line managers, make the resource allocation decisions (Taylor, 1990). One example of this is support for individuals. Many national coaches would claim that they are in the best position to allocate funds, having the knowledge to recognise the few participants with world-class potential and knowing precisely what financial support is needed to develop this potential.

Others (Riiskjaer, 1990) have argued that such an approach by government towards the voluntary sector destroys the essential nature of voluntary sector activity. It changes the voluntary sector from co-operative bodies with largely voluntary labour to neo-corporate bodies with paid officers, that are simply agencies of government. Riiskjaer sees the increasing direction of the voluntary sector by government, and the increasing financial dependency on government of the voluntary sector in sport as a dangerous development. However, he is discussing the situation in Denmark where it appears that there is much more government involvement at the level of the local sports club. It is not clear whether the argument also applies at the level of national governing bodies of sport, and in particular in the provision of the public good, sporting excellence. For the moment, we shall simply point out that some commentators do take the view that the move to centralisation in the production of sporting excellence does contain dangers. We will return to the topic again in the next chapter.

Direct funding by the Sports Council for governing bodies' excellence programmes is an important aspect of the relationship between government and the voluntary sector in sport but it is not the only one. We indicated in Chapter 2 that the Sports Council also owned National Sports Centres and 45 per cent of the Sports Council's expenditure on excellence is devoted to maintaining the direct supply of such facilities which are training facilities which governing bodies are expected to use. However there are problems with this government provision of National Centres for governing body use.

One major characteristic of the market for excellence in sport is prejudicial to the success of National Centres: demand for excellence training is very heterogeneous. As we have seen earlier in this chapter, typically the public sector is most comfortable dealing with fairly homogeneous product situations. Demand for excellence facilities is heterogeneous not only because of the differing needs of each sport, but also because of distinct demands within sports (eg the variety of surfaces which excellent tennis players have to cope with, and the different apparatus disciplines in gymnastics).

The result of diverse, fragmented demands for excellence training is that, whereas most governing bodies make use of the National Centres, many are unhappy with aspects of their use, and for a variety of reasons. In interviews with representatives of governing bodies (Taylor, 1990), the most common complaints about National Centres concerned access problems, in respect of both geographical access and bookings at peak times. The spatial distribution of National Centres is uneven but geographical access is even more restricted by the commitment of many governing bodies to one National Centre, giving their participants even less choice of location, and more travelling time. Of course, any single site national centre would suffer from these geographical access restrictions.

Basically the supply of Sports Council National Centres will always find difficulties in adequately catering for the diversity of demands presented by the very heterogeneous excellence market. This gives rise to the frustrating situation whereby most governing bodies make use of the National Centres, but many of these are continually threatening to reduce their use of them.

In addition to the Sports Council's National Centres there are some models for single-sport national centres, run by governing bodies, which demonstrate some of the benefits of such provision for excellence training. Such voluntary sector national facilities usually require substantial capital grants from the Sports Council to set up, but theoretically they may provide effective, efficient and economical facilities for excellence training.

The Squash Raquets Association (Telford) and the Badminton Association of England (Milton Keynes) have set up their own national centres and both stress the many benefits of this arrangement, similar to those demonstrated in the example above. The principles behind single-sport centres extends, interestingly, to the Sports Council's National Centres too, since the Sports Council offers governing bodies exclusive use of certain National Centre facilities ('dedicated space', such as the gymnastics centre at Lilleshall). It is likely that the capital cost of adding dedicated spaces to Sports Council National Centres would be cheaper than building a single-sport centre on a new site, particularly if complementary hotel and technical support facilities have the capacity to serve the new commitment. Operationally, dedicated spaces may have many of the advantages of the single-sport national centres.

Recently the Sports Council has moved towards tighter contractual relationships with governing bodies concerning the use of National Centres. Such contractual relationships will be discussed further in the next chapter.

The commercial sector and the voluntary sector in sport

Table 2.5 in Chapter 2 showed that it was the commercial sector, rather than the public sector that was the main source of finance for excellence in sport. The Table showed a figure of £109.5 million as sponsorship expenditure towards the funding of excellence, accounting for two-thirds of total expenditure on excellence. This figure itself is almost certainly an underestimate since it does not include the hidden costs to sponsors of administering sponsorship deals.

The importance of sponsorship in funding excellence may seem strange in the light of what we have said in Chapter 4, and in this chapter, that economic theory would suggest that the production of excellence would be in the hands of government or the voluntary sector, or both. Sporting excellence, however, attracts a wide television audience in some sports and this makes these sports, and their élite performers, attractive targets for the sponsors.

In Taylor (1990), one of the present authors not only indicated the rapid growth in sponsorship in sport (from £2.5 million in 1971 to £146 million in 1986), but also showed how sponsorship was the major link between the commercial sector and the voluntary sector. Analysis of the nature of sponsorship deals showed that most of the money goes to individual performers (or teams) and/or events, rather than to 'grass roots' developments and individual sports clubs. Consequently it is the governing bodies that deal to a large extent with the sponsors.

The reason for the concentration of sponsorship money on events and élite competitors is to do with the objectives of the sponsors. The rationale for private, commercial sponsors' involvement in the production of excellence in sport is a simple one – it generates a return for the sponsors. If a return for the sponsor is *not* expected then the deal is not sponsorship, but rather patronage or charity.

The expected return from sponsorship can take several forms.

First, sponsorship may be seen as an effective part of a portfolio of advertising techniques, and therefore the return is increased sales. Sponsorship often secures comparatively cheap media exposure, for example, through attachment to high profile national or international events. It can target particular market groups implicit in the membership or participation profile of a sport, or its spectators and followers. Less specifically, sponsorship can help to create or consolidate a corporate or brand image for the sponsor.

Second, sponsorship may perform a valuable public relations function for corporate purposes, such as entertaining important clients, suppliers, in-house staff, etc. Third, the return from sponsorship may be one that is personal to key managers in the sponsoring organisation through, for example, past and present affiliations with a sport. Thus the return from sponsorship may be part of a multi-dimensional set of factors contributing to managerial utility. Finally sponsorship may be seen as a way of reducing tax liability for the sponsor, although this is unlikely to be a return in its own right but is more probably a by-product of other returns.

In each of the cases above where a commercial return is expected, such returns from sponsorship are difficult to monitor accurately and in particular it is rarely possible to measure specific financial returns. Even formal assessment through such techniques as market research only give indicative results, rather than definitive measures of the financial return from sponsorship. From one point of view this elusive characteristic of sponsorship may be seen as an advantage to sports seeking sponsorship, since they are unlikely to have to prove themselves in terms of a tangible return to sponsors. However this is a very dangerous line of thinking, since increasingly sponsors are looking for evidence to justify their 'investment' in sponsorship deals. Sports need to help in the search for such evidence as part of the process of generating more finance from this important source.

Despite the growing importance of sponsorship, it is unfortunately the case that many of the characteristics of sponsorship are not conducive to effective or efficient production of excellence in sport as Taylor's (1990) evidence indicated.

First, sponsorship is ineffective in its distribution, being very 'hit and miss' with respect to both sports and individuals within sports. Some sports have characteristics which appeal directly to commercial sponsors; for them sponsorship is comparatively easy to generate. Squash, for example, has many members and participants who are in 'attractive' socio-economic groups for potential sponsors. Swimming is attractive because of the sheer size of its membership and participation.

Other sports, though, suffer from an intrinsic commercial disadvantage and administrators in these sports are uncertain about the prospects of attracting a greater amount or proportion of their revenues from sponsorship. Judo and wrestling, for example, are considered unsuitable for mass media interest; women's hockey is saddled with an outmoded 'jolly hockey sticks' image which is inappropriate for many sponsors. A different kind of problem faces the British Cycling Federation, which is unable to benefit from the major sponsorships available in cycling because these go to private, commercial events or individuals and clubs.

Within sports, too, the distribution of sponsorship is uncertain. It is likely where sponsorship is targeted directly to individuals, the ones to benefit are those at the very top of the performance structure and even then of course, not all the top-level performers in a sport will attract the same sponsorship monies. Other individuals, for instance those just below this top level, may have just as urgent financial needs but are much less likely to attract individual sponsorship.

Although sponsorship income is increasing very consistently on aggregate, this cannot be taken to imply that it is a reliable source of income at the level of the single governing body. Just as sponsorship is associated by sports with a virtuous circle of increasing income, media coverage, and participation, so one or two are increasingly worried by the reverse of this process. The English Ski Council, for example, suffered a big fall in sponsorship revenues in 1987 mainly because of the simultaneous, natural ending of key contracts. Women's athletics was obliged to suspend a sponsorship deal in 1987 because of the withdrawal of television coverage for a home international at short notice.

Volatility is bound to be a problem when most sponsorship deals are of fairly short duration. The effects of sponsorship volatility are not particularly harmful to the production of excellence in sport because it is directed mainly towards events. Should sponsorship finance spread in influence to more important inputs, then its volatility could upset longterm development programmes. An early example of this problem occurred at the All England Netball Association (AENA). When sponsorship of a coaching scheme ended, AENA was faced with a gap in their coaching development which, unless a replacement sponsor could be found, could only be filled by diluting the financing of other areas.

The keys to greater stability appear to be close relationships between governing bodies and sponsors, responsive servicing of sponsors' needs by governing bodies, professional marketing of sponsorship opportunities and a realistic expectation of the returns from sponsorship by the sponsors. In a relatively young source of finance, both sides need educating in best practice and there are some good examples of stable and innovative sponsorship arrangements to spotlight.

A third worrying characteristic is that sponsorship is primarily targeted at events. Whilst top-class competitive experience is important in the development of excellent sports people, it is not the most important of inputs, and is thus an ineffective means of producing excellence in sport. Furthermore, because events attract sponsorship, there is an incentive to create more events, which might be damaging to the production of excellence if top participants are 'overexposed' in too many events, harming their prospects for peak performance at the major competitions. This has been an issue in athletics in Britain particularly in years of major international competitions such as the Olympics. Little sponsorship is directed at other important areas of the production process – such as training, coaching, facilities and support services – although this is seen by optimists as an area of potential sponsorship development. Gymnastics, for example, has benefitted from a deal which supports Olympic trials, training camps and visiting foreign coaches.

Fourth, sponsorship is not necessarily an efficient means of financing excellence, since it generates high tied-in costs associated with administration of the deals and high quality servicing of events and sponsors. These administration and servicing costs are particularly high, of course, if the governing body handles sponsorship deals in-house. Often much of the time of the officers of the governing bodies are taken up 'chasing after sponsors'.

A final inefficiency of sponsorship is that much of it is in kind rather than cash. This can severely reduce the choice of equipment and clothing available to sportspeople and governing bodies, and equipment and clothing can sometimes have more than a marginal effect on performance – an example being skiing.

Against such disadvantages as these, however, may be set two advantages. First, sponsorships involving cash are a more or less pure form of transfer payment, and they probably involve much less control over the use of the money than is likely, for example, from government sources. This characteristic is considered desirable by recipients of transfer payments. Second, and of overriding importance to this discussion, it is impossible to ignore the scale of financial and in-kind contribution being made by sponsorships. For all the efficiency and effectiveness problems, therefore, sponsorship is an essential source of finance for excellence in sport, and in certain sports it is seen as a lifeline, eg skiing. Furthermore where some sports see little potential in sponsorship, others are optimistic about prospects for the future. Representatives from five of the seventeen governing bodies interviewed suggested that there was considerable growth potential for sponsorship in their sports.

The interrelationships between government, voluntary and commercial sectors

The discussion so far in this chapter has indicated that the voluntary sector interacts with both the public and commercial sectors. It is dependent on the public sector for finance for the collective benefits provided in the production of sporting excellence. Even where the product provided is essentially a private product benefitting mainly sports club members, the public sector normally supports these sports clubs by providing subsidised facilities or other benefits. Governing bodies of sport are also dependent on the commercial sector for the funding of excellence programmes. However, the motivation of the sponsor is completely different from that of the government. The sponsor is not normally interested in the collective benefits of international sporting success. He is much more interested in the image and marketing potential a sport can provide for his product. On the other hand, the voluntary sector in sport is often in direct competition with the commercial sector through its involvement in commercial activities which range from the staging of major spectator events to the selling of beer in the local rugby club. The interrelationships therefore between the voluntary, public, and commercial sectors in sport are, to say the least, complicated.

The question arises of how much of the output of the 'sports industry' is provided by government, how much by the commercial sector, and how much by government. In statistical terms, we attempted to answer this question in Tables 2.5 and 2.6 in Chapter 2. There we saw that expenditure on excellence was dominated by the commercial sector (67 per cent) with the public sector and the voluntary sector only providing ten per cent each (the rest coming from the expenditure of the individual competitors and their families). On the other hand, the market for mass participation is dominated by the voluntary sector (50 per cent of total expenditure in Table 2.6) with the public sector providing the bulk of the rest (38 per cent), and the commercial sector only providing twelve per cent.

In this section we investigate whether economics can help to explain why the supply of sports outputs is split between the different sectors in this way. Weisbrod (1978) provides us with a set of hypotheses that might be the first stage of an explanation. First of all he divides all outputs into three types: collective consumption goods, private good substitutes for collective goods, and pure private goods. Normally we expect to see government providing collective goods. However, he argues:

> the expectation is that supplementation of public sector provision (that is, financing) of any good, will either be overwhelmingly in the voluntary sector or overwhelmingly in the private, for-profit sector, depending on whether the publicly provided good is primarily a collective or an individual-type good. In addition to the extent of 'collectiveness' of the governmentally financed good, the relative size of the voluntary and private sectors in an industry will depend on the state of technology – specifically on the degree of similarity between collective goods and their private-good substitutes, and on the relative production costs.

The first element in the argument then is that consumers first look to the public sector for the provision of collective goods. For reasons discussed earlier in this chapter, it is likely that consumers are likely to be dissatisfied with the level of government provision for any particular collective good. As a result he looks for additional output in the voluntary sector and the commercial sector. The quote above suggests that the more collective the good the more likely it is to be provided in the voluntary sector. The more private the good, the more likely the commercial sector will provide the additional output demanded. However, relative production costs in the two sectors are also an important influence.

The second stage in Weisbrod's argument relates to the nature of demand, in particular the heterogeneity of demand. The smaller the heterogeneity, then the more likely it is that government will provide the major share of output. The greater the heterogeneity of demand, then the larger the share of total output provided by the voluntary and commercial sectors jointly. The reason for this is that government output is determined on the basis of a simple majority vote model. If consumers for a particular collective good are not big enough as a group to be an important influence on the voting process, they are unlikely to see government provision of the good.

The third element in Weisbrod's argument is what he calls his 'income hypothesis'. He argues that from the consumer's point of view there is likely to be an important disadvantage with the collective good compared with a private good substitute for it: the consumer will have a lower degree of individual control over its form, type of availability, and times of availability. He uses the example of a lighthouse, indicating that a particular lighthouse cannot be located differently for different users, nor turned on and off at different times to satisfy conflicting preferences. It we add to this a heterogeneity of demand for collective goods then we are likely to see various aspects of demand undersatisfied. Private market substitutes will cater more to specific consumer demands. Since the degree of individual control desired by the consumer is likely to be positively related to income, the private supplier is likely to 'skim' the market and cater to the demands of the higher-income consumer. The consumer who turns to the private-market option will expect to pay a higher charge and in return he will get a product closer to his individual demands. He is also likely to choose a form of the good that maximises his personal benefits, and probably minimises external benefits.

If we now turn to the sports market we can analyse to what extent Weisbrod's arguments are consistent with the evidence. In the market for participation, we have noted the dominance of provision by the public and voluntary sectors. And yet we have also noted that the nature of the product provided is more an individual-type good rather than a collective-type good. The benefits provided by public sector sports centres and swimming pools, and voluntary sector participation sports clubs are neither non-rival nor non-excludable. The good provided is essentially a private good although there are social benefits provided through the generation of health benefits to participants and possibly in the reduction in crime and vandalism as discussed in Chapter 4. According to Weisbrod's first hypothesis therefore we would expect undersatisfied demand to be met by the commercial sector rather than the voluntary sector. What we see is just the opposite.

The reason for this lies however in the 'relative production costs' of the two sectors. The voluntary sector, as indicated earlier, has the benefit of labour services provided at zero cost and the commercial sector cannot compete with this. In fact, there is more to it than that. For many, volunteerism is part of the product. That is to say that many people who offer their services free within the voluntary sector actually receive utility from their contribution to voluntary sector output. If, for example, we take an amateur football club we can see that there will be many tasks to be done to organise a match on a Saturday afternoon. A group of people will pick the team, contact the players, organise the fixtures and the referees, make certain the kit is washed, provide refreshments after the game, etc. Some of this will be done by the players, but much will be done by non-players. Many of these non-players receive positive enjoyment from this voluntary activity. Their interest in the sport is fed through the positive involvement in its organisation. And so all these labour services are provided free of charge and are even regarded as consumption rather than work by those providing it. Under such circumstances it is not surprising to see that the commercial sector cannot compete.

Weisbrod's second hypothesis indicates that the greater the heterogeneity of demand, then the greater the share of total output provided by the voluntary and commercial sectors. We have argued throughout this book that demand for sport is heterogeneous with different minority groups obtaining consumer satisfaction through sport in many different ways. It is not surprising therefore that over half this demand is satisfied by the voluntary and commercial sectors. The voluntary sector, however, possesses a further advantage to the commercial sector in this provision: that is, access to information.

The most rewarding sporting contests are those between equals or near equals since this fully engages their skills. As Scitovsky (1976) pointed out:

> (sport) seems the most pleasant when it fully engages our skill and prowess. In sports we usually try to do our best, not because of outside pressure, but for our own satisfaction. Playing tennis with an equally good partner is the most fun; playing with a weaker opponent is dull, because it is too easy, while playing with a much stronger one is discouraging, because it overtaxes one's capacity. Competitive sports and games are popular because the pleasantness of exercise is enhanced by the full exertion of our strength and skills called forth by competition.

Given this aspect of the nature of consumer satisfaction in sport, and given the heterogeneity of the demand for sport, the consumer is faced with an information problem. How can he or she find the right level of competition that allows this full enjoyment of competitive sport? The search costs involved may be prohibitive to the consumer and also to the commercial sector. The voluntary club has access to such relevant information through its own competitions and shares it amongst its members. A crucial input to the enjoyment of sport is common knowledge within the club, and this information advantage over the commercial sector is another reason for the importance of the voluntary sector in provision of sports participation.

The third element of Weisbrod's hypothesis is that the commercial sector will 'skim' the market and provide more to the higher-income consumer. If we look at the pattern of commercial provision for sport, this aspect can be identified. Golf is a sport that attracts high-income consumers and we see commercial provision of golf-courses and golf-driving ranges. Similarly, the commercial sector provides exclusive gym, weights and sauna clubs, often in the centre of cities, attracting businessmen with a greater range of customer services than would normally be seen in a voluntary or public sector club (and charging a much higher price as a result).

Thus we can see that all three elements of Weisbrod's argument can be identified in the market for sports participation services and his analysis is useful in explaining the relative shares of each of the three sectors in the market.

Turning now to the provision of sporting excellence, we can see that the issues here are substantially different. Rather than a minority, heterogeneous demand, the demand for international sporting success is probably a majority, fairly homogeneous demand (although there are derived demands from this overall demand that lead to heterogeneous demands for facilities as we saw earlier with National Centres). All we are saying here is that a majority of British consumers would like to see a British team win football's World Cup, a British tennis player win Wimbledon, and a British athlete win Olympic gold. All three of these have happened in the last quarter of a century. England won the World Cup in 1966, Virginia Wade won the Ladies Championship in 1977; and British athletes did particularly well at the Moscow Olympics in 1980 and the Los Angeles Olympics in 1984 with notable double successes by Sebastian Coe and Daley Thompson. The national euphoria generated by such successes suggests there is a majority demand for sporting excellence. Weisbrod's theory would therefore suggest a strong government commitment of resources to the production of sporting excellence, particularly since the experience of East Germany in the 1970s and 1980s has demonstrated that public sector domination of the production process can lead to very successful outcomes.

It is surprising then to see a relatively small commitment of public sector resources to the production of sporting excellence in this country. Finance for sporting excellence is, as we have seen, dominated by the commercial sector. The financial data we have presented, however, does not relate soley to the production of sporting excellence. Most of the commercial support for excellence is directed at the very top of the sporting hierarchy: the top events and the élite performers. It could be argued that government and the voluntary sector 'produce' the élite performers and the commercial sector steps in to finance them after they have proved their success (and hence their potential for marketing the sponsor's product). On the other hand such finance does mean that the government and voluntary sectors can concentrate their support on the 'grass roots' developments that generate the sporting excellence.

It is almost certainly the case, that sporting excellence is underprovided for in Britain. There are two major reasons for this. One is a lack of information on the strength of demand for this collective good. We have argued above that it is perhaps a demand shared by the majority of the population. Yet it is rarely raised in political discussions. It is a peculiar type of demand that only reveals itself after success has been achieved. The second reason, which is related to the first, is also an information issue: nobody has the relevant information on how international sporting success can be achieved. Information on the production function involved (ie the necessary inputs to produce the output of success) is difficult to acquire. It is perhaps not surprising then that sporting excellence is not often a political issue since no political party possesses the relevant information to improve performance over its rivals.

One input that is generally regarded as very important, and has certainly been a major influence on the success achieved in the recent past by both East Germany and the USSR, is the availability of national standard coaches.

Many governing bodies in British sport have indicated a chronic shortage of coaches at the top level. Further evidence of problems in the financing of coaching at the excellence level is the emigration by top British coaches to foreign jobs but little or no immigration by top foreign coaches into British sport. One of the fundamental causes of this is relatively low pay for top coaches in British sport. When employed full-time the salaries of national coaches in Britain are low by international standards. When employed by the hour coaches, like individual participants, sometimes have to lose pay and/or holiday entitlement.

Perhaps one major failing of British sport is the failure to retain élite international competitors as coaches once their competitive career is over. Such excellent participants provide a potentially rich source of the specialist skills required for coaching, and this is a common career route taken by competitors in other countries. In Britain, a major problem in realising this potential appears to be the lack of an organisational structure to nurture such participants through the transitory time period between playing at the top and coaching at the top. Finance is necessarily a part of this constraint.

Why is there such a shortage of finance for the development and pay of top coaches? Traditions of amateurism in British sport must take some of the blame, and the relatively poor financial state of many governing bodies must be a contributory factor. There are, however, some signs of improvement. For one thing, there is an increase in the number of full-time coaches employed in local authorities. The second development is the National Coaching Foundation which was set up with Sports Council funding in 1983 to co-ordinate and lead developments in coaching. The implication of their role is that when coaching is left to disparate and underfunded voluntary agencies it is neither effective nor efficient, and needs direction from a central organisation.

We see then, in the field of sporting excellence, a picture noticeably different from that we would expect on the basis of Weisbrod's hypothesis. The current organisation of excellence in Britain is also not one that generates a lot of confidence that Britain will continue to produce sporting champions throughout the 1990s and into the next century. Case histories of previous champions tend to indicate there has been a large chance element in the way such excellence has emerged. Often it depends upon above-average commitment by parents; in some sports we depend on the coaching and training facilities of other countries, most notably North American universities. The question arises why is sporting excellence so underfunded in Britain?

Part of the reason is historical. It was not until the executive Sports Council was set up in 1972 that government funds were directed to governing bodies specifically for excellence purposes. Since some funding for excellence was already in place through the voluntary and commercial sectors, inevitably government funding attempted to fill the gaps rather than to attempt a complete reorganisation. Also, public policy for excellence has never been clearly established as the quote we gave in Chapter 2 indicated (and is worth repeating here);

> Some countries invest vast public funds in specialist facilities, training programmes and financial and status rewards for élite athletes, in order to win prestige and trade internationally. It is neither tradition nor policy to treat top level sport in this way in Britain . . . . (*The Next Ten Years*, Sports Council, 1982).

This quote indicates two points. The tradition referred to is the tradition of amateurism in British sport. The country has depended on the voluntary sector to produce champions since the end of the nineteenth century and to some extent, up until fairly recently, the system has worked fairly well. The second point is that other countries have professionalised their approach to excellence by heavy investment in facilities for training and in payment of coaches. This has been a fairly recent phenomenon and whereas we could compete quite well with other countries when every country was operating on similar amateurish principles, it becomes increasingly difficult to compete with these countries now that they have made a clear commitment to sporting excellence by directing funds to this area.

Add to this the attitude of some government agencies, most notably some local authorities, that public funding for excellence is politically difficult because it is élitist, it is not surprising to see that the relative market shares of public, voluntary, and commercial sectors for the funding of sporting excellence in Britain shows a much smaller share for government than we would expect on the basis of the economic arguments put forward in this chapter.

Conclusions

The aim of this chapter has been to consider government intervention in the market for sport against contributions made by the other actors on the supply side, the voluntary sector and the commercial sector. We have concentrated on the voluntary sector because of its historical and current importance in the sports market. Analysis of the market shares of the three sectors involves very much an analysis of how the government and commercial sectors interact with the voluntary sector.

Weisbrod's economic analysis of the role of the voluntary sector provides a useful framework for considering how the voluntary sector in sport corrects for both market and government failures. His hypotheses concerning the role that each sector plays in sport are broadly confirmed by the evidence we have on funding for sports participation. However, when we examine funding for excellence, an area where we see a benefit provided that is very much at the collective end of the collective good-private good spectrum, we see a completely different picture than the one suggested by Weisbrod. The implication is that government underfunds excellence in Britain. The real effects of such underfunding, as with any lack of investment, will take time to materialise. The effects will be compounded by the fact that other European countries (both East and West) have made a much greater commitment to the production of sporting excellence than Britain. North America has an equal commitment to sporting excellence although the mechanism used is substantially different. It would be surprising indeed if these differing rates of investment in the production mechanisms for sporting excellence are not reflected in the results of major international sporting competitions in the years to come.

8 Government contracting of sport

Government, as we have seen, is an integral part of a system of sports supply, with implicit as well as explicit links with the private commercial and voluntary sectors. The way in which government intervenes in sports markets is currently undergoing a fundamental change, with the introduction of compulsory competitive tendering (CCT) for the maintenance of parks and open spaces and the management of sports and leisure facilities. The Sports Council, too, has decided to open the management of National Sports Centres to competitive tendering.

In this chapter we examine the whole area of contracting as it affects the relationship between the government and other suppliers of sports services. Competitive tendering is clearly a very topical issue for a discussion of contracting, and it is an important focus for our subsequent discussion. But contracting in sport does not start and end with CCT; this is merely the latest (and possibly the most conspicuous) example in a long line of explicit and implicit contractual arrangements which have affected the provision of sport. Other examples include the awarding of grants to governing bodies of sport, the joint provision of sports facilities by education and district authorities, and sponsorship deals.

Two contracting situations that are particularly relevant to excellence in sport will be discussed in this chapter – the problems arising from the grant aiding of governing bodies of sport by the Sports Council, and the problems with implicit and explicit contracts involving these governing bodies' use of National Sports Centres.

It is important to realise that analysis of CCT has a much broader context of contracting to call on. We therefore start this chapter with an examination of the key terms and concepts involved in contracting situations. These are then applied to sports-specific contracting situations.

Contracting principles

Wherever a transaction is carried out, there is a contracting situation. Sometimes, as Coase (1937) recognised, it is easier to administer the transactions contracts by internalising them within an organisation, for example a firm. Most transactions taking place within an organisation are unwritten, informal, *implicit*. In other situations it might be preferable to organise production externally rather than internally, using *explicit* contractual arrangements, for example to supply labour or goods. CCT is an example of moving from implicit to explicit contracts, involving in many cases contractors external to the organisation.

Any transactions generate costs – of specification, selection, administration, monitoring and control. At the heart of the contracting issue is the concept of *transactions costs* – ie choosing an organisational method which minimises these costs. This concept raises a veritable hornets' nest of problems which we now review.

One major problem is that information is not perfect – not all parties to a potential or actual contract have the same information relevant to the transaction concerned. This is part of the *bounded rationality* problem identified in Chapter 5. In fact it is commonly the case that one party has more relevant information than the other. This is termed 'asymetric information'. It may even be appropriate and in keeping with a party's objectives to conceal information – this is called 'impacted information'.

When a contract for a transaction is being drawn up and implemented, the existence of asymetric or impacted information can prejudice the operation of the contract. If the contractor has more information than the client there may well arise a problem of '*moral hazard*', whereby the contractor uses superior information to distort the operation of a contract without actually breaking its terms. Such a moral hazard is likely to occur when the terms of the contract have not been specified accurately enough, and when the client and contractor have different objectives. If the client has inferior information the contract will not be appropriately specified. If the contractor has superior information then this will encourage 'opportunism' in the contractor's behaviour, ie following their own interests rather than those of the client.

Thus moral hazard occurs. Of importance here is the issue of incentives. A contractor with different objectives needs incentives to comply with the client's objectives. Otherwise the moral hazard persists.

Another problem concerning transactions costs arises even before a contract is being carried out. This is 'adverse selection', whereby worthy bids for the contract are either not submitted or not selected. This is again the product of asymetric information. If the client is unable to specify accurately enough the objectives of a contract, because of inadequate knowledge, and therefore concentrates on inputs or processes rather than outputs, then the selection of contractors will be biased in favour of these inferior performance criteria. A 'good' contractor, meanwhile, may well have superior information concerning the relationship between inputs and outputs, but is in danger of either being put off by a specification which concentrates on inappropriate contractual details, or having a realistic bid rejected because of the relative ignorance of the client.

An important discipline on the contracting environment is competition. However, this discipline can be eroded by 'asset specificity', whereby physical assets and/or human skills have a use limited to one purpose. In such circumstances internal, implicit contracting is generally considered to be more appropriate than external explicit contracting.

Compulsory Competitive Tendering (CCT)

It is important to emphasise the differences between competitive tendering, contracting out and privatisation. Minogue and O'Grady (1985) demonstrate the difference between the last two:

> The term 'contracting out' is often used interchangeably with the expression 'privatisation'. The latter, however, is better used to refer to the decision by local authorities to rescind the welfare contract altogether – that is to cease to provide public moneys and regulation to back up the relationship between supplier and consumer. Contracting out on the other hand is more properly referred to as the act of choosing an alternative and commercially competitive supplier for a given unit of publicly supported service, not to the act of abandoning public commitment to it.

Competitive tendering, though, need not result in contracting out. It is a similar contracting process, but an in-house bid is likely to be tendered by the local authority's DSO (direct service organisation; DLO is direct labour organisation) and many in-house organisations will win contracts. Only if the competitive tendering contract is awarded to a company from outside the local authority is the situation one of contracting out.

Walsh (1988) gives the following description of the process of competitive tendering under the 1988 Local Government Act:

> The competitive process involves the local authority specifying in detail the service that is wishes to be delivered and allowing private firms to tender for the right to deliver it. The local authority's own work force, already employed to do the work, will only be allowed to continue to do so if they are selected in a competitive tendering process. The local

> authority must not treat its direct labour organisation (DLO) any differently from the private sector tenderers. In theory the authority might select the DLO to do the work even if it was not the lowest tenderer, but, in practice, it would need to have a very good reason for doing so.

The local authority will be forced to divide its activities into client and contractor roles, the contractor role carried out by the DSO or DLO if and when it wins the contract.

It is quite likely that many local authorities will 'favour' their DSO bids. Many client officers will, in fact, be involved in preparing the DSO bid. However, there is a limit to which this favouritism can be taken. The Act contains a requirement that local authorities do not behave in such a way as to 'restrict, distort or prevent competition'. Thus, if a local authority were to give the contract to its DSO even though it was not the lowest tenderer, private sector bidders may well claim that the authority was acting anti-competitively. The definition of such behaviour is in terms of such things as biased packaging of contracts (eg an 'exotic mix' of profitable, new facilities and unprofitable, old facilities); biased tendering procedures (eg unequal access to management information); onerous pre-tender enquiries of certain contractors; excessive performance bonds and default systems; and non-commercial considerations in the selection process.

In fact, and rather ironically in view of our subsequent discussion, anti-competitive behaviour is a clear example of moral hazard. Local authorities are, in many cases, reluctant agents of central government reform. The means by which this reform is to be implemented are imprecisely specified and monitoring them is very difficult. So local authorities have every opportunity to behave opportunistically in favour of their DSOs.

Compulsory competitive tendering was first introduced for building and highways construction and maintenance under the Local Government Planning and Land Act 1980. In the Local Government Act 1988, CCT was extended to a whole range of local government services including refuse collection, cleaning, catering, grounds maintenance (which included sports grounds and parks), and the repair and maintenance of vehicles. The Statutory Order adding the management of sport and leisure facilities was passed in late 1989, after an announcement in July 1988. The management of all relevant local authority leisure facilities will be contracted by 1992. There has been some apparent hesitancy by government over the addition of leisure management to the CCT legislation. Our later discussion of contracting problems in leisure management endorses this hesitation.

It is not the case that all leisure facilities are included under the Order. There are three main categories of facilities excluded: facilities provided by education authorities in schools and places of further and higher education; 'dual' or 'joint' use facilities; and facilities which are used principally for social objects rather than for sports and physical recreation objects (eg community centres and village halls where sport is a minor or secondary activity).

The four major facility types that are subject to CCT and that are likely to prove attractive to commercial (or voluntary sector) bidders are sports centres, leisure centres, swimming pools and golf courses, although the order also extends to skating rinks, tennis courts, squash courts, bowling centres, pitches for team games, athletics grounds, cycle tracks, putting greens, bowling greens, riding centres, artificial ski slopes, racecourses, centres for flying, ballooning or parachuting and centres for boating and water sports on inland and coastal waters. It is fairly obvious that the focus of the order is sport rather than more general recreation.

For the purposes of the Order, management of these facilities is taken to mean the following:

(a) providing instruction in the sport or other physical recreational activity provided;
(b) supervising the sport or activity;
(c) hiring of equipment for use at the facility;
(d) catering;
(e) providing refreshments;
(f) marketing and promoting the facility;
(g) taking bookings;
(h) collecting and accounting for fees and charges;
(i) assuming responsibility for heating, lighting and other service charges in relation to the facility;
(j) making the facility secure;
(k) cleaning and properly maintaining the facility (except for the external structure of buildings);
(Department of Environment, 1988).

Given the apparently comprehensive nature of the definition of the management function, it is pertinent to ask what control the local authority will still retain under CCT. In fact there are three clearly specified areas that will remain under local authority control after the introduction of CCT according to the explanatory letter accompanying the Draft Order: pricing, admissions and opening hours policies. The retention of control over these areas raises several interesting questions, which will be discussed later.

With respect to management decisions in sports and leisure facilities, local authorities appear to be free to do virtually anything they wish. However, one constraint is on anti-competitive behaviour in the selection process, as discussed above. Another constraint concerns accounting practices:

> If the DLO does win the right to carry out the work then it must keep a trading account for that activity. The only income that can be credited to that account will be payment for work done at a previously agreed price. The trading organisation – the DLO – will be governed by a special accounting code of practice. It will not be possible to cross-subsidise one trading account with another, though it will be possible to do so within an account. Thus local authorities will not be allowed to subsidise losses in catering with surpluses in grounds maintenance but it would be possible to subsidise costs at one leisure centre with surplus at another (Walsh 1988).

Will the introduction of CCT change the nature of public sector leisure provision? The first consideration in attempting to answer such a question is to analyse the differences between the management of sports facilities and other services included in the Local Government Act, 1988.

Is leisure contracting different?

Each of the differences identified in this section demonstrates that contracting in leisure management is more problematic than in other services. First of all, setting policy objectives for leisure services is much more complicated than for other service areas because public leisure provision cuts across several public policy areas which is not the case with a service such as refuse collection. As we pointed out in Chapter 4, public leisure provision is concerned with health, crime prevention, and improving the quality of life for the disabled, the elderly and other minority groups. It is also increasingly linked with economic development projects particularly in inner city regeneration. None of the other services included under the Local Government Act have such a complicated mixture of objectives. This is likely to make contract specification for leisure management particularly difficult.

Even in the narrow area of financial objectives, leisure is unusual. For the other activities, except cleaning, the financial target is a five per cent rate of return on capital employed. Since cleaning does not involve extensive capital equipment, the financial objective here is simply to break even. For the management of sports facilities it was considered inappropriate to set any financial target. The reason for this was that significant capital assets are unlikely to be employed in carrying out the managing activity, and that setting a financial target would be inconsistent with the intention that authorities should retain discretion over pricing policies.

The following statement appears in the explanatory letter accompanying the Draft Order:

> It is therefore intended that the financial objective (which applies only where the authority itself wins a managing contract) will be that income (including any subsidy) properly credited to the activity is at least as much as expenditure properly debited.

Since the authority has the choice of subsidy level this effectively means the authority sets the financial objective.

Setting objective standards of service delivery is much more difficult in leisure than in most other areas of local government service provision. We have seen that there is a multiplicity of objectives in public leisure provision but how can we tell if any of them has been achieved? Is the customer healthier? Have crime rates been reduced? Is there less vandalism and delinquency? Has quality of life been improved for specific target groups? In principle, answers to these questions can be obtained by appropriate measurement and monitoring. In practice, no local authority in Britain has attempted to answer these questions. Even throughput is measured imprecisely in many leisure facilities. Consequently we have little or no information on performance indicators that are relevant to social objectives. It will therefore be very difficult to specify contracts with particular targets for these social objectives.

Another important difference in leisure is identified in Chapter 3. There we argue that demand for leisure activities is likely to be particularly volatile. Skateboarding, for example, was very popular for a time in the mid-1970s. Many local authorities build skateboard parks in order to take skateboards off the pavements and roads. By the time many of the parks were constructed, most of the demand for the activity had disappeared. The important point is that leisure suppliers must be able to react to such fluctuation in demand. They must be flexible. This may be difficult if the supplier is constrained by a tight contract.

Finally, unlike most of the other service areas in the Local Government Act, it is the management of leisure *facilities* that is being put out to tender. These are facilities that have entailed substantial capital investment, and to maintain the quality of facilities further investment will almost certainly be required. With the local authority owning the facility and possibly a commercial contractor managing the facility, there will need to be an agreement over who pays for the investment. Since the local authority will retain ownership it may seem appropriate that it should pay. However, in such circumstances, the commercial contractor is likely to demand more and more investment since he has nothing to lose: to the extent that this is an excessive demand it is a form of opportunism. Furthermore, each new investment is an opportunity for recontracting between the two parties in the *absence* of open competition.

On the other hand, the contractor himself is unlikely to pay for new facilities he will not own, given that the contract will be up for renewal in four to six years and his investment could pass on to another contractor. Despite this, given the volatile nature of leisure demands and the need for the maintenance of quality, it is almost certain that new investment will be required for effective leisure service delivery. Thus the issue of capital investment is likely to prove a difficult area for leisure management contracts whereas such problems are not likely to arise in refuse collection, for example, where the contractor owns the capital equipment (ie the collection vehicles).

The consequences of CCT

Walsh (1988) analyses whether contracting out leisure services is likely to lead to greater efficiency using Williamson's (1975, 1985) behavioural ideas and theories. Williamson considers the question of whether it is more efficient to contract out or supply the service internally. The answer he argues depends on three of the factors introduced earlier in this chapter: 'bounded rationality', 'opportunism', and 'asset specificity'. Walsh summarises the argument:

> Williamson's transaction cost analysis can be understood more clearly if we consider the implications for organising contracts if one of the factors, bounded rationality, opportunism or asset specificity, is absent while the other two are present. If there is no bounded rationality, and the cost of gathering information is low, but there is asset specificity and opportunism then it is possible to operate on the basis of planning, because one can make provision for any contingency before it happens. Total knowledge can compensate for other difficulties. If there is no opportunism but only bounded rationality and asset specificity then we can rely upon 'promise' because we can be certain that people will keep their words and not pursue self-interest at the expense of others. Only the loosest form of contract is then necessary, because the contract does not have to deal with what should be done to accommodate changed circumstances. We can rely upon people's goodwill. There will be little need to police the contract since contractors will not be trying to gain advantage. If there is no asset specificity, but only uncertainty and opportunism, then we can rely upon the market because neither party will have a continuing dependence upon each other. The buyer can readily move to another supplier when problems arise. Suppliers can, equally, move to other markets.

However, if bounded rationality, opportunism, and asset specificity are all present then contracting out is likely to be economically inefficient. 'Planning' will be incomplete because of bounded rationality; we cannot rely on 'promise' because of opportunism; we cannot rely on competition because of asset specificity. Thus it is that when all three are present it is more efficient to, in Williamson's terms, organise on a hierarchical basis, that is to organise production of the service internally rather than contracting.

Walsh argues that in the case of leisure services, bounded rationality, opportunism, and asset specificity are all high, in particular because of the difficulties discussed above:

> Rationality is bounded because future leisure demands and patterns of activity are difficult to predict. The rate of innovation in the leisure industry is also high, partly driven by and partly driving the form of provision. It is relatively easy to know what the future patterns of refuse collection or cleaning will be. Leisure is much more difficult to predict. . . .
>
> The chances for opportunism in leisure and recreation are great because it involves a wide range of activities that are difficult to monitor. . . .
>
> The assets that are used in the leisure services are relatively specific and cannot easily be transferred to other uses. This is true of staff and capital resources.

The result is that the specification of contracts for the management of leisure services is likely to be much more difficult than for other services subject to CCT.

Opportunism causes the problem of moral hazard, and results from the contractor's objectives being different from the client's, as is likely. The contractor will have plenty of scope for opportunism because of the client's inadequate specification of objectives and service standards, and also their incomplete output monitoring information. The contractor will probably concentrate on the most profitable areas of leisure services provision at the expense of others. Thus social objectives are likely to be low priority compared to financial objectives, except where the two are not in conflict, eg the use of a sports centre or swimming pool during off-peak periods by the unemployed, the elderly and women with young children, at reduced prices. Incentives designed to encourage contractors to give social objectives serious consideration are difficult to devise because social outcomes are not likely to be specified or monitored.

There is a serious conflict between the need for flexibility in the contract on the one hand, due to the nature of leisure demands, and the need to control opportunism by the contractor on the other. A 'state-contingent' contract has flexibility, but different possible states or outcomes need to be specified clearly, and this is very difficult to do in leisure services. At the other extreme, a 'deterministic' contract, with tight specification of such matters as inputs, programmes and prices, is unlikely, in leisure services, to be precise enough to prevent opportunism.

Recontracting may, if anything, increase the opportunism and moral hazard. The first contractor will have what is termed 'ideosyncratic experience' of the management job, which puts them at an informational advantage over both the client and other potential contractors when recontracting occurs. At the moment this 'ideosyncratic experience' lies with in-house operations but their ability to exploit this advantage is hampered by a legacy of bureaucratic procedures and institutionalised manning and payment arrangements.

Whether the in-house operation or an outside contractor wins the first contract, in this situation of asymetric information it is vital for the client to encourage the contractor to reduce opportunism and behave as an *agent* of the client authority. One of the means of securing this co-operative agency behaviour is *instruction*; but this is ruled out in leisure services because of the imprecise specifications and consequentially weak policing potential. Any 'default systems' written into contract specifications are not likely to be very effective since they will probably relate to inputs rather than outcomes. The other main way to secure compatible contractor behaviour is through incentives but local authorities, with their institutional procedures, have a poor track record and little experience of providing meaningful incentives.

Opportunism, then, is a real danger to the success of CCT in leisure management. With a commercial contractor it is likely to take the form of financial opportunism, as described above. With a DSO another possible form of opportunism is 'shirking' – the inefficiency which many existing in-house operations have been accused of. Without sufficient monitoring or incentives there is no control mechanism to deal with such opportunism.

The capital intensive nature of leisure services investment (ie the sports centres and swimming pools) means that maintenance of this capital investment is a major issue. The Order suggests that this will be part of the contract, but the contractor may be prone to skimping on maintenance given the short-term nature of the contract. The very uncertainty as to who will run an authority's leisure facilities after 1993 is likely to lead to a reduction in new investment.

The real difficulty with contract specification for leisure services is the difficulty in specifying objectively the nature of the service to be provided. It is relatively straightforward to specify such things as opening hours or water temperature; it is much more difficult to specify objectively the quality of service provision desired and the nature of collective benefits to be generated. As far as the quality of service is concerned, it is reasonable to expect that the contractor's financial objectives will cause them to provide a high quality service. Given the nature of demand for leisure, provision of low quality is likely to lead to reduced demand, lower income and poor profitability, as well as the probability of incurring financial penalties under the contract.

Social objectives are the most problematic for CCT specification and policing. A real failure of government in the field of sport has been to tackle this question. It is only now, twenty years on from the beginning of the huge investment in indoor facilities, that local authorities are asking the relevant questions of what they are aiming to achieve through such provision. The imminent arrival of CCT is putting pressure on local government to find out exactly what is being achieved at the moment in order that they can decide a strategy for CCT. Very few authorities do know what social benefits are generated through their public sector leisure provision. Hence the difficulty in specifying a contract that would guarantee such benefits continuing to be produced in the future, if indeed they are currently produced.

Without adequate specification of outcomes, the contract is likely to concentrate on inferior parameters, in particular inputs. This will increase the likelihood of adverse selection, since it biases the selection process towards economy-orientated bids, rather than more effectiveness or efficiency-orientated bids. We saw in Chapter 5 how government cannot specify accurately what it wants sport and leisure services to achieve so it relies largely on inputs as pseudo performance measures. In such circumstances a contractor with more managerial knowledge could bid with a realistic level of service delivery or output in mind and fail to be considered by the local authority, because the authority has not the information to assess service delivery implications. Worse, a contractor who concentrates on inputs and ignores real outputs in the bid, may win the contract.

If a major set of social benefits generated through public sector sports provision is health benefits through increased participation, as Chapter 4 suggests, then there is every indication that such benefits will continue to be generated under CCT, probably even more so. For instance, City Centre Leisure, a company formed by former members of Westminster City Council's Recreation Department, took over the management of two of Westminster's leisure centres (the Seymour centre and the Queen Mother centre) in September 1988 (Westminster put its leisure facilities out to tender in March 1988, prior to the announcement of CCT). Within 10 months, attendances at the centres were twenty per cent higher than in the comparative period a year before. There will be a strong financial incentive under CCT to improve attendances and this is likely to be achieved through increases in quality, despite the difficulties of achieving agreements on the financing of quality improvements since they will normally require further capital investment.

There is a danger though that other social benefits will be ignored because they conflict with the self-interest of the contractor. These are the community benefits that are frequently talked about by public sector leisure managers and politicians but rarely if ever measured. An example of the sort of argument which is often put by both officers and political members is an extract of a comment by Peter Price of Sheffield City Council in response to a paper on 'Charging for Leisure' by N P Hepworth (1983):

> That was one of the most worrying and frightening speeches I have heard for a long time. It was certainly a great contrast to Denis Howell's talk in which he stressed the social provision aspects of sport and recreation .... We have a sports centre built in an area of 40 per cent unemployment. We can fill that sports centre with people willing to pay £2 or £5 a game for badminton; we can have rounds of golf at £8 or £10. People will pay to be exclusive but we are aiming at the underprivileged, the twenty per cent unemployed ....
>
> I believe Mr Hepworth has totally missed the point of what local government is about. It is about bringing services to people, people who need them ....
>
> We have recently introduced free charges for unemployed and that has doubled our uptake of sport ....
>
> We are not about making money, we are about providing services to people who need them, the people in deprived areas. We cannot shut the people out by a pricing policy.

The response by Hepworth is also worth quoting, since he could easily have been talking about a contracting situation but for the fact he was six years too early:

> I am not in favour of providing only for the well-off and doing nothing for the poor – far from it. My message is that you have to set down very clearly what it is you are trying to achieve. Mr Price said that he wants low charges in order to have a lot of unemployed people using his facilities. I would be quite happy to accept that, provided the pricing policy was the result of a clear and reasoned decision-making process. You have to determine precisely what it is you are trying to achieve. You have to ask the question: how much do I want use of the centres with which I am concerned by people who are unemployed. You have to put it down. You also have to put down what sort of use you are going to get and when you are going to get it. What is more you then have to analyse the situation and ask yourself whether you have got the kind of usage you intended. Now, you may have done all that at Sheffield but all the evidence is that in most places it is certainly not being done.

The evidence in Chapter 6 concerning the achievement of social objectives is mixed. Chapter 5 indicated that the state of management information in local authority leisure services is such that it is still not possible to establish what community benefits are achieved through public leisure provision.

If these social benefits are not to be ignored under CCT then authorities must tackle the difficult problem of measuring the effectiveness of their services in relation to these social objectives. This will involve a substantial change in the quality of information available.

Contracting for excellence in sport

We have noted in ealier chapters that the production of excellence in sport is not an easily quantifiable input-output relationship. There are many uncertainties in the production process; market failures mean that some of the outputs of excellence are collective and intangible; and the three principal supply sectors – commercial, voluntary and public – have an essential, if problematic interrelationship in the supply of excellence.

Any partnership in production involves a contracting situation, either implicit or explicit. In the excellence market the most conspicuous and long standing partnership is that between government (as represented by the Sports Council) and the voluntary sector's governing bodies. As we have suggested in Chapter 7, this partnership arrangement is moving towards more central control by the Sports Council. This involves more *explicit* contracting.

Two principal elements in the partnership to produce excellence serve to illustrate the changing contracting environment in which it functions: grant aiding of governing bodies by the Sports Council and use of the Sports Council's National Sports Centres by governing bodies. We examine the changing contracting circumstances to see if they are likely to increase either the effectiveness or efficiency of the production of excellence in sport.

Sports council excellence grants to governing bodies

The main source of grants from the Sports Council to governing bodies of sport has been subject to a change in allocation in recent years. Prior to 1985 governing bodies received annual grants for five years with little monitoring of the effectiveness or efficiency of the spending of these grants. Furthermore, over time governing bodies were becoming proportionally more reliant on grant-in-aid (and commercial sponsorship) and less reliant on their own internally derived revenues.

Since 1985 governing bodies have had to submit for approval by the Sports Council comprehensive development plans for the medium term – typically three to five years. Moreover, it was the intention of the Sports Council in implementing this 'New Approach' grant-in-aid system to monitor annually the governing bodies' success in meeting objectives specified in the development plans and make annual grant payments conditional on proven progress. As such this grant-in-aid is shifting ground from an implicit to an explicit contractual arrangement. The grants cover more than just excellence, of course, but the observations and analysis of the excellence element presented here is representative of other functional programmes too.

The 'New Approach' to grant-in-aid applications by governing bodies requires much more stringent functional specifications of development plans, which presumably have to fall in line with the Sports Council's corporate plan. So at the application stage the transfer payment is an increasingly heavily vetted one. This can be contrasted with the transfer payments administered by local authorities, which have very few conditions attached and little monitoring of results.

To tighten up on the contractual arrangements attached to grants involves very demanding information requirements in specification, selection and monitoring for contracts. The specification has to be a document which defines accountability. It must be possible to tell whether or not the specification looks like being met by the application, and it must also be possible to judge if the specification has been met by the contractor – in this case the governing body.

The detailed specifications for the Sports Council's grant aiding of governing bodies are actually provided by the contractor rather than the client. This is not unusual. To have the specification incorporated in the contractor's *proposal* recognises that asymetric information exists, ie that the governing body alone has sufficient information to provide details. Governing bodies submit detailed development plans, with only broadly defined guidance from the Sports Council.

One criticism of the nature of specifications/proposals is that the approved programmes under which funding is authorised are inappropriate for the effective production of excellence in sport. Broad headings such as 'excellence' or 'competition programmes' are not detailed enough to ensure a balanced expenditure programme *within* the programmes. For example:

Two specific excellence programme elements that seem to be continually deficient or absent from governing body proposals are 'individuals' and 'support services'. Only when explicit programme budgeting attention is drawn to these items will systematic attention be paid to relaxing any financial constraints to their development (Taylor 1990).

The selection process in grant-aiding governing bodies involves less the selection of who to award the grant to, although in a significant minority of cases this is a decision to be made. Rather, the most important selection decision concerns the amount of grant to be awarded, ie the contract price. A number of criteria for the selection of the contract price can be identified. Some of these are both measurable and employed by the Sports Council. Special cost considerations, such as expensive equipment, necessary travel and transport costs, and expensive competition requirements, are estimated. The amount of self-generated excellence income and/or cross-subsidisation of excellence programmes, from other functional areas such as membership and commercial activities, can be measured.

Other selection criteria, though, are less easy to measure and therefore very difficult to consider objectively in the selection process. These include a governing body's effectiveness in actually producing excellence, and the extent of any collective benefits arising from excellence – for example the degree of public awareness and appreciation of excellent performance in a sport, and the stimulation of a demonstration effect on participation.

An issue identified earlier as being of major importance in any contracting situation is *incentives*. The selection of grant awards and the financial criteria for doing so are important signals to governing bodies. The wrong signals would increase the danger of moral hazard, whilst appropriate incentives would reduce this danger. For example, if a governing body increases its revenue from commercial sponsorship and/or non-excellence programmes, what should the effect be on the grants awarded? A consequent grant *reduction* might be seen to be fair, on the grounds that the governing body is more able to sustain its total programme, including excellence, with its own resources.

The danger in reducing grants in such circumstances is that the signal being given to the governing body is that any work put in to increase money being placed into one hand is cancelled out by grant taken away from the other hand. The moral hazard here is that the governing body might deliberately seek *not* to generate more of the non-grant revenue in order to protect its claim on future grants.

In extreme cases, such as the Lawn Tennis Association with its large Wimbledon profits, the position is clearcut – no excellence grant can be justified when internal funds are so large and reliable.

Unfortunately for the Sports Council such cases are the exception rather than the rule; non-grant sources of revenue are often quite unpredictable, for example from sponsorship and events. So the grant allocation criteria have to maintain an incentive to governing bodies to reduce their dependency on Sports Council grant-in-aid and yet take into account the resource constraints and equity objectives of the grant system.

A precedent for maintaining incentives in the excellence 'contract' has been set by the Sports Council, in the context of unexpected surpluses on programmes which are grant-aided:

> In such cases the grant is reclaimed to the point where the programme breaks even, to ensure that the grant is the minimum needed for the programme to exist. The Sports Council recognises, though, that this procedure might appear to penalise 'good housekeeping' and it looks constructively at opportunities to divert surplus grant to other programmes or new developments (Taylor 1990).

Monitoring excellence grant awards is made difficult by the uncertainties of the production process. There is very little systematic, time series evidence collected or presented in support of applications, and none required in monitoring processes. Within the Sports Council, monitoring of excellence programmes is negligible. To an extent this is understandable: it would be a complicated exercise to generate empirical evidence on the relationship between expenditures (inputs) to the excellence production process on the one hand and achievements (output) on the other hand. But the consequences of a lack of monitoring for the contracting process are severe – allocating grant according to excellence performance criteria becomes infeasible. A simple listing of medals, competitions, etc. recently won is a poor substitute for a proper evaluation of excellence achievements and their relationship to governing body activity.

Another basic problem with the excellence contract between the Sports Council and governing bodies is that it is in danger of not being flexible enough to cater for the instability of important non-grant sources of revenue, especially from events and sponsorship. Sponsorship deals typically last two or three years, whilst Sports Council grant-in-aid development contracts cover three to five years. Under such circumstances there is a danger of a medium-term downward adjustment in Sports Council grant-in-aid coinciding with the termination of an important sponsorship deal. Contingency grant arrangements would give the process more flexibility and ensure the stability of overall funding necessary for continuity in the excellence production process.

It is clear that contractual arrangements between the Sports Council and governing bodies for the production of excellence in sport are riddled with problems, uncertainties and information gaps. By implication the transactions costs incurred in any improvement in accountability are significant, as both the Sports Council and governing bodies have discovered in the process of operating the 'New Approach' to grant allocation.

Furthermore, where the production process involves intangible and collective outputs and uncertain relationships between inputs and outputs there is little likelihood of the client (the Sports Council) having sufficient information about the precise, detailed requirements of the production process. One important consequence of this is that grant-aiding by the Sports Council has been and will continue to be determined primarily by the objectives of economy and equity between sports. This results from the lack of adequate information in the grant application process with which to assess effectiveness or efficiency, and the likelihood that in the Sports Council matters of equity between governing bodies are bound to be high on the political agenda.

It would seem that the tightening of contractual arrangements between the Sports Council and governing bodies concerning excellence grant-in-aid is likely to have uncertain and unproven results. However, the 'catch' to this rather gloomy conclusion is that there is no viable 'market' alternative and it is impossible to 'internalise' these transactions (eg by the Sports Council taking over governing bodies). Therefore the choice lies between the proverbial devil and the deep blue sea: between implicit or explicit contracts. If the latter cost more in transactions costs, without the possibility of measuring the results properly, then a move in that direction is, quite simply, a gamble.

Governing bodies' use of national sports centres

One of the fundamental purposes of National Sports Centres is for use by governing bodies for training and other functions in the pursuit of excellence in sport. To this effect, there has been an implicit contract operating, whereby governing bodies have been expected to use the Centres. Recently the Sports Council has conducted both internal and external reviews of the operations of its National Centres, largely because of concern over their net expenditures, or operating deficits, which totalled over £2 million in 1985–6. The reviews have resulted, among other things, in the probable tightening of contractual relationships between National Centres and governing bodies. This change parallels developments in grant-in-aid discussed above.

One form of explicit contractual relationship has existed for some time and encourages the 'brand loyalty' of governing bodies of National Centres. This is the formal adoption of a National Centre by a governing body as a 'committed user'. This sometimes involves a formal contractual arrangement whereby the governing body contributes to certain costs at the Centre and commits itself to a certain level of use, in return for financial assistance and privileged access to the Centre. More than fifteen sports are attached to one or more of the National Centres as committed users.

The Sports Council's recent reviews of their National Sports Centres concluded by reaffirming that the priority use of National Centres is for excellence training. However, lower deficit financing of the Centres also became a priority objective. The Sports Council further agreed, unanimously:

> In pursuit of excellence, the Centres would depend upon a partnership with the governing bodies and there should be a clear link between governing body programme funding and the use of the National Centres (Sports Council minutes, 2nd meeting 1987).

The clear implication of this statement is that grant-in-aid to governing bodies is to be somehow conditional upon their use of National Centres in a much more explicit contractual manner than has been the case in the past.

The Sports Council wants tighter contractual relationships with governing bodies concerning the use of National Centres, especially when reinvestment in National Centres is undertaken for defined sports, increasing asset specificity. The most obvious means of achieving this explicit contract would be to designate part of any grant-in-aid for excellence training to be used only in payment for time and space at National Centres, and to be clawed back if the specified use of the Centres was not made.

This contractual arrangement seems to have the necessary characteristics to operate successfully, with few additional transactions costs. The incentive is clear enough, so opportunism and moral hazard is very unlikely. Monitoring of use is easy, so there is not a serious bounded rationality problem. The main problem, if only a short-term one, is the contractual specification of the amount of use and the price. The quantity of use of National Centres to be specified is that which governing bodies *should* be budgeting for out of any excellence grant. This could only be decided by bargaining, since it is not possible to logically determine the amount of National Centre use that should be made, compared with use of other facilities and with expenditure on other inputs to the excellence production process.

As for the price to be specified for governing body use, the new financial imperative may drive the prices charged up towards the full-cost level. If so, grant-in-aid for excellence training would have to rise correspondingly, or else use would fall below the current level. If governing bodies paid National Centres full cost prices with use-specific grants, then the subsidy for this element of excellence production would be clear. This compares with the present situation where unquantified, hidden subsidies are given to governing bodies through price discounts.

Whether a more explicit contractual relationship concerning use of National Centres will increase the effectiveness or efficiency of excellence production is uncertain. On the one hand the governing body is a contractor for whom the client, the Sports Council, wishes to provide excellence. If the Sports Council considers efficiency to be served by specialised provision (ie National Centres) then it may require a long term collective responsibility of governing bodies, in partnership with the Sports Council, to utilise National Centres such that economies of scale and specialisation are achieved. The use of National Centres by governing bodies for training and competition purposes is increasingly under competitive threat from other suitable facilities, particularly in local authorities. To allow this competition between National Centres and local authorities is, according to the Sports Council, inefficient because of the wasteful duplication of specific public sector assets.

On the other hand, though, governing bodies are not just contractors. They are also, at the same time, *consumers* in the excellence market, wishing to secure the best value for money in the facilities which they use for excellence training. If governing bodies are moving away from using National Centres for sound reasons then to have their choices distorted by the threat of financial penalties is inefficient, in the short run at least. This argument depends crucially on the rationality of the governing bodies' free choice of training facilities. If their decisions to use non-National Centre facilities are just to save money, they may be judged to be false economy, and branded as opportunists demonstrating moral hazard. On the other hand, if they are using the facilities of local authorities because they do not have very asset specific demands and they are searching rationally for the best deal, then they need to use competition to achieve it.

The question is: which serves efficiency best – the fulfilling of collective obligations to specialised production facilities or the free choice of consumers between competing facilities? This is really an empirical question and unfortunately it is not one for which there is conclusive evidence one way or the other.

Another complicating factor is that the management of National Centres is also being made the subject of competitive tendering (although this is not part of the CCT legislation). In principle this increases the danger of moral hazard since it is the *secondary* users of the Centres, the non-excellence markets, that are the most profitable. If this potential for opportunism is in any way a threat to excellence production, then it might be more appropriate to think in terms of direct capital and revenue funding of *voluntary* sector National Sports Centres. Examples of this already exist in badminton, squash and wrestling. However, for many of its 'committed users' the Sports Council has already implemented a policy which reduces the scope for opportunism. This is the provision of 'dedicated spaces' within National Centres, for the permanent use of one sport only.

Conclusions

In all of the preceding discussion of contracting one requirement has continually forced its way into the analysis: information. Indeed, information has been identified as a key resource throughout this book, whether it is information on the changing nature of leisure demands; information on the scale and importance of market failures; the information needed for government to make sensible decisions; the information that the voluntary sector rather than the other sectors is best equipped to handle; or the information essential to the specification, selection and monitoring of contracts.

In a private sector market mechanism, the 'invisible hand' relegates information to a requirement implicit in a countless number of agents in the market – consumers, producers, distributors, etc. There is less need for a guiding hand to co-ordinate information in such a market. Each agent supposedly has sufficient incentive to ensure not only that they have the optimum amount of information, but also that the other agents with whom they conduct transactions are informed about their requirements.

Government cannot imitate the market and take information for granted. It has to generate information explicitly and use it to ensure that partnerships and contracts, both implicit and explicit, work effectively and efficiently. Since information requirements are important to all issues of government intervention in sports markets, not just contracting, we conclude the chapter and the book simultaneously by drawing together implications for the use of this pervasive yet often neglected resource, information.

Information audit

For government to intervene successfully in markets such as sport, it is necessary to map out what information exists and what information is needed to make appropriate decisions and monitor consequent results. To this end we consider it essential that the relevant arms of government, especially local authorities and the Sports Council, conduct an *information audit*. This audit should be structured in such a way as to assist the formulation of clearer objectives, specific policy targets, and an appropriate set of performance indicators. It would be the basis for an *information plan*, which would assess the usefulness of information to planning, contracting and management decisions, against the costs and feasibility of acquiring the information.

The first category of information to be audited is costs. However, whereas this may sound like a straightforward financial audit, our intention goes beyond this. To assist management decisions such as contracting, rather than just to ensure financial accountability, it is necessary to arrange cost information accordingly. Cost centering, by functions or programmes, is a prerequisite to making decisions such as pricing and programming of facilities – essential elements to contract specification. It is difficult when many costs are common across programmes or facilities, and sometimes arbitrary decisions have to be made. But an approximate awareness of the cost of a particular activity or space is better than no knowledge at all. Also, once cost centering is attempted, experience is gained and improvement can be made on an incremental basis. Furthermore, where practicable, cost information should be arranged such that it records not only totals, but also average (or unit) and marginal (or incremental) costs.

Demand data, or usage, is another fundamental information requirement. For built sports facilities, local authorities typically collect aggregate data, although this often does not include accurate usage data for block bookings. To assist again with such decisions as pricing and programming it would be desirable to record usage by time of day, week, and year, by types of activity, and by different (target) groups of people – including accurate estimates of group use such as schools, clubs and lessons. Such details are seldom all available to public sector leisure managers. For resource-based amenities such as parks and outdoor pitches, usage recording is more problematic, although regular sample counts by on-site staff are possible.

Taking demand data to another level of sophistication would involve monitoring capacity utilisation and excess demand. Capacity utilisation data is difficult to generate because it depends crucially on the programming of a facility; it is rarely attempted except for single activity spaces. Excess demand is rarely recorded systematically.

Decision consequences have been poorly monitored in the public sector in the past. Whether this is because of a lack of motivation, a lack of training or a lack of information is not really the point here. What is needed to assist in contract specification and monitoring and to inform management decision-making, are systematic attempts to identify the consequences of decisions taken. This applies to changes in prices, programming, marketing, investment and grant-aiding, to name but a few.

Attitudes to leisure provision are changing rather than static. This important message from the analysis of Chapter 3 carries with it the implication that accurate information on changing consumer attitudes is vital if provision is to match customer expectations. The obvious mechanism here is market research, which sadly is still at best a one-off, *ad hoc* activity in most local authorities. Furthermore, sports facility market research is often dominated by questions concerning user characteristics rather than a detailed examination of user attitudes concerning such areas as values, motives, aspirations, quality of facilities, and satisfaction levels. Market research can also, of course, be directed to non-users in order to identify the major factors that are acting as barriers to participation.

Finally, the bottom line in the government provision or support of sport is too often unidentified and unquantified. This is not surprising, since the bottom line is not simply a financial profit, but more typically a complex and interdependent set of outputs and impacts. Chapter 4 identified a number of impacts expected from government intervention in sports markets. Contracts issued by local authorities and the Sports Council have such impacts as their implicit or explicit bottom line. Yet is is normal for these impacts to be assumed, rather than monitored.

Bovaird (1988) suggests that there should be more emphasis in 'impact indicators'. He specifies several categories of such indicators including changes in client state and changes in welfare of indirectly affected people. Changing client state refers to changes in the client's welfare as a result of using public sports facilities. One aspect to this is the change in health status as a result of participation in sport, as discussed in Chapter 4. It is not that difficult to devise methods of measuring such an impact indicator. However, at the moment no local authority does so.

Changes in the welfare of indirectly affected people refers to welfare improvements of non-participants, through such means as reduced vandalism and increased productivity. Given the wide-ranging nature of such benefits, measurement of them in the context of sports provision presents numerous problems. However, an imperfect measure is better than no information at all and only by attempting to devise an indicator of such impacts will the experience be acquired to devise superior indicators.

Information planning

A lack of management information is likely to prevent local authorities from writing contracts with sufficient detail to ensure satisfactory outcomes. One example illustrating the danger is the pricing decision. A typical pricing specification is likely to take the form of institutionalising existing prices, with annual 'rate of inflation' increases. The implicit assumption behind such a specification is that the existing level and structure of prices is in some sense correct. It also suggests that demand and costs for the various activities will remain the same throughout the contract, except for general inflation. This seems unlikely, especially given what has been said in Chapter 3 about the nature of leisure demands. It is pertinent to ask the question 'what would a local authority need to know in order for it to be confident that its pricing policy were rational?'

It is impossible to make sensible pricing decisions without systematic and accurate information on a number of considerations. First, the costs of provision for a facility or service, and preferably for each activity, is arguably the most important reference point for pricing – one that requires detailed cost centering. An estimate of marginal costs is particularly important for a facility suffering the peak load problem, as many sports facilities do – ie regular excess demand at peak times and low demand at off-peak times. Second, accurate information on the use of facilities or services, preferably by type of user, by activity and by time of day, week and year is needed to determine both the level of 'normal' prices and the scope and levels of price discrimination. Ideally this use should be expressed in terms of capacity utilisation for each facility and time of day. Third, the extent to which there is excess demand at peak times will demonstrate the potential for premium pricing as an alternative to rationing by a queue. Finally, the attitudes of customers to prices, in relation to other related factors influencing their decision to use the facility or service, needs to be documented.

To implement an information plan requires both the means of recording and processing information and the *motivation* to use the information in decisions, contracts, and business plans. The means are usually seen to be technological, from computer linked tills and databases to 'smart cards'. Manpower training is crucial, though, in order to fulfill the potential that technology has to offer. Manpower is also an essential complement to technology in the acquisition of market research information.

As we suggested in Chapter 5, motivation is at present a constraint to the improvement of management information in government supply of and support for sport. A precondition for information planning, therefore, is to offer sufficient incentives for administrators and managers to *want* improved information. This may come partly from the contracting process itself, since managers may be part of the DSO bidding process and therefore keen to prove their worth in terms of service provision. Local authority contract administrators may well favour the DSO bid in principle, and the desire to ensure that the DSO bid receives due attention may lead to more explicit social performance specification. Motivation would also be boosted by more performance-related pay at the institutional and personal levels. The monitoring of performance by the *service* (as well as by the individual) is both an input to and a consequence of performance-related pay.

An information plan will also have to consider transactions costs. Information is not a free resource and some types of information will be too costly to acquire. In chapter 7 we noted that the voluntary sector may have a much more effective and cheaper access to information about certain people's leisure needs, which is why voluntary clubs are a cost effective form of provision for sports participation. It would be impractical and wasteful for the government to attempt to duplicate the collection of such information.

Time for change

Improving information is seen as a foundation for the success of contracting in the relationship between government and other providers in the sports market. The opportunity to develop information systems is certainly with local authorities and the Sports Council now. CCT and the tighter contractual relationships between the Sports Council and governing bodies of sport have been shown to have stringent information requirements.

Bovaird (1988) argues that unless attempts are made to measure such community impacts *before* CCT is implemented then it may be impossible to specify contracts in such a way that the private contractor will be constrained to deliver such benefits. CCT under this argument will founder on the potential for opportunism created by inadequate information.

We are inclined to be more optimistic about the opportunities for developing information systems and subsequently improving not just contracting, decision-making and planning by government, but also, ultimately, the sports services with which government is involved. Quite simply, every time a contract is due for renegotiation then there is an opportunity for a client to impose sharper requirements on the contractor, based on better information. These opportunities will occur regularly – every three to five years for both CCT contracts and governing body grants from the Sports Council. They will also occur periodically as new circumstances demand recontracting, eg new investment, or if the existing contract is terminated early for whatever reason.

If local authorities continue to operate on the same basis as previously, with the same level of management information, then tender contracts will be written in such a way that opportunistic behaviour is likely. Local authorities will be unable to write in clauses to set quantitative targets for social objectives since they will have insufficient information either to set such targets or to show that the current in-house service is achieving them. Consequently, if they try to set such targets they will be open to the attack that they are acting anti-competitively. They will be asking a private contractor to achieve objectives that the authority's own recreation department cannot prove is being achieved through current provision.

Alternatively, contracting can be the catalyst for better management. Under the right information conditions it increases accountability and gives contractors a clear direction to take. This 'improvement scenario' is a radical change from what has been described in Chapter 5. However, to *not* take this course would be to invite a deterioration in sports services supported or supplied by government. In a situation of implicit contracts or internal transactions, which government has implemented in the past, trust and public service attitudes are subsidised with little accountability but with mutually compatible objectives likely to an extent.

In a poorly informed explicit contracting situation the contractor, not being influenced by public service objectives and with a clear motive to make profit from the contract, will probably exploit the situation to the detriment of social objectives. As Walsh (1988) argues:

> The contract and specification will be crucial to the success of the competitive approach. If the local authority creates too loose a contract, it will lose control of the service. Anything that is significant must be specified, because if it is not in the specification there is no guarantee that the contractor will provide it.

It is the inability of the government agencies involved in sport to specify clearly what it is they are trying to provide that is the major element of government failure in the market for sport in the recent past.

References

Arrow K J (1951) *Social Choice and Individual Values*, Wiley, New York

Arrow K J (1963) *Social Choice and Individual Values*, 2nd Edn, Yale University Press

ASA (1987) *The Teaching of Swimming*

Audit Commission (1989) *Sport for Whom? Clarifying the Local Authority Role in Sport and Recreation* HMSO

Benington J and White J (1988) *The Future of Leisure Services* Longman

Boulding K (1956) *The Image: Knowledge in Life and Society* University of Michigan Press

Bovaird A G (1988) 'Evaluation in Leisure — A Review of Major Approaches' in *Proceedings of the 1988 ILAM National Seminar, 'A Question of Balance'*

Buchanan J M (1965) *An Economic Theory of Clubs* Economica, 32.

Bureau of Outdoor Recreation (1976) *Evaluation of Public Willingness to Pay User Charges for Use of Outdoor Recreation Areas and Facilities*, US Department of Interior, Washington DC.

Butson P (1983) *The Financing of Sport in the UK* Sports Council

CIPFA (1981) *Leisure and Recreation Statistics: Estimates 1981/82.*

Clarke J and Critcher C (1985) *The Devil Makes Work: Leisure in Capitalist Britain,* Macmillan

Coalter F, Long J and Duffield B (1986) *Rationale for Public Sector Investment in Leisure* The Sports Council

Coase R H (1937) 'The Nature of the Firm' *Economica*, Vol 4.

Coe S (1985) *Olympic Review: Preparing for '88*, Sports Council

Coopers and Lybrand Associates (1981) *Service Provision and Pricing in Local Government,* (for The Department of the Environment), HMSO, London.

Cowling D, Fitzjohn M, Tungatt M (1983) 'Identifying the Market' *Sports Council Study 24*

Csikszentmihalyi M (1975) *Beyond Boredom and Anxiety* Jossey-Bass Ltd

Culyer A J *(1976) Need and the National Health Service* Martin Robertson

Culyer A J (1980) *The Political Economy of Social Policy* Martin Robertson

Cyert R M and March J G (1963) *A Behavioural Theory of the Firm,* Prentice Hall

Davies, B (1968) *Social Needs and Resources in Local Services* Michael Joseph

Department of the Environment (1975) *Sport and Recreation* HMSO, Cmnd 6200

Department of the Environment (1977a) *Policy for Inner Cities* HMSO, Cmnd 6845

Department of the Environment (1977b) *Recreation and Deprivation in Urban Areas* HMSO

Department of the Environment (1988) *Draft Statutory Instrument, 1988*, Local Government England and Wales, Local Government Scotland

Dower M, Rapoport R, Stretlitz Z, and Kew S (1981) *Leisure Provision and People's Needs*, HMSO

Driver B L and Rosenthal D H (1981) *Measuring and Improving Effectiveness of Public Outdoor Recreation Programs* George Washington University

Earl P (1983) *The Economic Imagination: Towards a Behavioural Analysis of Choice,* Wheatsheaf

Earl P (1986) *Lifestyle Economics: Consumer Behaviour in a Turbulent World*, Wheatsheaf

Fentem P H and Bassey E J (1978) *Exercise and Health*, Sports Council Working Paper No 8, 1978

Fentem P H and Bassey E J (1981) *Exercise: The Facts* Oxford University Press

Fine B (1990) *Consumer Behaviour and the Social Sciences: A Critical Review* Queen Mary College, London

Gratton C (1984) 'Efficiency and Equity Aspects of Public Subsidies to Sport and Recreation', *Local Government Studies*, March/April.

Gratton C and Taylor P (1985) *Sport and Recreation: An Economic Analysis,* E and F N Spon Ltd

Gratton C and Taylor P (1987) 'Indoor Arenas: The Missing Market', *Leisure Management*, Vol 7, No 10.

Gratton C and Tice A (1987) 'Leisure Participation, Lifestyle and Health', paper delivered to the International Conference on The Future of Adult Life, Leeuwenhorst Conference Centre, Holland, April.

Gratton C and Tice A (1989) 'Sports Participation and Health', *Journal of Leisure Studies*, January.

Greenley D A, Walsh R G, and Young R A (1982) *Economic Benefits of Improved Water Quality: Perceptions of Options and Preservation Values* Westview Press.

Grossman M (1972) 'On the Concept of Health Capital and the Demand for Health', *Journal of Political Economy*, 80

Heal K and Laycock G (1987) *Preventing Juvenile Crime: The Staffordshire Experience,* Crime Prevention Unit, Paper 8, Home Office.

Health Education Council (1987) *The Health Divide: Inequalities in Health in the 1980s,* A review by Margaret Whitehead.

Heilbroner R L (1972) *The Worldly Philosophers* Simon and Schuster

Hepworth N P (1983) 'Charging for Leisure' in *Proceedings of the Institute of Baths and Recreation Management 1983 Conference*

Hosseini H (1990) 'The Archaic, the Obsolete and the Mythical in Neoclassical Economics', *American Journal of Economics and Sociology*

House of Lords Select Committee (1973) *Report on Sport and Leisure*

Iso-Ahola S E (1982) *The Social Psychology of Leisure and Recreation* Wm C Brown Company

Jackson P M (1982) *The Political Economy of Bureaucracy*, Philip Allan

Jones S G (1986) *Workers at Play: a Social and Economic History of Leisure, 1918–1939* Routledge, and Kegan Paul

Judd M (1983) 'The oddest combination of town and country: popular culture and the London Fairs, 1800–60', in Walton J K and Walvin J (1983) *Leisure in Britain, 1780–1939*, Manchester University Press.

Kelly G A (1955) *The Psychology of Personal Constructs* Norton

Krutilla J V (1967) 'Conservation Reconsidered', *American Economic Review*, Vol. 57.

Leibenstein H (1933) 'Competition and X-efficiency: Reply' *Journal of Political Economy*

London Borough of Waltham Forest (1981) *Working Party Report on Vandalism*

MacNulty W K (1985) 'UK Social Change Through a Wide-Angle Lens', *Futures,* August

Malcolmson R W (1973) *Popular Recreations in English Society, 1700–1850* Cambridge University Press.

Maslow A (1952) *Management and Motivation* Prentice Hall.

Maslow A (1970) *Motivation and Personality* Harper and Row

Mason S (1981) *Conspicuous Consumption* Gower

Mason T (1980) *Association Football and English Society, 1863–1915* Harvester Press

McGuire I, Henderson J and Mooney G (1988) *The Economics of Health Care* Routledge and Kegan Paul

McIntosh P and Charlton V (1985) *The Impact of 'Sport for All' Policy, 1966–1984, And A Way Forward,* The Sports Council

Menger K (1871) *Principles of Economics* Free Press, Glencoe, Illinois

Minogue M and O'Grady J (1985) 'Contracting Out Local Authority Services in Britain' *Local Government Studies,* May/June

Morris J N, and Heady J A, P A B, Roberts C G, and Parks J W (1953) 'Coronary Heart Disease and Physical Activity of Work', *Lancet*, 2

Morris J N, Chave S P Adam C et al (1973) 'Vigorous Exercise in Leisure-Time and the Incidence of Coronary Heart Disease', *Lancet*, 1.

Morris J N, Everitt M G Pollard R, Chave S P and Semmence A M (1980) 'Vigorous Exercise in Leisure-Time: Protection Against Coronary Heart Disease', *Lancet*, 2.

Niskanen W A (1971) *Bureaucracy and Representative Government* Addine-Atherton.

Office of Health Economics (1987) *Women's Health Today*

Paffenbarger R A, and Wing A L (1969) 'Chronic disease in former college students. The effects of single and multiple characteristics on risk of fatal coronary heart disease', *American Journal of Epidemiology*, 90.

Paffenbarger R S and Loughlin M E Sina A S et al (1970) 'Work Activity of Longshoremen as related to death from coronary heart disease and stroke', *New England Journal of Medicine*, 282.

Paffenbarger R S, Wing A L, and Hyde R T, (1978) 'Physical activity as an index of heart attack risk in college alumni', *American Journal of Epidemiology*, 108.
Paffenbarger R S, Hyde R S, Wing A L, and Hsich C C (1986) 'Physical Activity, All Cause Mortality and Longevity of College Alumni', *New England Journal of Medicine*, 314.
Pannell Kerr Forster Associates (1983) *Development and Operation of Leisure Centres: Selected Case Studies,* (for The Audit Inspectorate), HMSO, London.
Rawls J (1971) *A Theory of Justice,* The Belkings Press
Reid D A (1967) 'The Decline of Saint Monday, 1766–1876' *Past and Present,* 71.
Riiskjaer S (1990) 'Economic Behaviour and Cultural Perspectives in Voluntary Sport', *Sport Science Review*, Vol 13.
Rosenthal S R (1980) 'Risk Exercise', *Stress*, pp. 37–40.
Rosenthal S R (1982) 'The Fear Factor', *Sport and Leisure* No. 23, p. 61.
Scitovsky T (1976) *The Joyless Economy,* Oxford University Press.
Scitovsky T (1981) *The Desire for Excitement in Modern Society,* Kyklos
Scitovsky T (1986) *Human Desire and Economic Satisfaction* Wheatsheaf
Shepherd R J (1990) 'Sport, Physical Fitness, and the Costs of Sport', *Science Review*, Vol 13.
Simon H A (1957) *Models of Man* Harper and Row
Sports Council (1972) *Provision for Sport*
Sports Council (1982) *Sport in the Community . . . The Next Ten Years*
Sports Council (1983) *Swimming in the Community*
Sports Council (1986) *A Digest of Sports Statistics for the UK* 2nd Edition
Sports Council (1988) *Sport in the Community: Into the 1990s*
Sports Council (1989) *Solent Sports Counselling Project: Special Report on the Evaluation of the Project's Work, April 1987-March 1989*, North West Sports Council.
Taylor P (1990) *The Financing of Excellence in Sport,* Sports Council.
Thomas G S, Lee P R, Franks S P and Paffenbarger R S (1981) *Exercise and health: The Evidence and the Implications*, Oelgeschlager, Gunn and Hain
Thompson E P (1967) 'Time, Work-discipline and Industrial Capitalism', *Past and Present*, 38
US Department of Interior (1979) *The Third Nationwide Outdoor Recreation Plan*, Washington D C
Veal, A J (1981) 'Sports Centres in Britain: A Review of', *User Studies* (unpublished report to Sports Council).
Veblen T (1899) *The Theory of the Leisure Class* The Modern Library, New York
Walsh K (1988) 'The Consequence of Competition' in Bennington J and White J
Walsh R G (1986) *Recreation Economic Decisions* E & F N Sport Ltd.
Walvin J (1978) *Leisure and Society, 1830–1959,* Longman

Weisbrod B A (1978) *The Voluntary Non-Profit Sector* Lexington Books
Weisbrod B A (1988) *The Non-Profit Economy*, Harvard University Press
Williamson O E (1975) *Markets and Hierarchies: Analysis and Antitrust Implications* Free Press, New York
Williamson O E (1985) *The Economic Institutions of Capitalism: Firms, Markets and Relational Contracting,* Free Press, New York
Wolfenden Committee (1960) *Sport and the Community*, Central Council for Physical Recreation, London

Appendix I

Figure A.1 – Pools built before 1870

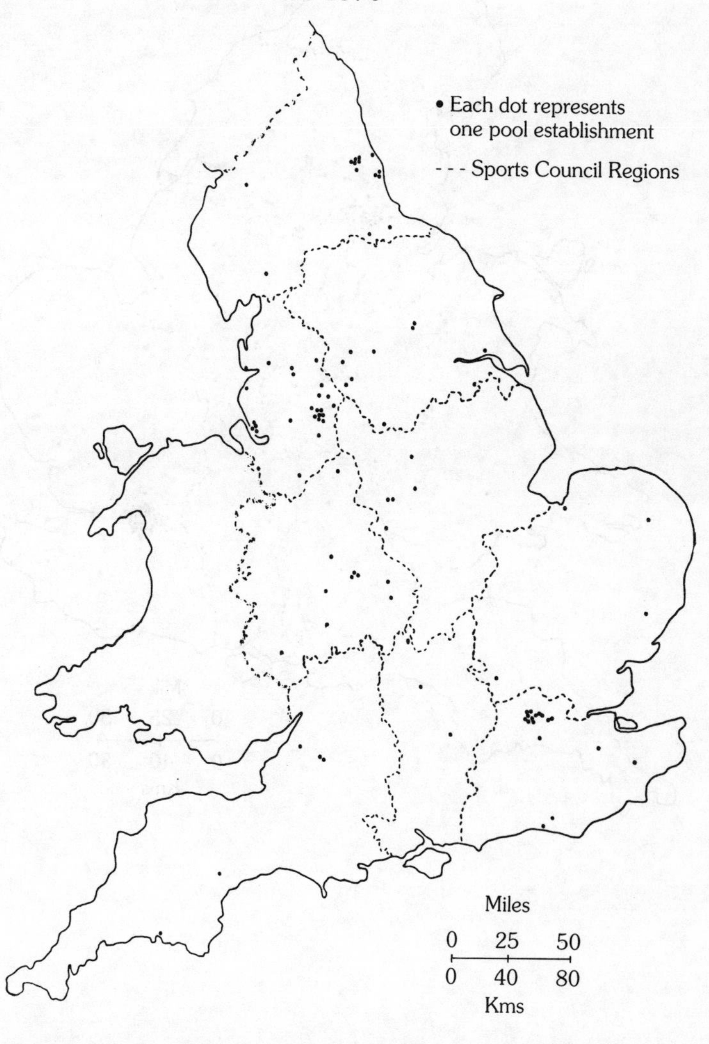

Figure A.2 – Pools built 1870–1899

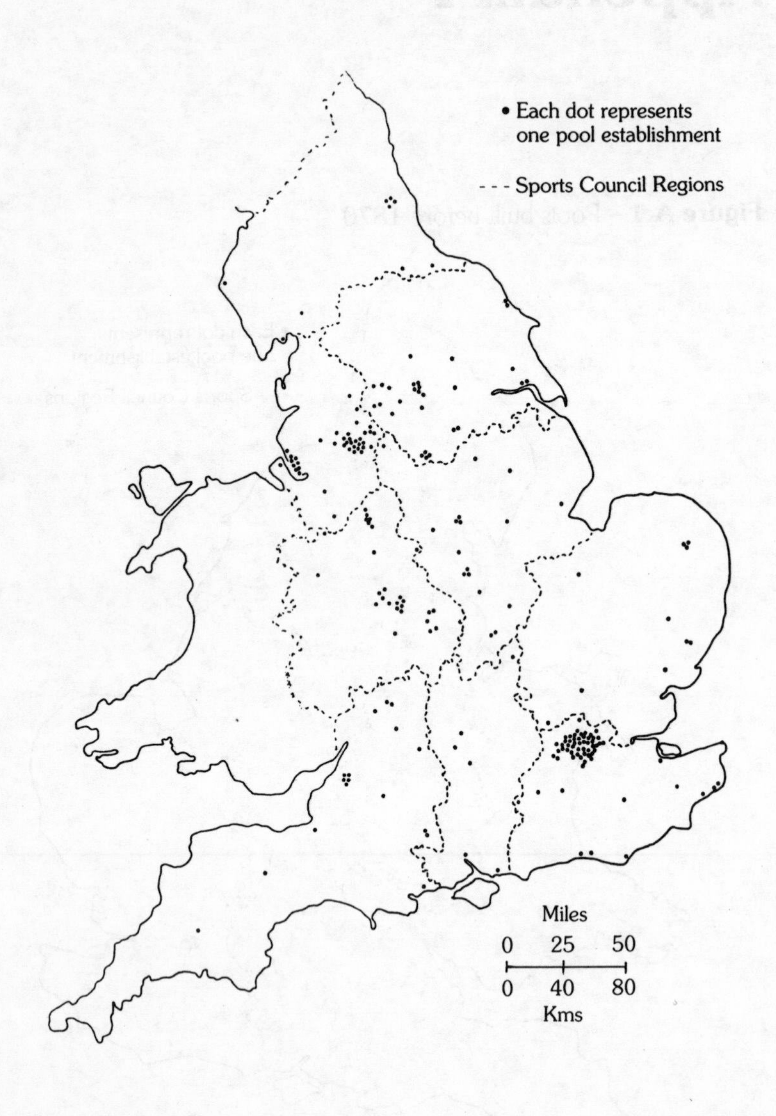

Figure A.3 – Pools built 1900–1914

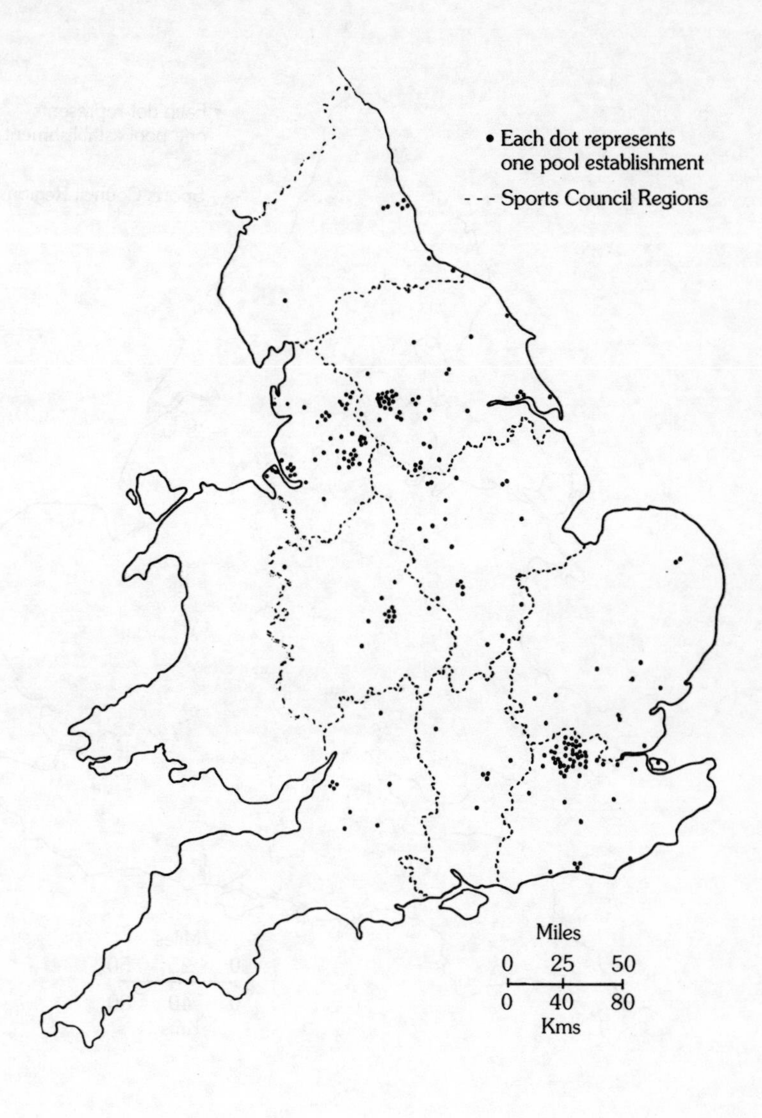

Figure A.4 – Pools built 1915–1929

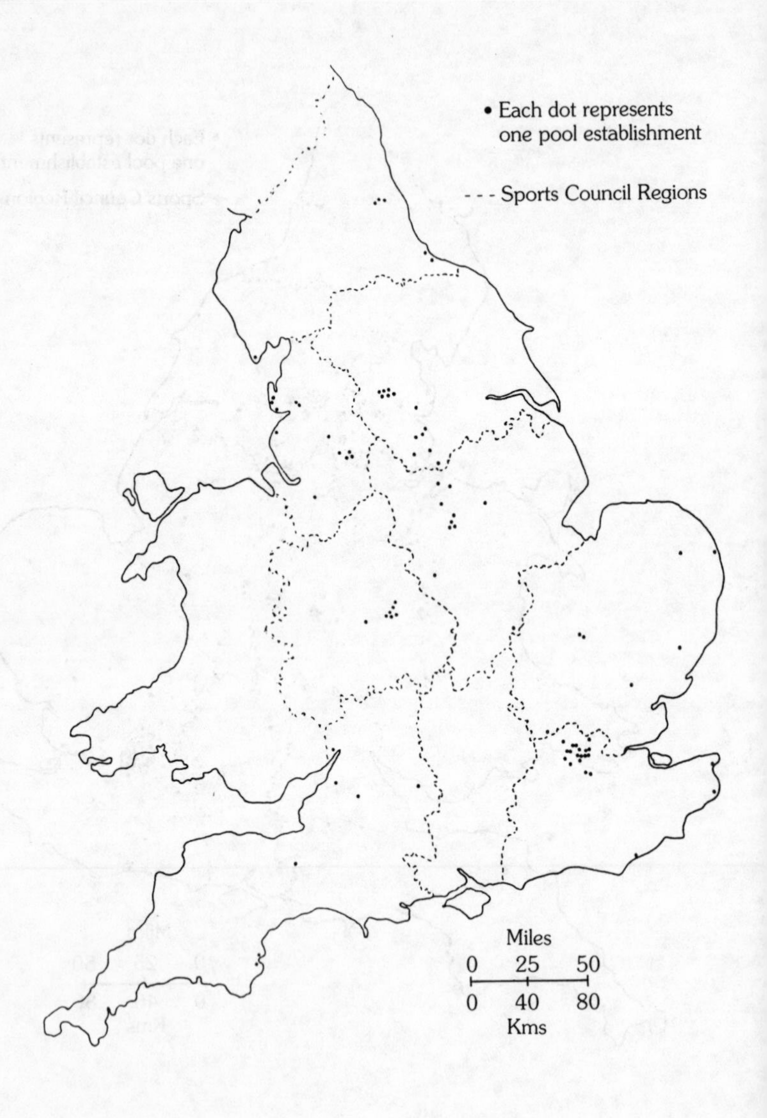

Figure A.5 – Pools built 1930–1945

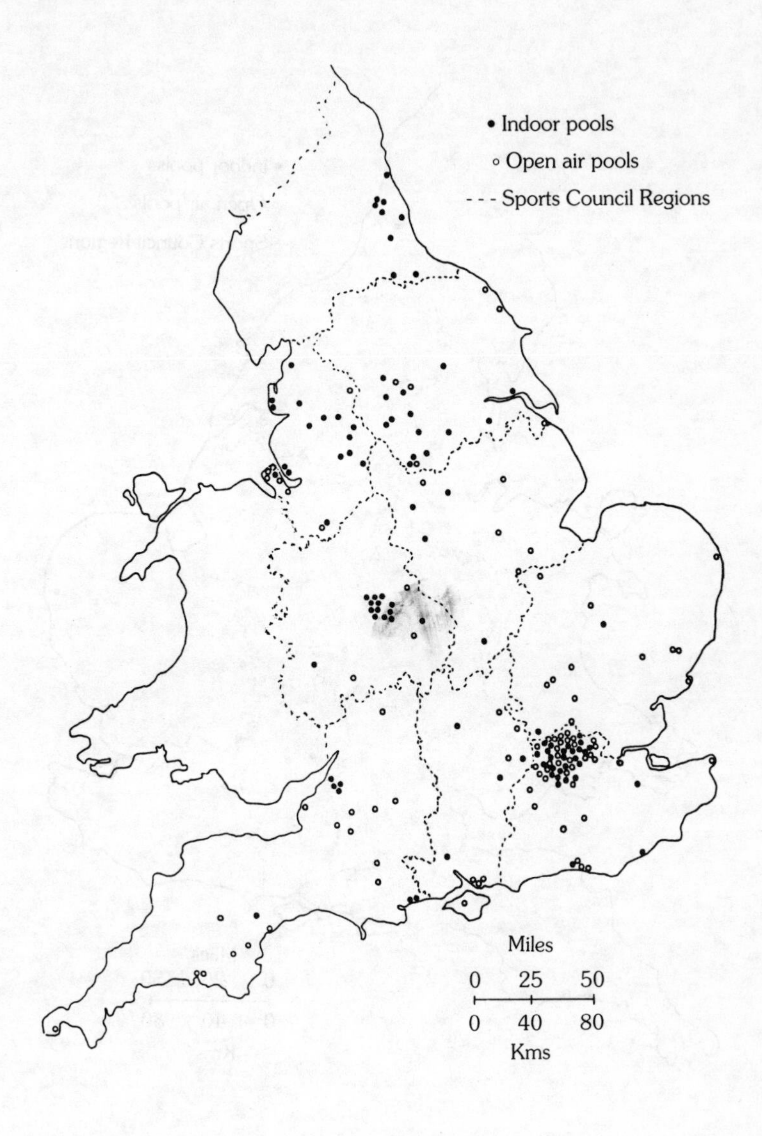

Figure A.6 – Pools built 1946–1959

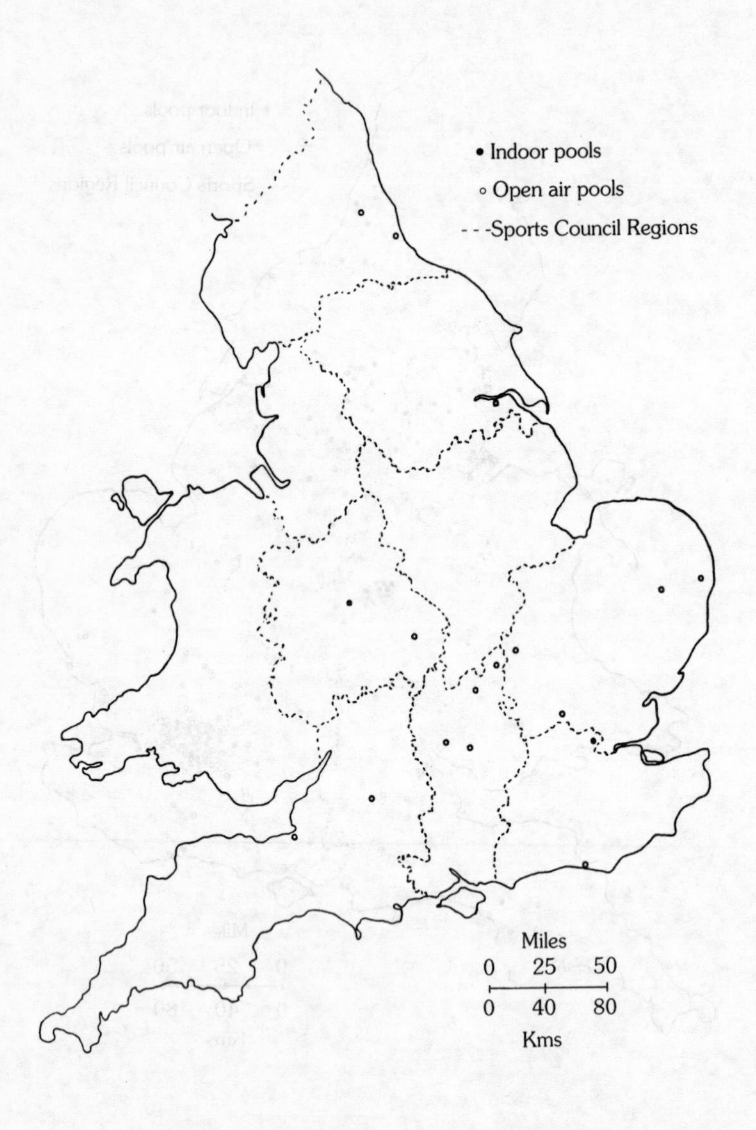

Figure A.7 – Pools built 1960–1969

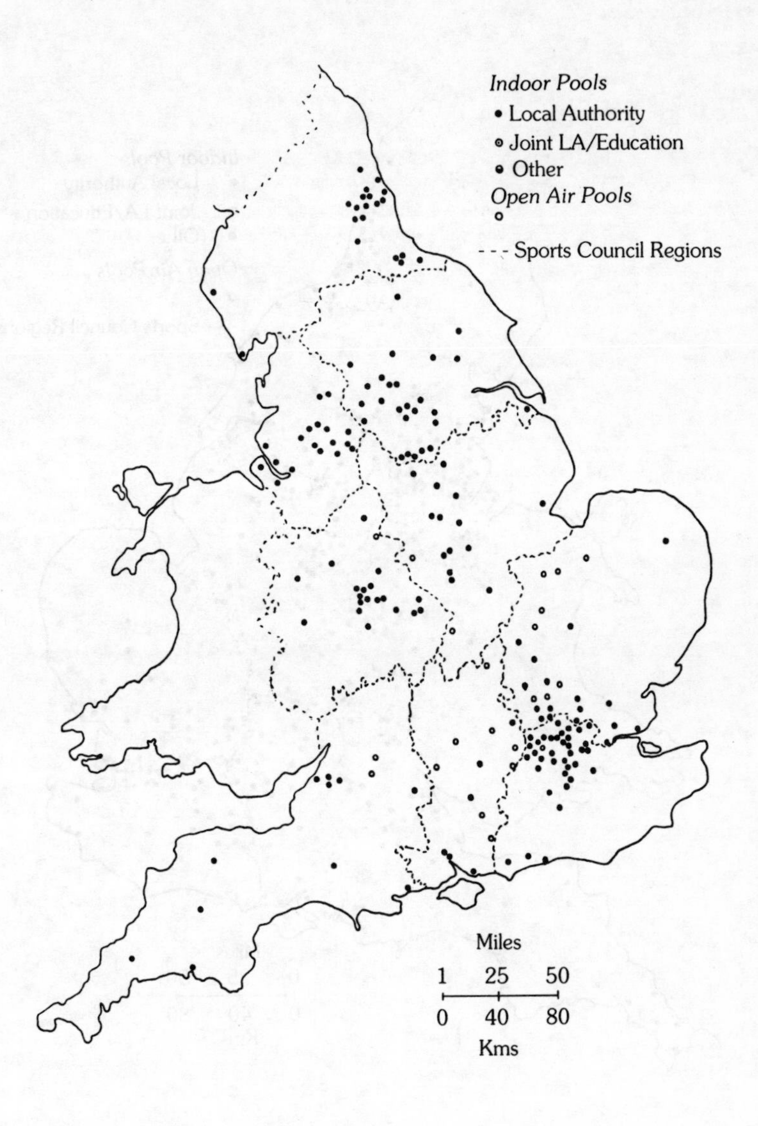

Figure A.8 – Pools built 1970–1977

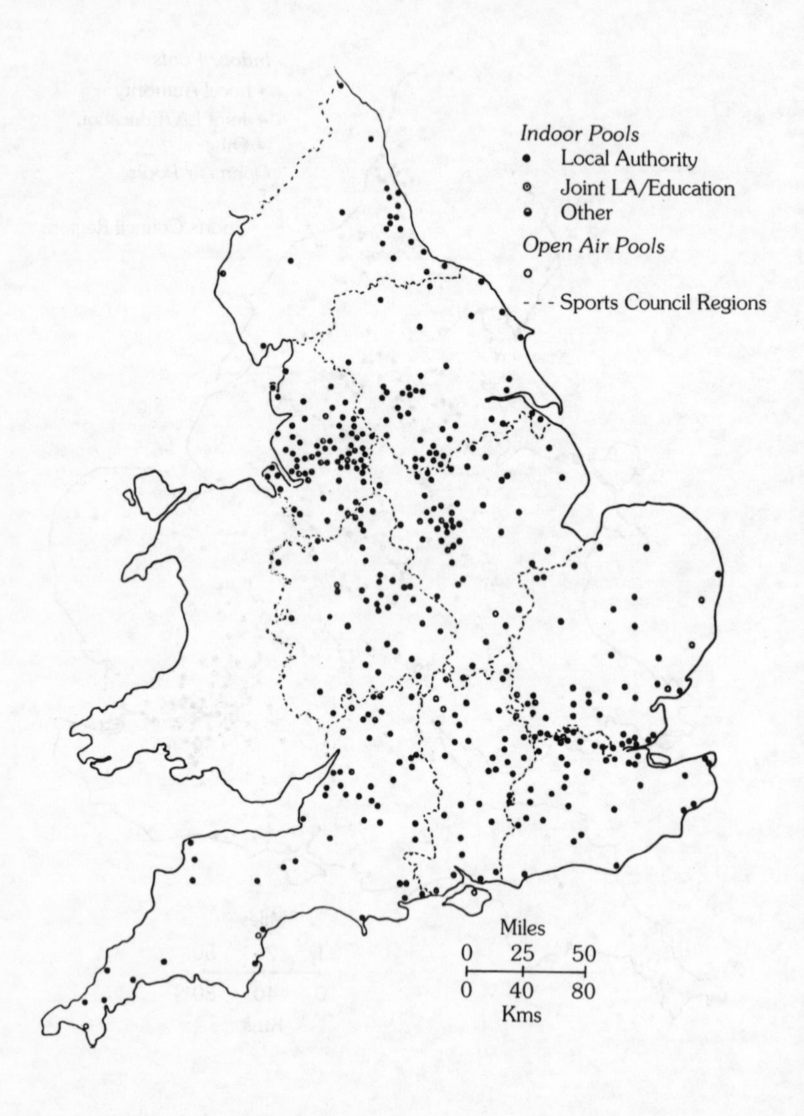

Source: Sports Council (1983)

Appendix II

Governing bodies

The following governing bodies were approached to provide information on club and individual membership for *A Digest of Sports Statistics*. Those who responded are marked *

Sport	Governing bodies	
ANGLING	*NAC	— National Anglers Council
	*NFA	— National Federation of Anglers
	*NFSA	— National Federation of Sea Anglers
	*SANA	— Scottish Anglers National Association
	*SFCA	— Scottish Federation for Coarse Angling
	*SFSA	— Scottish Federation of Sea Anglers
	*STA	— Salmon and Trout Association
	UAF	— Ulster Angling Federation
	*UCFF	— Ulster Coarse Fishing Federation
	*UPCIFSA	— Ulster Provincial Council of the Irish Federation of Sea Anglers
	*WAC	— Welsh Anglers Council
	WFCA	— Welsh Federation of Coarse Anglers
	WFSA	— Welsh Federation of Sea Anglers
	WSTAA	— Welsh Salmon and Trout Angling Association
ARCHERY	*GNAS	— Grand National Archery Society
	*NIAS	— Northern Ireland Archery Society
	NWAS	— North Wales Archery Society
	*SAA	— Scottish Archery Association
	*SFAA	— Scottish Field Archery Association
	SWAS	— South Wales Archery Society
	*WAF	— Welsh Archery Federation
ASSOCIATION FOOTBALL	*FA	— Football Association
	FAOW	— Football Association of Wales
	*IFA	— Irish Football Association
	NIWFA	— Northern Ireland Women's Football Association

Sport	Governing bodies	
	*SFA	— Scottish Football Association
	*SWFA	— Scottish Women's Football Association
	WFA	— Women's Football Association
ATHLETICS	*AAA	— Amateur Athletic Association
	*BAAB	— British Amateur Athletics Board
	ECCU	— English Cross Country Union
	NIAAA	— Northern Ireland Amateur Athletics Association
	NIAACC	— Northern Ireland Amateur Athletics Coaching Committee
	*NIWAAA	— Northern Ireland Women's Amateur Athletics Association
	RWA	— Race Walking Association
	SAAA	— Scottish Amateur Athletics Association
	SAAJCC	— Scottish Amateur Athletics Joint Coaching Committee
	*SCCU	— Scottish Cross Country Union
	*SGA	— Scottish Games Association
	SWAAA	— Scottish Women's Amateur Athletics Association
	SWCCU	— Scottish Women's Cross Country Union
	*WoAAA	— Women's Amateur Athletics Association
	WAAA	— Welsh Amateur Athletics Association
	WCCA	— Women's Cross Country Association
	WCCU	— Welsh Cross Country Union
	WWAAA	— Welsh Women's Amateur Athletic Association
BADMINTON	*BAE	— Badminton Association of England
	*SBA	— Scottish Badminton Association
	UBBUI	— Ulster Branch Badminton Union of Ireland
	*WBU	— Welsh Badminton Union
BALLOONING	*BBAC	— British Balloon and Airship Club
BASEBALL and SOFTBALL	BABSF	— British Amateur Baseball and Softball Federation
	EBA	— English Baseball Association
	WBU	— Welsh Baseball Union
BASKETBALL	*BAW	— Basketball Association of Wales
	*EBBA	— English Basketball Association

Sport	Governing bodies		
	*SBA	—	Scottish Basketball Association
	UCABBI	—	Ulster Council Amateur Basketball Association of Ireland
	WLBA	—	Welsh Ladies Basketball Association
BOWLS	*BCGBA	—	British Crown Green Bowls Association
	*EBA	—	English Bowling Association
	*EBC	—	English Bowls Council
	*EBF	—	English Bowling Federation
	*EIBA	—	English Indoors Bowling Association
	*EWBA	—	English Women's Bowling Association
	*EWBF	—	English Women's Bowling Federation
	*EWIBA	—	English Women's Indoor Bowling Association
	*IBA	—	Irish Bowling Association, Northern Ireland Region
	*IIBA	—	Irish Indoor Bowling Association
	*IWBA	—	Irish Women's Bowling Association
	*IWIBA	—	Irish Women's Indoor Bowling Association
	*SBA	—	Scottish Bowling Association
	*SIBA	—	Scottish Indoor Bowling Association
	*SWBA	—	Scottish Women's Bowling Association
	*SWIBA	—	Scottish Women's Indoor Bowling Association
	*WBA	—	Welsh Bowling Association
	WCGBA	—	Welsh Crown Green Bowling Association
	*WIBA	—	Welsh Indoor Bowling Association
	*WLIBA	—	Welsh Ladies Indoor Bowling Association
	*WWBA	—	Welsh Women's Bowling Association
BOXING	*ABA	—	Amateur Boxing Association
	SABA	—	Scottish Amateur Boxing Association
	*UCIABA	—	Ulster Council Irish Amateur Boxing Association
	WABA	—	Welsh Amateur Boxing Association
CAMPING AND CARAVANNING	*CACC	—	Camping and Caravanning Club
CANOEING	*BCU	—	British Canoe Union

Sport	Governing bodies		
	CANI	—	Canoe Association of Northern Ireland
	*SCA	—	Scottish Canoe Association
	*WCA	—	Welsh Canoe Association
CAVING	*CCC	—	Cambrian Caving Council
	ISA	—	Irish Speleological Association
	*NCA	—	National Caving Association
CRICKET	*CC	—	Cricket Council
	*NCA	—	National Cricket Association
	NICA	—	Northern Ireland Cricket Association
	NWCUoI	—	Northern Women's Cricket Union of Ireland
	SCU	—	Scottish Cricket Union
	SWCA	—	Scottish Women's Cricket Association
	*WCA	—	Welsh Cricket Association
	*WCA	—	Women's Cricket Association
CROQUET	*CA	—	Croquet Association
	*SCA	—	Scottish Croquet Association
	*UCA	—	Ulster Croquet Association
CURLING	ECA	—	English Curling Association
	*RCCC	—	Royal Caledonian Curling Club
	WCA	—	Welsh Curling Association
CYCLING	BCCA	—	British Cycle Cross Association
	*BCF	—	British Cycling Federation
	BPAGB	—	Bicycle Polo Association of Great Britain
	*CSC	—	Cycle Speedway Council
	*CTC	—	Cyclists Touring Club
	NICF	—	Northern Ireland Cycling Federation
	*NBMXA	—	National Bicycle Motocross Association
	*RTTC	—	Road Time Trials Council
	*SBMXA	—	Scottish Bicycle Motocross Association
	*SCU	—	Scottish Cyclists Union
	UKBMXA	—	United Kingdom Bicycle Motocross Association
	WCU	—	Welsh Cycling Union
DARTS	*BDO	—	British Darts Organisation
	NDAGB	—	National Darts Association of Great Britain

Sport	Governing bodies	
	*NIDO	— Northern Ireland Darts Organisation
	*SDA	— Scottish Darts Association
	WDO	— Welsh Darts Organisation
FENCING	*AFA	— Amateur Fencing Association
	LAFU	— Ladies Amateur Fencing Union
	NIAFU	— Northern Ireland Amateur Fencing Union
	SAFU	— Scottish Amateur Fencing Union
	WAFU	— Welsh Amateur Fencing Union
FIVES	*EFA	— Eton Fives Association
	*RFA	— Rugby Fives Association
FLYING	AOPA	— Aircraft Owners and Pilots Association
GAELIC SPORTS	CA	— Camogie Association
	GAA	— Gaelic Athletic Association
GLIDING	*BGA	— British Gliding Association
	*SGA	— Scottish Gliding Association
	UGC	— Ulster Gliding Club
GOLF	*EGU	— English Golf Union
	*ELGA	— English Ladies Golf Association
	GUIUB	— Golfing Union of Ireland Ulster Branch
	*ILGUNE	— Irish Ladies Golfing Union, Northern Executive
	*LGU	— Ladies Golf Union
	*R&A	— Royal and Ancient Golf Club of St. Andrews
	*SGU	— Scottish Golf Union
	*SLGA	— Scottish Ladies Golfing Association
	*SOAG	— Society of One Arm Golfers
	*WGU	— Welsh Golf Union
	*WLGU	— Welsh Ladies Golf Union
GYMNASTICS	*BAGA	— British Amateur Gymnastics Association
	*NIAGA	— Northern Ireland Amateur Gymnastics Association
	*SAGA	— Scottish Amateur Gymnastics Association
	WAGA	— Welsh Amateur Gymnastics Association

Sport	Governing bodies	
HANDBALL (OLYMPIC)	*BHA	— British Handball Association
	*SHA	— Scottish Handball Association
HANG GLIDING	*BHGA	— British Hang Gliding Association
	SHGA	— Scottish Hang Gliding Association
	*UHGC	— Ulster Hang Gliding Club
	*WHGF	— Welsh Hang Gliding Federation
HOCKEY	*AEWHA	— All England Women's Hockey Association
	*HA	— Hockey Association
	*SHA	— Scottish Hockey Association
	*SWHA	— Scottish Women's Hockey Association
	*UBIHU	— Ulster Branch Irish Hockey Union
	UWHU	— Ulster Women's Hockey Union
	*WHA	— Welsh Hockey Association
	*WWHA	— Welsh Women's Hockey Association
HUNTING	*BFSS	— British Field Sports Society
	*BFSSSB	— British Field Sports Society Scottish Branch
ICE HOCKEY	*BIHA	— British Ice Hockey Association
	EIHA	— English Ice Hockey Association
	SIHA	— Scottish Ice Hockey Association
ICE SKATING	NSAGB	— National Skating Association of Great Britain
	SIFSA	— Scottish Ice Figure Skating Association
	SSSU	— Scottish Speed Skating Union
JUDO	*BJA	— British Judo Association
	*NIJF	— Northern Ireland Judo Federation
	*SJF	— Scottish Judo Federation
	*WJA	— Welsh Judo Association
KARATE	BKF	— British Karate Federation
	EKC	— English Karate Council
	*NIKB	— Northern Ireland Karate Board
	*SKBC	— Scottish Karate Board of Control
	WKF	— Welsh Karate Federation
LACROSSE	*AEWLA	— All England Women's Lacrosse Association
	*AWLLA	— All Wales Ladies Lacrosse Association

Sport	**Governing bodies**	
	*ELU	— English Lacrosse Union
	*SLA	— Scottish Lacrosse Association
RACKET AND REAL TENNIS	*T&RA	— Tennis and Rackets Association
	BEF	— British Equestrian Federation
	*BHS	— British Horse Society
	BHS-NIR	— British Horse Society-Northern Ireland Region
	BSJA	— British Show Jumping Association
	*RDA	— Riding for the Disabled Association
	STRA	— Scottish Trekking and Riding Association
ROLLER HOCKEY	*NIRHA	— Northern Ireland Roller Hockey Association
	*NRHAGB	— National Roller Hockey Association of Great Britain
ROLLER SKATING	NSA	— National Skating Association
ROUNDERS	NSA	— National Rounders Association
ROWING	*ARA	— Amateur Rowing Association
	IARU	— Irish Amateur Rowing Union Ulster
	*SARA	— Scottish Amateur Rowing Association
	*WRC	— Welsh Rowing Council
RUGBY	*BARLA	— British Amateur Rugby League Association
	*IRFU	— Irish Rugby Football Union Ulster Branch
	*RFL	— Rugby Football League
	*RFU	— Rugby Football Union
	SRU	— Scottish Rugby Union
	*WRU	— Welsh Rugby Union
SHINTY	*CA	— Camanachd Association
SHOOTING	*BASC	— British Association for Shooting and Conservation
	*CPSA	— Clay Pigeon Shooting Association
	ESSA	— English Small Bore Shooting Association
	NIPA	— Northern Ireland Pistol Association

Sport	Governing bodies		
	NISSU		Northern Ireland Small Bore Shooting Union
	*NRA	—	National Rifle Association
	*NSRA	—	National Small Bore Rifle Association
	*SCPA	—	Scottish Clay Pigeon Association
	*SFNI	—	Shooting Federation of Northern Ireland
	*SPA	—	Scottish Pistol Association
	*SRA	—	Scottish Rifle Association
	*SSC	—	Scottish Shooting Council
	*SSRA	—	Scottish Small Bore Rifle Association
	*UCPSA	—	Ulster Clay Pigeon Shooting Association
	*UCSSA	—	Ulster County Small Bore Shooting Association
	URA	—	Ulster Rifle Association
	*WCTSA	—	Welsh Clay Target Shooting Association
	WPA	—	Welsh Pistol Association
	WRA	—	Welsh Rifle Association
	*WSC	—	Welsh Shooting Council
	WSBRU	—	Welsh Small Bore Rifle Union
SKATEBOARDING	*ESA	—	English Skateboarding Association
	*NISA	—	Northern Ireland Skateboarding Association
	*SSA	—	Scottish Skateboarding Association
SKIING	BBA	—	British Bobsleigh Association
	BRTA	—	British Racing Toboggan Association
	*BSF	—	British Ski Federation
	*ESC	—	English Ski Council
	*SCW	—	Ski Council of Wales
	*SNSC	—	Scottish National Ski Council
	*USF	—	Ulster Ski Federation
SNOOKER, BILLIARDS AND POOL	*BSCC	—	Billiards and Snooker Control Council
	NIBSCC	—	Northern Ireland Billiards and Snooker Control Council
	SBACC	—	Scottish Billiards Association and Control Council
	*SNPC	—	Scottish National Pool Council
	WBSA	—	Welsh Billiards and Snooker Association
SQUASH	*SRA	—	Squash Rackets Association

Sport	Governing bodies	
	*SSRA	— Scottish Squash Rackets Association
	*USRA	— Ulster Squash Rackets Association
	UWSRA	— Ulster Women's Squash Rackets Association
	*WSRA	— Welsh Squash Rackets Association
	*WoSRA	— Women's Squash Rackets Association
LAND YACHTING	*BFSLYC	— British Federation of Sand and Land Yacht Clubs
	*SSYC	— Sandpipers Sand Yacht Club
LAWN TENNIS	*LTA	— Lawn Tennis Association
	*ILTAUC	— Irish Lawn Tennis Association Ulster Council
	*SLTA	— Scottish Lawn Tennis Association
	*WLTA	— Welsh Lawn Tennis Association
MARTIAL ARTS	*MAC	— Martial Arts Commission
MODEL AIRCRAFT FLYING	NIAA	— Northern Ireland Association of Aeromodellers
	*SAA	— Scottish Aeromodellers Association
	*SMAE	— Society of Model Aircraft Engineers
MOTOR SPORTS – FOUR-WHEELED	*ANICC	— Association of Northern Ireland Car Clubs
	*ASKC	— Association of Scottish Kart Clubs
	*RAC	— RAC Motor Sports Association Ltd
	*WAMC	— Welsh Association of Motor Clubs
MOTOR SPORTS – TWO-WHEELED	ACU	— Auto Cycle Union
	*CCWMCG	— Cambrian Council of Welsh Motor Cycle Clubs
	MCUI	— Motor Cycle Union of Ireland
	SACU	— Scottish Auto Cycle Union
	SCB	— Speedway Control Board
MOUNTAINEERING	*BMC	— British Mountaineering Council
	*FMCI	— Federation of Mountaineering Clubs of Ireland
	*MCS	— Mountaineering Council of Scotland
MOVEMENT, DANCE AND FITNESS ACTIVITIES	BADA	— British Amateur Dance Association
	*BWoY	— British Wheel of Yoga
	DS	— Dalcroze Society
	EFDSS	— English Folk Dance and Song Society

Sport	Governing bodies	
	*KFA	— Keep Fit Association
	KFANI	— Keep Fit Association of Northern Ireland
	KFAW	— Keep Fit Association of Wales
	*LAMG	— Laban Art of Movement Guild
	*MMM	— Margaret Morris Movement
	*MS	— Medau Society of Great Britain and Northern Ireland
	*NIYF	— Northern Ireland Yoga Fellowship
	*RSCDS	— Royal Scottish Country Dance Society
	*RSCDSNI	— Royal Scottish Country Dance Society — Northern Ireland
	SABDA	— Scottish Amateur Ballroom Dancers Association
	*SBTA	— Scottish Baton Twirling Association
	SKFA	— Scottish Keep Fit Association
	*SOBHD	— Scottish Official Board of Highland Dancing
	SYA	— Scottish Yoga Association
	WADA	— Welsh Amateur Dancers Association
	WFDS	— Welsh Folk Dance Society
	*WLHB	— Women's League of Health and Beauty
NETBALL	*AENA	— All England Netball Association
	*NINA	— Northern Ireland Netball Association
	*SNA	— Scottish Netball Association
	*WNA	— Welsh Netball Association
ORIENTEERING	*BOF	— British Orienteering Federation
	*NIOA	— Northern Ireland Orienteering Association
	*SOA	— Scottish Orienteering Association
	*WOA	— Welsh Orienteering Association
PARACHUTING AND PARASCENDING	*BAPC	— British Association of Parascending Clubs
	*BPA	— British Parachuting Association
	*SSPA	— Scottish Sport Parachuting Association
PENTATHLON AND TRIATHLON	*MPAGB	— Modern Pentathlon Association of Great Britain
	BTA	— British Triathlon Association
PÉTANQUE	*BPA	— British Pétanque Association
	*SPA	— Scottish Pétanque Association

Sport	Governing bodies	
POLO	*HPA	— Hurlingham Polo Association
	SPA	— Scottish Polo Association
SUB AQUA	*BSAC	— British Sub-Aqua Club
	NIFSAC	— Northern Ireland Federation of Sub-Aqua Clubs
	*SSAC	— Scottish Sub-Aqua Club
	*WASAC	— Welsh Association of Sub-Aqua Clubs
SURFING	*BSA	— British Surfing Association
	SSF	— Scottish Surfing Federation
	WSF	— Welsh Surfing Federation
SWIMMING	*ASA	— Amateur Swimming Association
	RLSS	— Royal Life Saving Society
	RLSSUB	— Royal Life Saving Society — Ulster Branch
	*SASA	— Scottish Amateur Swimming Association
	*UBIASA	— Ulster Branch Irish Amateur Swimming Association
	*WASA	— Welsh Amateur Swimming Association
TABLE TENNIS	*ETTA	— English Table Tennis Association
	*STTA	— Scottish Table Tennis Association
	*TTAW	— Table Tennis Association of Wales
	*UBITTA	— Ulster Branch Irish Table Tennis Association
TENPIN BOWLING	*BTBA	— British Tenpin Bowling Association
TRAMPOLINING	*BTF	— British Trampolining Federation
	NITA	— Northern Ireland Trampolining Association
	*STA	— Scottish Trampolining Association
	WTA	— Welsh Trampolining Association
TUG-OF-WAR	*NITOWA	— Northern Ireland Tug-of-War Association
	*STOWA	— Scottish Tug-of-War Association
	*TOWA	— Tug-of-War Association
	*WTOWA	— Welsh Tug-of-War Association
VOLLEYBALL	*EVA	— English Volleyball Association
	*NIVA	— Northern Ireland Volleyball Association

Sport	Governing bodies
	*SVA — Scottish Volleyball Association
	*WVA — Welsh Volleyball Association

Source: *A Digest of Sports Statistics* (Sports Council, 1986)

Index